The Golden Book of

CHOCOLATE

The Golden Book of
CHOCOLATE

First English language edition
for the United States and Canada
published in 2008 by Barron's Educational Series, Inc.

© 2006 McRae Books S.r.l.

The Golden Book of Chocolate
was created and produced by McRae Books S.r.l.
Via Umbria, 35 – 50145 Florence, Italy
info@mcraebooks.com
www.mcraebooks.com
Publishers: Anne McRae, Marco Nardi

Project Director Anne McRae
Art Director Marco Nardi
Photography Alan Benson
Introduction Kate Singleton
Texts Carla Bardi, Claire Pietersen
Food Styling Claire Pietersen
Project Editor Gabriella Greco
Layouts Los Tudio
Repro Puntoeacapo

All inquiries should be addressed to:
Barron's Educational Series, Inc.
250 Wireless Boulevard
Hauppauge, New York 11788
www.barronseduc.com

ISBN-13: 978-0-7641-6157-5
ISBN-10: 0-7641-6157-1

Library of Congress Control Number: 2007940664

9 8 7 6 5 4 3

Printed in China

The level of difficulty for each recipe is given on a scale from
1 (easy) to 3 (complicated).

CONTENTS

INTRODUCTION
TO THE SUBLIME

Over the ages and in different parts of the globe, various comestibles have been hailed as the food of the gods: honey, truffles, hallucinogenic mushrooms, wine. None more so, however, than chocolate, if names are anything to go by. For the fragrant, dark brown substance many people around the world feel they could hardly live without derives from a plant whose official botanical appellation is *Theobroma cacao*: *Theo* = Gods; *broma* = food. The Latin definition was provided in 1753 by the great Swedish scientist Linnaeus, himself a chocolate-lover. The binomial system he invented for the classification of all living things replaced unwieldy descriptive Latin sentences. In this case Linnaeus clearly let his taste buds prevail over his appreciation of a distant culture: cacao, a word of early pre-Columbian origin, hardly takes pride of place.

Linnaeus was writing when chocolate had already gained numerous devotees throughout Europe. In many respects it was quite unlike the sort of chocolate we are accustomed to today, yet it was clearly an enticing product. So what is it exactly that makes a food suitable for divine consumption? Arguably, not so much its rarity as its ability to provoke states of otherworldly understanding, to induce wellbeing not commonly associated with our mortal toils, to aid the accomplishment of superhuman feats. Chocolate ranks highly in this regard, as centuries of popular credence reveal.

Since ethereal pleasure is deemed to encompass all the senses, little wonder that many early consumers believed

chocolate to be endowed with aphrodisiac properties. This conviction is well established. In fact it had already gained credit before chocolate actually made it to the West. It was certainly common by the early 1520s among the Spanish conquistadores of Mexico, as they grew accustomed to the potent dark beverage beloved of the Aztec society they were about to decimate. They would have tasted it late in the evening, in keeping with local ceremony, served by their Mexican wives, concubines, and domestic servants. Given the circumstances, it is easy to imagine how what started out as a rumor in time became gospel truth.

It is surely this belief that quietly underlies the time-honored choice of chocolate as the quintessential gift in courtship. Men, in particular, have long invested chocolate with expressive powers. It has become the classic token of love for Valentine's Day, conveying affection along with desire. Of course, the festivity itself is a modern custom driven by commercial interests. Yet the pre-eminence of chocolate is interesting in the way it reflects earlier conventions. In bygone ages it was commonly considered beneficial for breeding women. One 18th century English health expert described how, by the use of chocolate, his wife "was brought to bed of twins, three times."

When chocolate first spread through Europe in the early 1600s, it was in fact considered a drug, a medicine. Taken in liquid form, its agreeable taste must have come as a pleasant surprise, especially when compared with many of the medicinal potions concocted at the time. Such unusual delectability no doubt contributed to the spread of chocolate and to the range of theories concerning its beneficial properties. Samuel Pepys, the great 17th century English diarist, was a keen frequenter of the chocolate houses that had sprung up in London by the mid 1600s. In his diary for 24 April 1661, he relates how two days earlier he had risen at four o'clock in the morning to celebrate the coronation of Charles II. The festivities continued well into the night, with plentiful libations. "Waked in the morning with my head in a sad taking through last night's drink, which I am very sorry for." Pepys ruefully admits. "So rise and went out with Mr Creed to drink our morning draught, which he did give me in chocolate to settle my stomach."

Writing a decade later, the illustrious letter-writer Marie de Rabutin-Chantal, marquise de Sévigné, was among those who wavered considerably in their opinion of the drink. In the end, however, the benefits prevailed, and the marquise declared: "I have reconciled myself to chocolate. I took it the day before yesterday to digest my dinner, to have a good meal, and I took it yesterday to nourish me so that I could fast until evening: it gave me all the effects I wanted. That's what I like about it: it acts according to my intention."

This latter statement hints at an intuitive grasp of the psychological attractions of chocolate. Today the craving for chocolate has spawned the neologism "chocoholic" to refer to those who fear to keep a box of chocolates in the fridge because they know they cannot resist wolfing them down in one sitting. So what fires that compulsion? Modern research has shown chocolate to be a complex product that can influence our sense of wellbeing in subtle ways. It comprises approximately 380 known chemicals, though processing must alter and, alas, adulterate that original rich composition.

Adam Drewnowski, a researcher at the University of Michigan, has looked into the way chocolate can trigger the production of opioids. Opioids are chemicals, such as those found in opium, which produce a feeling of mild euphoria. Drewnowski found that eating chocolate causes the brain to produce natural opiates, which dull pain and increase feelings of wellbeing.

Similarly, scientists at the Neurosciences Institute in San Diego have identified three substances in chocolate that could act on the brain, directly or indirectly, in ways that are similar to the effects of cannabis. They refer to this as a "cannaboid mimic," explaining how receptors on the surface of cells interact with certain chemicals by locking themselves to proteins that trigger reactions inside the cell. Now, the active chemical in marijuana is called tetrahydrocannabinol, or THC. When receptors in the brain bind to THC, the person feels "high." Chocolate does not contain THC, but it does comprise anandamide, an analogous compound that the brain also produces. Since anandamide is broken down quickly, it doesn't hang around long enough in the brain to induce a permanent smile. However, research has shown that there are two chemicals in chocolate that inhibit the natural breakdown of anandamide. And this might explain, to some extent, the feel-good factor.

Chocolate also contains theobromine, which belongs to a class of alkaloid molecules known as methylxanthines. These substances occur in as many as sixty different plant species. They include caffeine, the primary methylxanthine in coffee, and theophylline, the primary methylxanthine in tea. Theobromine is the primary methylxanthine found in products of the cocoa tree. Theobromine's effect on the human brain is similar to that of caffeine, but on a much smaller scale. As well as being mildly diuretic, it is a moderate stimulant and can relax the smooth muscles of the bronchi in the lungs. The fact that theobromine levels in the body are halved by six to ten hours after consumption may help explain the unrelenting attractions of the chocolate box.

The cacao beans from which chocolate is derived contain theobromine in notably varying quantities, ranging from 300 to 1200 milligrams per ounce. Nowadays *Theobroma cacao* is more widely cultivated in West Africa than it is in its native Mexico and Guatemala. Though the varietals grown worldwide are basically only two, plus the hybrids they have generated, soil and microclimate inevitably play their part in creating variety. The outcome of this diversification is that different types of chocolate contain different amounts of theobromine. Levels are higher in dark chocolates than in milk chocolates, where the concentration of cacao has been reduced through the introduction of milk solids and sugar. But even within the more rarefied spheres of dark chocolate there are remarkable differences in the chemical compounds of the finished product. Just why this is so should become clear from the following pages.

The cacao tree is indigenous to the region of Latin America that lies between southern Mexico and the northern Amazon basin. It requires a constant climate that never drops below 60°F (16°C), considerable humidity, and protection from the blazing sun. The rain forests that were once its natural habitat also ensured another element essential to the prosperity of the *Theobroma cacao*: midges, which are entirely responsible for pollination.

The cacao tree bears its leaves, flowers, and fruit simultaneously throughout the year. The blossoms grow from small cushions on the trunk and larger branches, though only a few develop into fruit, or pods. These are shaped like large oval melons, saffron yellow or red in color, depending on the variety. It is easy to imagine how the sight of the trees, bedecked with such colorful excrescences, must have surprised those first European invaders. They referred to the phenomenon as "cauliflory," meaning "flowering on the stem," from the Greek word *caulos*, a stem or stalk. The pods themselves require four to five months to reach full size, and then another month to ripen completely. Each pod contains 30 to 40 leathery, bean-shaped seeds, surrounded by a sweet, mucilaginous white pulp that is slightly acidic, but refreshing to the taste. Harvesting must be done with care, so as not to damage the cushions, which continue to produce flowers, and therefore fruit.

The cacao beans obtained from a ripe pod are attractive, brightly colored, and veined. Among the peoples of pre-Columbian Mexico they were used as a currency and traded as a commodity. As for the word "cacao" itself, it can be traced back to the term *kakawa* found in the culture of the Olmec, who flourished in the hot and humid Veracruz and Tabasco provinces of Mexico between 1500–400 BC. Thus it now seems almost certain that *Theobroma cacao* was first domesticated by the Olmec.

No doubt in the first instance ripe cacao pods that had fallen to the forest floor would have burst open, so that

the seeds fermented spontaneously in their own juices. A passer-by might then pick up a handful of fermented seeds and dry them out before roasting them in the home fire. Once the fire died down, he would discover his beans to have changed color and become more friable. At which point they could be ground. Whatever the level of technology involved, to this day the process of extracting chocolate from cacao beans calls for those same steps. The beans must be left to ferment for just under a week. As fermentation progresses, the pulp becomes liquid and drains away as the temperature steadily rises. At a certain point, the seeds germinate, only to be killed by high temperatures and increased acidity. Short-lived though the germinal moment may be, it is essential in providing the finished product with its characteristic chocolate flavor.

Once fermentation is completed, the drying process can begin, traditionally using mats or trays left in the sun. During exsiccation, which takes from one to two weeks, the beans lose over half their weight, while the enzymatic action initiated by the fermentation continues. Roasting then follows, at temperatures from 210°F–219°F (99°C–104°C) for chocolate and 241°–250°F (116°C–121°C) for cocoa powder. This part of the process is vital for the development of flavor and aroma. Finally, winnowing frees the nibs of their thin, dry husk so that they can be ground into the substance known in the trade as "cacao liquor," or chocolate mass.

The Spanish first encountered chocolate at the Aztec court, which had learned the secrets of processing and preparation from the earlier Mayan civilization, in its turn indebted to the Olmec. In all three it was consumed as a beverage. Since cacao beans are rich in fat, simply to mix the ground cacao with water would soon have led to separation, with the cacao gradually settling in an unpleasant sludgy sediment at the bottom of the cup. To avoid this the pre-Columbian inhabitants of Mexico made *xocolatl* from the *cacahuatl* by adding cold water and stirring vigorously (*xoco* means bitter, and *atl* means water), then pouring the liquid from one container to another from a certain height to create the froth that was held to be the finest feature of the whole sensorial experience.

A LITTLE HISTORY

Among the Aztecs the drinking of chocolate was confined to the elite: the royal house, the lords and nobility, the long-distance merchants and the warriors. The ceremonial importance of the substance was profound. Not only was it provided at banquets at which noblemen and merchants displayed their wealth. It was also offered to the gods, and was used to anoint newborn children on the forehead, face, fingers, and toes.

A report by Bernial Diaz del Castillo noted that Montezuma drank *xocolatl* several times a day from beakers made of pure gold, and that warriors and nobles of the court kept the ground cacao in golden containers, which they carried around with them. The local dignitaries spiced the drink with native vanilla, wild honey, pita juice, and occasionally chili, whereas the Spanish officers preferred aniseed, cinnamon, almonds, and hazelnuts. Moreover, they increasingly chose to make their drink with hot water, and to sweeten it with the cane sugar they had introduced to the New World. Instead of obtaining the coveted froth with pouring, their slaves used a wooden whisk called a *molinello* to stir the hot beverage until it foamed invitingly.

Fortunately for the Spaniards, the Church recognized the new drink as a beverage rather than a food, which meant it could be enjoyed during periods of fasting. This must have encouraged them to bring chocolate back to Spain in the late 1500s. A hundred years later it had become the new national drink, a fashionable pastime to be enjoyed in airy assembly rooms. Madame D'Aulnoy, an aristocratic Frenchwoman visiting the Spanish court in Madrid in those years, described silver dishes filled with gold-wrapped candied fruits and accompanied by the new beverage. "Each porcelain cup stood on an agate saucer with a gold border, each with a matching sugar bowl," she declared with almost breathless wonder. "There was iced chocolate, warm chocolate, and some with eggs and milk. There are even women who can drink six cups in succession."

The product soon spread further a field, and by 1668 *cioccolato* was being sold in Florence "in little earthenware beakers, hot as well as cold, according to taste," as a local chronicler relates. In fact the Florentines added some remarkable aromas to the drink. The much praised speciality of Grand Duke Cosimo III's court was jasmine chocolate, the production of which was kept secret until well after its inventor's death. Interestingly, it was first concocted by Francesco Redi, scientist, poet, philologist, and physician to his Medici patrons, and has only recently been rediscovered.

Even in Europe, however, chocolate remained a prerogative of the wealthy until well into the 1700s. And this despite the fact that systematic planting of cacao trees in various parts of the Dutch, English, and French colonies meant that the raw material was more readily available and at better prices than ever before. The problem lay with the processing, which had changed little since the Aztecs and required considerable labor.

The Spanish had returned to their homeland not only with supplies of cacao, but also with the time-honored method for turning the fermented and roasted nibs into chocolate paste. This involved the painstaking use of a metate, or grinding stone, made of grey or black porous basalt. This essential object was shaped like a low, sloping, three-legged stool. The chocolate purveyor would kneel at the top end and with a flat-sided stone rolling pin work the nibs back and forth until they were reduced to a powder. Heating the metate slightly would soften the fat known as cocoa butter that is a major constituent part of the raw material, thereby permitting the amalgamation of sugar and other ingredients such as roasted almonds. Once the mixture had become malleable, it could be pressed into cakes or bars, or shaped into balls. In the 1700s there were 150 chocolate grinders plying their trade from house to house in Madrid alone.

There is an art to working the metate, and it requires time as well as muscle. It Spain and in Italy it was still in use well into the 20th century among artisan chocolate makers. Elsewhere it was soon replaced by mechanization. Fry and Sons of Bristol established the first chocolate factory in Britain in 1728. Less than thirty years later, the Prince of Lippe decided to return to his native Germany after years of serving as an officer with the Portuguese. Fearing withdrawal from what had become a most enjoyable habit, he opened a chocolate factory there that was the first of many. By 1782, there were eight factories in Munich alone. And in France in 1776 a hydraulic machine was invented to grind chocolate into paste. In recognition of his technical acumen, its inventor, a certain M Doret, was authorized to give his factory the title of Chocolatérie Royale.

The most interesting and influential side effect of the increased availability of chocolate was the spread of chocolate and coffee houses in London during the 18th century. More than centers of gastronomic indulgence, these were like clubs whose members could discuss topical affairs in relative freedom over a pleasurable cup of the delectable beverage. In time certain establishments gained a name for a particular political allegiance; others for the degree of gambling that took place there; others still for the philosophical debates favored by patrons. Curiously, this public airing of ideas in chocolate houses, so typical of the English Enlightenment, was never transferred to the North American colonies. The leisured classes in Virginia took their chocolate at home.

In 1828 a Dutch chemist by the name of C.J. van Houten patented a process for separating the cocoa butter from the basic brown mass. This allowed him to produce a powdered chocolate with a very low fat content: more or less, what we know as cocoa. To make this product mix well with water, van Houten treated it with alkaline salts in a process that came to be known as "Dutching." Darker in color and milder in flavor, the product was more digestible and easily prepared.

The most significant outcome of this discovery was arguably not the gradual demise of the thick, foamy beverage the Spanish had brought back from Mexico. Rather, it was the production of chocolate bars. In 1847 the Fry firm in Bristol found a way of mixing cocoa powder and sugar with melted cacao butter to produce a thinner, less viscous paste which could be cast into a mold. This was the world's first eating chocolate. The convenience of the new product was truly revolutionary. It could travel, was easily consumed, and required no bulky paraphernalia. By the late Victorian age, J.S. Fry & Sons were the largest chocolate manufacturers in the world, not least because they were the sole suppliers of chocolate and cocoa to the Royal Navy.

The Fry's greatest rivals were the Cadburys of Birmingham, who in 1853 acquired the royal privilege as purveyors of chocolate to Queen Victoria. The Cadburys duly installed a model of Van Houten's machine in their own factory and in 1868 came out with the world's first chocolate box. Next came a Valentine's Day candy box, which predated the famous Perugina Baci confections by several years. By curious coincidence the Frys, the Cadburys, and the prominent Rowntree family near York were all Quakers who maintained a social conscience even as their fortunes accrued. They built housing and communal facilities such as libraries for their workers, and boycotted cacao from colonial plantations in which conditions of near slavery prevailed. By the same token, they also avoided the sort of industrial malpractice that has tainted the name of other heavyweights on the world stage for chocolate.

THE WORLDWIDE BUSINESS

Fine chocolate as we know it today is smooth, suave, and mellow. Texture must to some extent impinge upon taste, which suggests that what we enjoy now is a substantially different product to what was consumed until the late 1800s, when eating chocolate was usually coarse and gritty (grittiness is a treasured feature of the chocolate made in Modica, Sicily, but this is a variation in style that we shall address later). The transformation of the product and our expectations of it are almost entirely due to the Swiss.

In 1867 a Swiss chemist by the name of Henri Nestlé discovered a method of making powdered milk by evaporation. This was truly a pivotal event, not least because his company has since grown into the world's largest food corporation. It also inspired his fellow countryman Daniel Peter to experiment with the production of chocolate using the powdered milk. The outcome in 1879 was the world's first milk chocolate bar. The basic concept was simple: by drying out the moisture in the mix and adding cacao butter, the liquefied substance could be poured into a mold.

That same year Rudolphe Lindt, another Swiss chocolate manufacturer, increased the amount of cacao butter in his formula and developed the process referred to as "conching." This involves subjecting the chocolate liquor to constant rolling and pressing until the friction and heat thus produced bring the mass to the desired flavor and degree of smoothness. The outcome was so satisfactory that to describe it Lindt borrowed the term "fondant" from the confectionary industry, where it referred to smooth sugar creams.

Further improvements implemented in Switzerland put that country at the technological and financial forefront of the business. A familiar case in point is "Toblerone," introduced in 1899 by Jean Tobler, whose company merged with Suchard in 1970. The consistently shiny, dark quality of Toblerone was achieved through tempering, a term borrowed this time from metallurgy. Here it meant first heating the mass, then carefully lowering the temperature, thereby destroying the crystal structure of the fat which would otherwise tend to create blotchy surfaces. Toblerone, the triangular sweetmeat composed of almond and honey nougat in a chocolate shell, was the first real fusion of the concepts of chocolate and candy bar. It expressed an early stage in the transition from luxury fare to popular snack, collective rite to individual indulgence.

For the apotheosis of this process we must turn to the USA, where solitary snacking has become a way of life. Here, among the rolling hills of south-eastern Pennsylvania, a caramel confectioner named Milton Snavely Hershey redirected his manufacturing interests into chocolate after visiting the World's Columbian Exposition in Chicago in 1893. The long-term fruit of this Pauline conversion was the foundation and development of "Hershey, the Chocolate Town," the dimensions of which made Cadbury and Rowntree's achievements pale into matchbox scale by comparison. The several thousand employees could count on schools, libraries, churches, a hospital, a fire department, a park, a zoo, a golf course, and other amenities. Moreover, alongside the milk chocolate and cocoa factories there were 8000 acres (3237 hectares) of Hershey-owned dairy farms and a sugar plantation in Cuba.

From the outset, mechanization and automation were the keywords in production and company image. By the 1980s, 25 million of the individually wrapped milk chocolates known as Kisses dropped off the conveyor belt into boxes each day. Everything was clean, modern, and healthful. It was a farsighted paternalistic empire that lives on as the Hershey Foods Corporation, with annual sales of over two billion dollars. Together with its arch-rival the M&M/Mars Company, it controls around 70 percent of the vast American candy market.

Clearly the industrialization of chocolate production depended not only on improved technology, but also on greater availability of the raw material. This has meant a move away from the high quality but low yielding Criollo variety of cacao bean to the more prolific Forastero, and the development of the Trinitario hybrid that combines the delicate savor of the former and the force of the latter.

World demand has also promoted the intensive cultivation of cacao throughout the area known as the "Cacao belt:" the humid, tropical regions between 10° north and 10° south of the equator. Apart from Mexico and Guatemala, these include Nicaragua, Panama, Brazil, Venezuela, Ecuador, Colombia, Bolivia, Peru, the Caribbean islands, Jamaica, Malaysia, Indonesia, and Sri Lanka. More importantly, however, they also comprise West Africa, which currently produces over 67 percent of the world's crop of cacao beans. Of this total, an astonishing 43 percent comes from Cote d'Ivoire alone, with countries such as Ghana, Nigeria, Cameroon, and Madagascar also playing an important role.

Intensive growing has brought problems of its own, however. *Theobroma cacao* is a delicate creature easily beset by fungal infections, especially where genetic diversity has been radically reduced. In the past ten years, the production of cacao beans in Brazil has dropped by 75%, largely as the result of blight by the fungus *Crinipellis perniciosa*, which has now spread into Peru, Ecuador, Venezuela, and Colombia in South America, and Panama in Central America. Another noxious microorganism is called Black Pod, which is currently devastating production in West and Central Africa.

Smallholders account for two-thirds of the cacao produced worldwide. In poor countries, these farmers labor in isolation and have no hope of acquiring the equipment to take their product to the market, or indeed the nearest port. They are thus entirely at the mercy of the brokers and the major food conglomerates who establish prices. World cacao prices fluctuate substantially and have dipped well below production costs in the last decade. Though they have risen slightly in recent years, the producers themselves are mired in debt. As a result, many of them resort to exploitative labor, including the enslavement or indenture of children.

In June of 2001, the US House of Representatives voted to consider a labeling system to assure consumers that slave labor was not used in the production of their chocolate. The US chocolate industry initially responded with an intense lobbying effort to ward off this legislation, declaring that it would hurt the people of West Africa by leading to a boycott of all cacao from that region. Following some critical newspaper coverage, however, it changed its tune and agreed to a Protocol and Joint Statement aimed at eliminating child and forced labor in cacao producing countries, especially in West Africa.

The intention may have been good enough, but its effects are likely to be limited. For, as the then Prime Minister of Cote d'Ivoire pointed out, the multinational chocolate manufacturers who encouraged developing countries to grow cacao, thereby forcing the prices down, would have to pay about ten times as much for cacao as they currently do if they want to end unethical labor practices.

Fortunately it is the consumers who now have the power to bring about change. They can purchase a range of different styles of chocolate and cocoa powder made by manufacturers who buy Fair Trade cacao from Fair Trade Certified producer groups. These are collectives made up of democratically managed farms. There are 20 of them

in nine countries: Ghana, Cameroon, Bolivia, Costa Rica, Nicaragua, Dominican Republic, Ecuador, Belize, and Peru. Moreover, because organic farms are subject to an independent monitoring system that checks labor practices, organic chocolate is also considered "slave free."

The rise in the demand for organic produce that has characterized Western consumer trends in recent years is particularly important in the case of chocolate. In the first instance because organic cacao beans have higher levels of immunity-enhancing flavonoids because they are grown without chemicals. Pesticides such as Lindane, long outlawed as a health hazard in Europe and Canada, are still used in cacao producing countries. Just as importantly, however, organic chocolate confections can never contain hydrogenated fat.

Many people who quietly enjoy a square of chocolate or two from time to time may wonder what hydrogenated fat is doing in their candy bar. Well, if they read the small print on the ingredient labels of their chosen confection they are likely to discover that it also contains starch, nuts, animal fats, emulsifiers (usually soy lecithin), glucose syrup, and perhaps gum arabic as a thickener too. They should check the sugar content as well, since excess here is likely to undo any benefits the small amount of chocolate it contains may offer.

Even with cacao world prices as low as they are, for multinational manufacturers the partial replacement of this essential ingredient with cheaper surrogates represents an obvious increase in profit margins. If this sounds like a sickly version of conspiracy theory, suffice it to recall that in March of 2000 the EU, well primed by the European chocolate heavyweights, authorized the addition of 5% of vegetable fats other than cacao butter for the production of chocolate. It is calculated that this seemingly small percentage will save the manufacturers who pressed for it around 200 million dollars a year. By the same token, it will also further impoverish the producer countries.

Sadly but unsurprisingly, the adulteration of chocolate is nothing new. In the early 1800s unscrupulous French manufacturers were adding powdered dried peas, flour made from rice or lentils, and potato starch to their chocolate mixtures. In Britain a few decades later a health commission on food safety found 39 out of 70 chocolate samples had been colored with red ochre from ground bricks, to say nothing of the extraneous starches they found in practically every product they analyzed. Common additives across the Atlantic were "earthy or other solid substances," red or yellow ochre, red lead and vermilion. Just as growing awareness of such practices ultimately led to legislation aimed at protecting the consumer's health and pocket, so it is to be hoped that more evident and exhaustive labeling will help today's chocolate lovers to make informed purchases. Happily, there are some encouraging signs in this direction.

DE GUSTIBUS...

Over the past decade, artisan chocolate makers have come to the fore throughout the Western world. Gourmet chocolate accounts for roughly 10 percent of overall chocolate sales in the USA and is growing faster than the chocolate market. It is estimated that total gourmet chocolate sales reached $1.3 billion in 2005, and will reach $1.8 billion in 2010.

Similar trends are evident in Europe. Valrhona, the prestigious French chocolatier founded in 1925, now produces a connoisseur's dream named Manjari, which is made from 100 percent Criollo beans grown at a single plantation in the Indian Ocean, the location of which is a house secret. Only 20 tons of Manjari are available worldwide, most of it finding its way to exclusive restaurants for the creation of desserts and pastries.

Another eloquent case in point is the introduction of cacao plantations to the Hawaiian Islands. This was the brainchild of former advertising and travel executive Jim Walsh, who moved there from Chicago with family in 1984. He also opted for the Criollo variety, and in 1986 planted his first 18,000 trees, carefully regulating the amount of water each tree received to create the kind of stress that results in concentration of flavor, just as it does in vine and grape cultivation. The results have been remarkable, with hugely increased output compared with other growing regions. Walsh attributes this fortune to the abundant and varied midge

population on the islands. While fermentation and drying are carried out in situ, the beans are sent to a plant in northern California for roasting, grinding, mixing, conching, and tempering. Singularly smooth and concentrated, Hawaiian Vintage Chocolate commands premium prices on the gourmet market.

Renowned for its inventive use of chocolate in a wide range of culinary preparations during the 1700s, Italy is also currently enjoying a renaissance in artisan chocolate production. Labels like Domori and Amedei now have far flung admirers who seek out fine chocolate just as they would fine wine. Interestingly, many excellent producers of both commodities are located in Tuscany. Not all of them, however. Ten years ago in the handsome Sicilian town of Modica there was only one producer left of the traditional gritty chocolate introduced to the island during the Spanish domination of the 15th and 16th centuries. Fortunately it was the Antica Dolceria Bonajuto, run by Franco Ruta, writer, publisher, and chocolate activist supremo. While Ruta now heads the Italian association of artisan chocolate producers that is pressing for EU recognition of quality chocolate, Modica is enjoying a revival of its historic product, with numerous artisans setting up shop to supply to increasingly discerning visitors.

Perhaps the most promising sign of a changing tide occurred in 2005 in England, where quality chocolate was a rarity until a decade ago. It all started back in 1991 when Craig Sams, founder of Whole Earth—the pioneering organic food company—was sent a sample of dark 70% chocolate made from organic cocoa beans. His wife, Josephine Fairley, environment columnist for The Times and confirmed chocoholic, also sampled the product, and was bowled over by the intensity of flavor. Convinced other chocolate lovers would likewise

39

appreciate it, the couple set about making the world's first organic chocolate. Green & Black's, the final product, was a high-quality, bittersweet dark chocolate bar containing 70% cocoa solids—enough to make chocolate fans sit up and take notice. As the brand began to gain a loyal following, in 1994 Maya Gold was added to the range. Aware that cocoa farmers were suffering from falling cacao prices, Sams and his wife agreed to pay the farmers a fair price for their crops, which subsequently earned them the UK's first Fair Trade mark.

In 2002, Cadbury Schweppes bought a 5 percent stake in the company, completing its takeover in 2005. No doubt many admirers must have viewed this acquisition with a degree of perplexity. However, Green & Black's is operated as a stand alone business with founder Craig Sams remaining as Chairman. Moreover, the unaltered product line is much more widely distributed, thereby introducing quality chocolate to a broader customer base. Clearly Cadbury Schweppes had seen the writing on the wall. And that should be comforting for consumers and producers.

Block chocolate, for eating or incorporation into other foods or drinks, comes in two basic types: plain or dark, which is a mixture of chocolate mass, cacao butter and sugar; and milk chocolate, which includes milk solids, greater sugar content, and a lower proportion of chocolate mass. Purists would disallow the inclusion of milk chocolate as "real" chocolate. As for white chocolate, it is not really chocolate at all since it contains no mass, but is a mixture of cacao butter, milk solids, sugar, and flavorings.

That said, such chocolate can be used to create individual sweetmeats known as pralines in parts of continental Europe, or chocolates in the English speaking world. They are made by coating small pieces of sugar confectionery or nuts with melted chocolate. This can be achieved by hand dipping, which is an elusive skill, or by mechanical enrobing or molding. Popular fillings include fruit, coffee, or mint creams, toffee, and marzipan.

All this is a far cry from the subtly enticing world of fine and organic chocolate, however, which increasingly tends to be plain. In this way it is easier to appreciate the particular aromas that chocolate lovers have come to associate with their favorite producers, who in their own turn may favor chocolate mass from a specific region. Again, the analogy with wine production can be helpful. Chardonnay grapes grown in California will produce wines that are subtly different to those made from the same grape variety in Australia, France, or Italy. Part of this variety is due to soil and microclimate, and part to methods of cultivation, fermentation, and production. Likewise, Criollo or Forastero grown in different regions of the world will vary in their aromas, and such differences will be further accentuated by processing, especially roasting and conching.

Happily for those whose taste buds have been fired by savoring some of the many excellent chocolates that are now available on the market, tasting events have become a relatively common occurrence. By comparing chocolates of different provenance, the palate grows more discerning. Gourmet chocolate still accounts for only a small percentage of overall world sales, but it is growing. Now that many small quality producers the world over have helpful websites and will post their wares to their aficionados further afield, it is to be hoped that the confectionery giants react by improving their product and adopting sourcing practices that guarantee a decent livelihood for the growers.

COOKIES

CHEWY CHOCOLATE CHIP COOKIES

Preheat the oven to 350°F (180°C/gas 4). • Line two baking sheets with parchment paper. • Mix the flour, baking powder, baking soda, and salt in a medium bowl. • Beat the butter and both sugars in a large bowl with an electric mixer on high speed until creamy. • Add the eggs one at a time, beating until just combined after each addition. • With mixer on low, beat in the vanilla, mixed dry ingredients, and oats. • Stir in both types of chocolate chips and the walnuts by hand. • Shape the dough into cookies the size of golf balls and place about 3 inches (7 cm) apart on the prepared baking sheets.
• Bake until lightly browned, about 10 minutes.
• Cool on the baking sheets for 10 minutes, then transfer to wire racks to cool completely.

2 cups (300 g) all-purpose (plain) flour

1 teaspoon baking powder

1 teaspoon baking soda

¼ teaspoon salt

1 cup (250 g) butter, softened

1 cup (200 g) granulated sugar

1 cup (200 g) firmly packed dark brown sugar

2 large eggs

1 teaspoon vanilla extract (essence)

2½ cups (375 g) old-fashioned rolled oats

1 cup (180 g) bittersweet (dark) chocolate chips

½ cup (90 g) white chocolate chips

1 cup (100 g) coarsely chopped lightly toasted walnuts

Makes: about 24
Preparation: 20 minutes
Cooking: 10 minutes
Level: 1

HAZELNUT MOCHA BISCOTTI

Preheat the oven to 325°F (170°C/gas 3). • Spread the hazelnuts on a baking sheet. Toast until lightly golden, about 7 minutes. Transfer to a large cotton kitchen towel. Fold the towel over the nuts and rub them to remove the thin inner skins. Pick out the nuts. • Increase the oven temperature to 350°F (180°C/gas 4). • Butter a baking sheet. • Mix the flour, cocoa, baking soda, and salt in a medium bowl. • Beat the eggs, sugar, and vanilla in a large bowl with an electric mixer at high speed until pale and creamy. • With mixer at low speed, gradually beat in the mixed dry ingredients, coffee granules, chocolate chips, and hazelnuts to form a stiff dough. • Divide the dough in half. Form into two 12-inch (30-cm) logs and place 2 inches (5-cm) apart on the prepared baking sheet, flattening them slightly. • Bake until firm to the touch, 25–30 minutes. • Transfer to a cutting board to cool for 10 minutes. • Lower the oven temperature to 325°F (170°C/gas 3). Line two baking sheets with parchment paper. • Cut the cookies on the diagonal into 1/2-inch (1-cm) thick slices. • Arrange the slices cut-side down on the prepared baking sheets and bake until crisp, 10–15 minutes. • Transfer to wire racks and let cool completely.

3/4 cup (125 g) hazelnuts

2 cups (300 g) all-purpose (plain) flour

1/2 cup (75 g) unsweetened cocoa powder

2 teaspoons baking soda (bicarbonate of soda)

1/8 teaspoon salt

3 large eggs

1 cup (200 g) granulated sugar

1/2 teaspoon vanilla extract (essence)

2 teaspoons freeze-dried coffee granules

1/3 cup (60 g) semisweet (dark) chocolate chips

8 oz (250 g) white chocolate, coarsely chopped

Makes: about 48
Preparation: 35 minutes
  + 10 minutes to cool
Cooking: 45 minutes
Level: 2

CHOCOLATE CHIP COOKIES

48

Preheat the oven to 375°F (190°C/gas 5). • Butter three baking sheets. • Mix the flour, baking soda, and salt in a large bowl. • Beat the butter and both sugars in a large bowl with an electric mixer at high speed until creamy. • Add the eggs one at a time, beating until just combined after each addition. • With mixer at low speed, gradually add the vanilla and mixed dry ingredients. Stir in the chocolate chips by hand. • Shape the dough into balls about the size of a golf ball and place about 3 inches (7 cm) apart on the prepared baking sheets. • Bake until pale golden brown, about 10 minutes. • Cool on the baking sheets for 5 minutes, then transfer to wire racks to cool completely.

3½ cups (525 g) all-purpose (plain) flour

1 teaspoon salt

2 teaspoons baking soda (bicarbonate of soda)

14 oz (400 g) butter, softened

3 cups (600 g) firmly packed light brown sugar

1 cup (200 g) granulated sugar

4 large eggs

2 teaspoons vanilla extract (essence)

1½ cups (250 g) semisweet (dark) or milk chocolate chips

Makes: about 50
Preparation: 20 minutes
Cooking: 10 minutes
Level: 1

■■■ *This recipe produces about 50 big, flat, crisp cookies. Be sure to space them well apart on the baking sheets so that they don't all melt into one during cooking!*

GLAZED CHOCOLATE PRETZELS

50

Mix the flour, cocoa, baking powder, and salt in a medium bowl. • Beat the butter and sugar in a large bowl with an electric mixer at high speed until pale and creamy. • Add the egg and almond extract, beating until just blended. • With mixer at low speed, gradually beat in the mixed dry ingredients and almonds. • Divide the dough in half. Press into disks, wrap each one in plastic wrap (cling film), and chill in the refrigerator for 30 minutes. • Preheat the oven to 350°F (180°C/gas 4). • Butter two baking sheets. • Form the dough into 1½-inch (4-cm) balls and roll each one into a 12-inch (30-cm) rope. • Make each rope into a pretzel shape by twisting the two ends around each other, then bringing both back near to the center of the strip, about 1 inch (2.5 cm) apart. • Bake until firm, 10–12 minutes. • Cool on the baking sheet for 5 minutes. Transfer to wire racks and let cool completely. • Melt the white chocolate in a double boiler over barely simmering water. • Drizzle the cool cookies with the chocolate and let stand for 30 minutes until set.

2 cups (300 g) all-purpose (plain) flour
2 tablespoons unsweetened cocoa powder
1 teaspoon baking powder
½ teaspoon salt
¾ cup (180 g) butter, softened
1 cup (200 g) granulated sugar
1 large egg
½ teaspoon almond extract (essence)
½ cup (50 g) finely ground almonds
4 oz (125 g) white chocolate, coarsely chopped

Makes: about 22
Preparation: 40 minutes + 1 hour to chill and set
Cooking: 10–12 minutes
Level: 2

WHITE CHOCOLATE AND PECAN COOKIES

Preheat the oven to 350°F (180°C/gas 4). • Butter a baking sheet. • Mix the flour, baking soda, and salt in a medium bowl. • Beat the butter and raw sugar in a large bowl with an electric mixer at high speed until creamy. • Add the vanilla and egg, beating until just blended. • With mixer at low speed, beat in the mixed dry ingredients, white chocolate, and pecans. • Form the dough into balls the size of walnuts and place 2 inches (5 cm) apart on the prepared baking sheet. Press half a pecan lightly into the top of each cookie. • Bake until just golden, 10–12 minutes. • Cool on the baking sheet for 5 minutes. Transfer to wire racks and let cool completely.

1⅓ cups (200 g) all-purpose (plain) flour

½ teaspoon baking soda (bicarbonate of soda)

⅛ teaspoon salt

½ cup (125 g) butter, softened

¾ cup (150 g) raw sugar (Demerara or Barbados)

1 teaspoon vanilla extract (essence)

1 large egg

4 oz (125 g) white chocolate, coarsely chopped

½ cup (50 g) finely chopped pecans

10 pecans, cut in half, to decorate

Makes: about 20
Preparation: 20 minutes
Cooking: 10–12 minutes
Level: 1

SPICY CHOCOLATE CHIP COOKIES

Cookies: Preheat the oven to 350°F (180°C/gas 4).
• Line a baking sheet with parchment paper. • Mix
the flour, baking powder, red pepper flakes, and salt
in a small bowl. • Heat the raisins and coffee
liqueur in a small saucepan over low heat. • Melt
the chocolate with the butter in a double boiler over
barely simmering water. Set aside to cool. • Beat
the eggs and sugar in a large bowl with an electric
mixer at high speed until very pale and creamy,
about 5 minutes. • With mixer at medium speed,
beat in the chocolate and vanilla. • With mixer at
low speed, beat in the mixed dry ingredients, and
then the raisin mixture and chocolate chips. • Drop
tablespoons of the dough 1 inch (2.5 cm) apart on
the prepared baking sheet. • Bake until risen
slightly, 10–12 minutes. • Cool on the baking sheet
for 5 minutes. • Transfer to wire racks and let cool
completely. • Glaze: Melt the white chocolate and
red pepper flakes in a double boiler over barely
simmering water. Drizzle over the cooled cookies
and let rest until set, about 30 minutes.

Cookies

- 2/3 cup (100 g) all-purpose (plain) flour
- 1/2 teaspoon baking powder
- 1/2 teaspoon red pepper flakes
- 1/8 teaspoon salt
- 1/2 cup (60 g) raisins
- 2 tablespoons coffee liqueur
- 8 oz (250 g) semisweet (dark) chocolate, coarsely chopped
- 1/4 cup (60 g) butter
- 2 large eggs
- 3/4 cup (150 g) granulated sugar
- 2 teaspoons vanilla extract (essence)
- 1 cup (180 g) semisweet (dark) chocolate chips

Glaze

- 3 oz (90 g) white chocolate
- 1/2 teaspoon red pepper flakes

Makes: about 18
Preparation: 15 minutes
    + 30 minutes to set
Cooking: 12 minutes
Level: 1

CHOCOLATE HAZELNUT HEARTS

Mix the flour, finely ground hazelnuts, cocoa, and salt in a medium bowl.• Beat the butter and brown sugar in a large bowl with an electric mixer at high speed until creamy. • Add 1 whole egg and 1 egg yolk, beating until just blended. • With mixer on low speed, beat in the mixed dry ingredients and ground hazelnuts to form a smooth dough. • Press the dough into a disk, wrap in plastic wrap (cling film), and chill in the refrigerator for 30 minutes. • Preheat the oven to 350°F (180°C/gas 4). • Butter two baking sheets. • Discard the plastic wrap. Roll out the dough on a lightly floured work surface to $1/4$-inch (5-mm) thick. • Use a $1^1/_2$-inch (4-cm) heart-shaped cookie cutter to cut out the cookies. Gather the dough scraps, re-roll, and continue cutting out cookies until all the dough is used. • Use a spatula to transfer the cookies to the prepared baking sheets, placing them 1 inch (2.5 cm) apart. • Use a wire whisk to beat the remaining egg white in a small bowl until frothy and brush over the tops of the cookies. Sprinkle with the chopped hazelnuts. • Bake until firm to the touch, 10–15 minutes. • Transfer to wire racks to cool.

$1^1/_3$ cups (200 g) all-purpose (plain) flour

$1/2$ cup (75 g) finely ground hazelnuts

$1/3$ cup (50 g) unsweetened cocoa powder

$1/8$ teaspoon salt

$1/2$ cup (125 g) butter, softened

$3/4$ cup (150 g) firmly packed dark brown sugar

2 large eggs, 1 separated

$1/2$ cup (50 g) finely chopped hazelnuts

Makes: about 30
Preparation: 40 minutes
  + 30 minutes to chill
Cooking: 10–15 minutes
Level: 1

CHOCOLATE MADELEINES

Butter two 12-cup madeleine pans. • Preheat the oven to 400°F (200°C/gas 6). • Melt the butter in a small saucepan over medium-low heat until light brown. Remove from the heat and add the chocolate. Stir until smooth. • Mix the flour and cocoa in a small bowl. • Beat the eggs, sugar, and honey with an electric mixer at high speed until pale and creamy. • Stir in half the chocolate mixture by hand. Gently fold in the flour and cocoa and then add the remaining chocolate mixture, stirring until well combined. • Spoon the batter into the prepared madeleine pans. • Bake until springy to the touch, 10–12 minutes. • Cool the madeleines in the pan for 10 minutes. Transfer to wire racks and let cool completely.

½ cup (125 g) butter,

4 oz (125 g) bittersweet (dark) chocolate, chopped

1 cup (150 g) all-purpose (plain) flour

⅓ cup (50 g) unsweetened cocoa powder

3 large eggs

½ cup (100 g) granulated sugar

1 tablespoon honey

Makes: about 40
Preparation: 25–30 minutes
Cooking: 10 minutes
Level: 1

CHOCOLATE ROSE COOKIES

Rose Leaf Decorations: Melt the chocolate in a double boiler over barely simmering water. Use a small pastry brush to paint the melted chocolate onto the underside of each rose leaf. • Reserve a small amount of chocolate in the double boiler. Leave the decorations to set at room temperature for at least 30 minutes—do not refrigerate. When the chocolate has set, carefully peel off the rose leaves. Cookies: Preheat the oven to 400°F (200°C/gas 6). • Butter two baking sheets. • Mix the flour, cocoa, baking powder, and salt in a medium bowl. • Beat the butter and sugar in a large bowl with an electric mixer at high speed until creamy. • Add the egg, beating until just blended. • With mixer at low speed, beat in the mixed dry ingredients to form a stiff dough. • Form the dough into two logs $1^1/_2$ inches (4 cm) in diameter. Wrap in plastic wrap (cling film) and chill in the refrigerator for 30 minutes. • Discard the plastic wrap. Slice the dough $1/_4$ inch (5 mm) thick. • Transfer the cookies to the prepared baking sheets, placing them about 3 inches (7 cm) apart. • Bake until golden, 8–10 minutes. • Transfer to wire racks to cool. • Melt the remaining chocolate in the double boiler over barely simmering water. Use a teaspoon to place a little of the chocolate on each cookie. Lay a rose leaf decoration on top.

Rose Leaf Decorations

6 oz (180 g) bittersweet (dark) chocolate, coarsely chopped

30–32 green rose leaves, washed and dried

Cookies

$1^1/_2$ cups (225 g) all-purpose (plain) flour

1 tablespoon unsweetened cocoa powder

1 teaspoon baking powder

$1/_8$ teaspoon salt

$1/_2$ cup (125 g) butter, softened

$3/_4$ cup (150 g) granulated sugar

1 large egg

Makes: about 30
Preparation: 40 minutes
  + 30 minutes to chill
Cooking: 8–10 minutes
Level: 2

DOUBLE CHOCOLATE CHIP COOKIES

Preheat the oven to 350°F (180°C/gas 4). • Butter two baking sheets. • Mix the flour, baking soda, and salt in a large bowl. • Beat the butter and both sugars in a large bowl with an electric mixer at high speed until creamy. • Add the eggs one at a time, beating until just combined after each addition. • With mixer on low speed, gradually beat in the vanilla and mixed dry ingredients. • Stir in the dark and white chocolate chips by hand. • Drop tablespoons of batter about 3 inches (8 cm) apart on the prepared baking sheets. • Bake until pale golden brown around the edges and set in the middle, 10–12 minutes. • Cool on the baking sheets for 5 minutes, then transfer to wire racks to cool completely.

$2\frac{1}{3}$ cups (375 g) all-purpose (plain) flour

$\frac{1}{2}$ teaspoon baking soda (bicarbonate of soda)

$\frac{1}{4}$ teaspoon salt

$\frac{3}{4}$ cup (200 g) butter, softened

$\frac{3}{4}$ cup (150 g) granulated sugar

$\frac{1}{4}$ cup (50 g) firmly packed light brown sugar

2 large eggs

2 teaspoons vanilla extract (essence)

1 cup (180 g) semisweet (dark) chocolate chips

1 cup (180 g) white chocolate chips

Makes: about 36
Preparation: 15 minutes
Cooking: 10–12 minutes
Level: 1

CHEWY CHOCOLATE SPICE COOKIES

Melt the chocolate in a double boiler over barely simmering water. • Mix the flour, cocoa, and ginger, cinnamon, cloves, nutmeg, and salt in a large bowl. • Beat the butter and ginger root in a large bowl with an electric mixer at high speed until pale, about 4 minutes. • Add the brown sugar and beat until smooth. • Add the molasses and beat until combined. • Dissolve the baking soda in the boiling water in a small bowl. • With mixer on low speed, beat half of the mixed dry ingredients into the butter mixture. Add the baking soda mixture, then the remaining mixed dry ingredients. • Stir in the chocolate. • Shape the dough into a ball then press into a disk shape, about 1 inch (2.5 cm) thick. Wrap in plastic wrap (cling film) and chill in the refrigerator for at least 3 hours. • Preheat the oven to 325°F (170°C/gas 3). • Butter two baking sheet. • Roll the dough into $1^1/_2$-inch (4-cm) balls. Place on the prepared baking sheets about 2 inches (5 cm) apart. Refrigerate for 30 minutes. • Roll each cookie in the granulated sugar and replace on the baking sheets. • Bake until the surfaces crack slightly, 10–12 minutes. • Let cool on the sheets for 5 minutes. Transfer to wire racks to cool completely.

8 oz (250 g) semisweet (dark) chocolate, coarsely chopped

1½ cups (225 g) all-purpose (plain) flour

2 tablespoons unsweetened cocoa powder

1 teaspoon ground ginger

1 teaspoon ground cinnamon

¼ teaspoon ground cloves

¼ teaspoon ground nutmeg

¼ teaspoon salt

½ cup (125 g) butter, softened

1 tablespoon freshly grated ginger root

½ cup (100 g) firmly packed dark brown sugar

½ cup (125 g) molasses

1 teaspoon baking soda (bicarbonate of soda)

2 teaspoons boiling water

¼ cup (50 g) granulated sugar

Makes: about 24
Preparation: 15 minutes
+ 3 hours 30 minutes
to chill
Cooking: 10–12 minutes
Level: 1

CHOCOLATE CHIP AND CANDIED CHERRY COOKIES

Preheat the oven to 375°F (190°C/gas 5). • Butter two baking sheets. • Mix the flour, baking powder, and salt in a large bowl. • Beat the butter, sugar, and vanilla in a large bowl with an electric mixer at high speed until pale and creamy. • With mixer on low speed, beat in the dry ingredients, cherries, and chocolate. • Drop rounded teaspoons of the dough 1 inch (2.5 cm) apart on the prepared baking sheets. • Bake until just golden, about 15 minutes. • Cool on the baking sheets until the cookies firm slightly, about 5 minutes. Transfer to wire racks to cool completely.

³/₄ **cup (125 g) all-purpose (plain) flour**

½ **teaspoon baking powder**

⅛ **teaspoon salt**

½ **cup (125 g) butter, softened**

¼ **cup (50 g) granulated sugar**

½ **teaspoon vanilla extract (essence)**

½ **cup (50 g) coarsely chopped candied cherries**

2 **oz (60 g) semisweet (dark) chocolate, coarsely chopped**

Makes: about 18
Preparation: 20 minutes
Cooking: 15 minutes
Level: 1

DOUBLE CHOCOLATE DROPS

<u>Cookies</u>: Preheat the oven to 400°F (200°C/gas 6).
• Butter three baking sheets. • Mix the flour, baking soda, and salt in a large bowl. • Melt the chocolate in a double boiler over barely simmering water.
• Beat the butter, sugar, and melted chocolate in a large bowl with an electric mixer at high speed until creamy. • Add the vanilla and egg, beating until just blended. • With mixer on low speed, beat in the mixed dry ingredients and milk until well blended. • Drop teaspoons of the dough 1 inch (2.5 cm) apart on the prepared baking sheets.
• Bake until slightly risen, 10–12 minutes. • Cool on the sheets until the cookies firm slightly, about 5 minutes. Transfer to wire racks to cool completely.
<u>Chocolate Frosting</u>: Melt the chocolate in a double boiler over barely simmering water. • Add the butter and stir until smooth. Beat in the confectioners' sugar. • Spread the cookies with frosting and top each one with half a pecan.

Cookies

1⅓ cups (200 g) all-purpose (plain) flour

½ teaspoon baking soda (bicarbonate of soda)

⅛ teaspoon salt

2 oz (60 g) semisweet (dark) chocolate, coarsely chopped

½ cup (125 g) butter, softened

1 cup (200 g) granulated sugar

1 teaspoon vanilla extract (essence)

1 large egg

2 tablespoons milk

Chocolate Frosting

2 oz (60 g) semisweet (dark) chocolate, coarsely chopped

¼ cup (60 g) butter, softened

1⅓ cups (200 g) confectioners' (icing) sugar

About 18 pecans, halved

Makes: about 36
Preparation: 25 minutes
Cooking: 10–12 minutes
Level: 1

CHOCOLATE HAZELNUT COOKIES

Preheat the oven to 325°F (170°C/gas 3). • Set out three baking sheets. • Spread the hazelnuts on a baking sheet. Toast until lightly golden, 7–8 minutes. • Let cool completely. Transfer to a food processor, add $1/2$ cup (100 g) of the granulated sugar and process until coarsely chopped. • Mix the flour, baking powder, and salt in a medium bowl. • Beat the butter and remaining granulated sugar and brown sugar in a large bowl with an electric mixer at high speed until creamy. • Add the eggs one at a time, beating until just combined after each addition. Add the vanilla. • With mixer at low speed, beat in the mixed dry ingredients and enough orange juice to make a smooth dough. • Stir in the chocolate and hazelnut mixture by hand. • Drop teaspoons of the dough 1 inch (2.5 cm) apart on the baking sheets. • Bake until golden brown, 10–12 minutes. • Cool on the baking sheets until the cookies firm slightly, about 5 minutes. Transfer to wire racks to cool completely.

$3/4$ cup (90 g) hazelnuts

1 cup (200 g) granulated sugar

2 cups (300 g) all-purpose (plain) flour

1 teaspoon baking powder

$1/8$ teaspoon salt

1 cup (250 g) butter, softened

$1/2$ cup (100 g) firmly packed light brown sugar

2 large eggs

1 teaspoon vanilla extract (essence)

1–2 tablespoons freshly squeezed orange juice

8 oz (250 g) semisweet (dark) chocolate, coarsely chopped

Makes: about 45
Preparation: 30 minutes
Cooking: 10–12 minutes
Level: 1

PEANUT BUTTER CHOCOLATE CHIP COOKIES

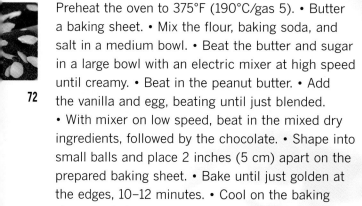

Preheat the oven to 375°F (190°C/gas 5). • Butter a baking sheet. • Mix the flour, baking soda, and salt in a medium bowl. • Beat the butter and sugar in a large bowl with an electric mixer at high speed until creamy. • Beat in the peanut butter. • Add the vanilla and egg, beating until just blended. • With mixer on low speed, beat in the mixed dry ingredients, followed by the chocolate. • Shape into small balls and place 2 inches (5 cm) apart on the prepared baking sheet. • Bake until just golden at the edges, 10–12 minutes. • Cool on the baking sheet until the cookies firm slightly, about 5 minutes. Transfer to wire racks to cool completely.

$1\frac{1}{4}$ cups (180 g) all-purpose (plain) flour

$\frac{1}{2}$ teaspoon baking soda (bicarbonate of soda)

$\frac{1}{8}$ teaspoon salt

$\frac{1}{2}$ cup (125 g) butter, softened

$\frac{1}{2}$ cup (100 g) raw sugar (Demerara or Barbados)

$\frac{1}{2}$ cup (125 g) smooth peanut butter

1 teaspoon vanilla extract (essence)

1 large egg

4 oz (125 g) semisweet (dark) chocolate, coarsely chopped

Makes: about 16
Preparation: 20 minutes
Cooking: 10–12 minutes
Level: 1

CHOCOLATE PUMPKIN COOKIES

Preheat the oven to 375°F (190°C/gas 5). • Set out two baking sheets. • Mix the flour, baking powder, baking soda, cinnamon, and salt in a large bowl. • Use a pastry blender to cut in the butter until the mixture resembles fine crumbs. • Stir in the sugar, pumpkin, and orange zest. • Stir in the chocolate chips. • Drop teaspoons of the dough 2 inches (5 cm) apart on the baking sheets. • Bake until golden, 8–10 minutes. • Cool on the baking sheets until the cookies firm slightly, about 5 minutes. Transfer to wire racks to cool completely.

1   cup (150 g) all-purpose (plain) flour

½   teaspoon baking powder

½   teaspoon baking soda (bicarbonate of soda)

½   teaspoon ground cinnamon

⅛   teaspoon salt

¼   cup (60 g) butter, softened

½   cup (100 g) granulated sugar

½   cup (125 ml) canned pumpkin purée

½   tablespoon finely grated orange zest

½   cup (90 g) semisweet (dark) chocolate chips

Makes: about 22
Preparation: 20 minutes
Cooking: 8–10 minutes
Level: 1

CHOCOLATE ALMOND THINS

Preheat the oven to 325°F (170°C/gas 3). • Spread the almonds on a large baking sheet. • Toast until lightly golden, about 7 minutes. • Butter four baking sheets. • Set out two rolling pins. • Mix the flour, cocoa, and salt in a small bowl. • Use a wooden spoon to mix the egg and egg white and sugar in a large bowl. • Stir in the mixed dry ingredients and butter. • Drop tablespoons of the mixture 2 inches (5 cm) apart on the prepared baking sheets. Do not place more than five cookies on one sheet. Spread the mixture out into thin circles. Sprinkle with the almonds. • Bake until firm at the edges, 8–10 minutes. • Working quickly, use a spatula to lift each cookie from the sheet and drape it over a rolling pin. • Let cool completely.

1   cup (100 g) flaked almonds

2   tablespoons all-purpose (plain) flour

2   tablespoons unsweetened cocoa powder

1/8 teaspoon salt

1   large egg + 1 large egg white, lightly beaten

1/2 cup (100 g) granulated sugar

2   tablespoons butter, softened

Makes: about 20
Preparation: 30 minutes
Cooking: 8–10 minutes
Level: 3

DIPPED CHOCOLATE ORANGE COOKIES

Mix the flour and salt in a large bowl. • Cut in the butter until the mixture resembles fine crumbs. • Mix in the ground almonds, sugar, and orange zest. • Add the egg yolk and orange juice and stir until smooth. • Press the dough into a ball and wrap in plastic wrap (cling film). Chill in the refrigerator for 30 minutes. • Preheat the oven to 350°F (180°C/gas 4). • Butter two baking sheets. • Roll out the dough to $1/4$ inch (5 mm) thick. • Use a 2-inch (5-cm) cookie cutter to cut out the cookies. Re-roll the dough scraps and continue cutting out cookies until all the dough is used. • Transfer the cookies to the prepared baking sheets, placing them 1 inch (2.5 cm) apart. • Bake until golden, 10–15 minutes. • Cool on the baking sheets for 5 minutes, then transfer to wire racks to cool completely. • Melt the chocolate in a double boiler over barely simmering water. • Dip the cookies halfway into the chocolate and let stand for 30 minutes until set.

1   cup (150 g) all-purpose (plain) flour

$1/8$ teaspoon salt

$1/3$ cup (90 g) butter, cut up

$1/3$ cup (50 g) finely ground almonds

$1/4$ cup (50 g) granulated sugar

1   tablespoon finely grated orange zest

1   large egg yolk, lightly beaten

2   tablespoons freshly squeezed orange juice

4   oz (125 g) semisweet (dark) chocolate, coarsely chopped

Makes: about 30
Preparation: 45 minutes
   + 1 hour to chill and set
Cooking: 10–15 minutes
Level: 1

MINTY CHOCOLATE KISSES

Cookies: Mix the flour, cocoa, and salt in a medium bowl. • Beat the butter and sugar in a large bowl with an electric mixer at high speed until pale and creamy. • Add the mint extract and egg, beating until just blended. • With mixer on low speed, beat in the mixed dry ingredients. • Press the dough into a disk, wrap in plastic wrap (cling film), and chill in the refrigerator for 30 minutes. • Preheat the oven to 350°F (180°C/gas 4). • Butter two baking sheets. • Roll out the dough on a lightly floured surface to 1/8 inch (3 mm) thick. • Use a 2-inch (5-cm) cookie cutter to cut out the cookies. Gather the dough scraps, re-roll, and continue cutting out cookies until all the dough is used. • Use a spatula to transfer the cookies to the prepared baking sheets, placing them 1 inch (2.5 cm) apart. • Bake until just golden at the edges, 6–8 minutes. • Cool on the baking sheets for 5 minutes, then transfer to wire racks to cool completely. • Filling: Bring the cream to a boil in a small saucepan over low heat. • Remove from the heat and stir in the white chocolate. Stir in the mint extract. • Cool until firm but not set, about 30 minutes. • Stick the cookies together in pairs with the filling. • Glaze: Melt the chocolate and butter in a double boiler over barely simmering water. • Spread on top of the cookies. Chill in the refrigerator until set, about 30 minutes.

Cookies

- 1 cup (150 g) all-purpose (plain) flour
- 2 tablespoons unsweetened cocoa powder
- 1/8 teaspoon salt
- 1/2 cup (125 g) butter, softened
- 1/4 cup (50 g) granulated sugar
- 1 teaspoon mint extract (essence)
- 1 large egg

Filling

- 1/2 cup (125 ml) heavy (double) cream
- 8 oz (250 g) white chocolate, coarsely chopped
- 1 teaspoon mint extract (essence)

Glaze

- 5 oz (150 g) bittersweet (dark) chocolate, coarsely chopped
- 1/3 cup (90 g) butter

Makes: about 24
Preparation: 40 minutes + 90 minutes to chill
Cooking: 8–10 minutes
Level: 2

PIPED BUTTER AND CHOCOLATE COOKIES

Preheat the oven to 350°F (180°C/gas 4). • Butter three baking sheets. • Mix the flour and cornstarch in a medium bowl. • Beat the butter and confectioners' sugar in a large bowl with an electric mixer at high speed until pale and creamy. • Add the egg, beating until just blended. Stir in the vanilla and lemon extracts. Continue beating until pale and fluffy. • With mixer on low speed, beat in the mixed dry ingredients. • Divide the dough evenly between two bowls. • Mix the cocoa and oil in a small bowl. Stir the cocoa mixture into one bowl of the dough. • Fit a pastry bag with a $1/4$-inch (5-mm) star tip. Fill the pastry bag with the plain batter, twist the opening tightly closed, and pipe out small rings, hearts, circles, and swirls, spacing $1^1/2$ inches (4 cm) apart on the prepared baking sheets. • Repeat with the chocolate batter. • Bake, one sheet at a time, until the plain cookies are golden brown, 10–15 minutes. • Cool the cookies on the baking sheets for 2 minutes. Transfer to wire racks to cool completely.

2 cups (300 g) all-purpose (plain) flour

$1/3$ cup (50 g) cornstarch (cornflour)

1 cup (250 g) butter, softened

$2/3$ cup (100 g) confectioners' (icing) sugar

1 large egg

$1/2$ teaspoon vanilla extract (essence)

$1/4$ teaspoon lemon extract (essence)

2 tablespoons unsweetened cocoa powder

1 teaspoon vegetable oil

Makes: about 25
Preparation: 25 minutes
Cooking: 10–15 minutes
Level: 2

CHOCOLATE OATY KISSES

Cookies: Preheat the oven to 350°F (180°C/gas 4). • Butter two baking sheets. • Mix the flour, cocoa, baking powder, and salt in a medium bowl. • Beat the butter, lard, and sugar in a large bowl with an electric mixer at high speed until pale and creamy. • With mixer on low speed, beat in the mixed dry ingredients, followed by the oats and corn syrup mixture. • Form the dough into balls the size of walnuts and place 1 inch (2.5 cm) apart on the prepared baking sheets, flattening them slightly. • Bake until firm to the touch, 20–25 minutes.
• Cool on the baking sheets for 5 minutes. Transfer to wire racks to cool. • Filling: Beat the butter and confectioners' sugar in a small bowl until creamy.
• Mix in the cocoa and vanilla. • Stick the cookies together in pairs with the chocolate filling.

Cookies

1½ cups (225 g) all-purpose (plain) flour

2 tablespoons unsweetened cocoa powder

½ teaspoon baking powder

⅛ teaspoon salt

½ cup (125 g) butter, softened

½ cup (125 g) lard or vegetable shortening, softened

½ cup (100 g) granulated sugar

1 cup (150 g) old-fashioned rolled oats

¼ cup (60 g) light corn syrup (golden syrup) dissolved in 1 tablespoon hot water

Filling

¼ cup (60 g) butter, softened

⅓ cup (75 g) confectioners' (icing) sugar

2 tablespoons unsweetened cocoa powder

½ teaspoon vanilla extract (essence)

Makes: about 16
Preparation: 25 minutes
Cooking: 20–25 minutes
Level: 1

WHITE FLORENTINES

Preheat the oven to 325°F (170°C/gas 3). • Line four baking sheets with parchment paper. • Heat the cream with the vanilla pod, butter, and sugar in a medium saucepan over medium heat, stirring constantly, until the sugar has dissolved. Bring to a boil and remove from the heat immediately. Discard the vanilla pod and let cool. • Mix the almonds, hazelnuts, candied peel, cherries, angelica, and flour in a large bowl. • Add the cooled cream mixture and mix well. • Drop tablespoons of the mixture 4 inches (10 cm) apart on the prepared baking sheets, flattening them to make 2-inch (5 cm) circles. Do not place more than five cookies on each sheet. • Bake, one sheet at a time, until golden around the edges, 10–12 minutes. • Cool on the sheets until the cookies firm slightly, about 5 minutes. Transfer to racks and let cool completely. • Melt the white chocolate in a double boiler over barely simmering water. • Lay the cooled florentines flat-side upward on a sheet of waxed paper, and spread the chocolate over them with a pastry brush. For a thick coating, paint the cookies several times.

½ cup (125 ml) heavy (double) cream

¼ vanilla pod

2 tablespoons butter

½ cup (100 g) granulated sugar

½ cup (50 g) coarsely chopped almonds

¼ cup (30 g) coarsely chopped hazelnuts

1 cup (100 g) finely chopped mixed candied peel

¼ cup (25 g) finely sliced red candied cherries

1 tablespoon finely chopped candied angelica

3 tablespoons all-purpose (plain) flour

8 oz (250 g) white chocolate, coarsely chopped

Makes: about 20
Preparation: 45 minutes
Cooking: 10–12 minutes
Level: 3

HAZELNUT FLORENTINES WITH WHITE CHOCOLATE

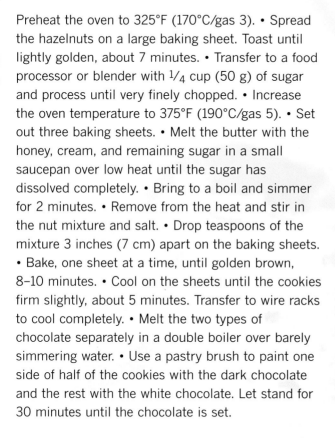

Preheat the oven to 325°F (170°C/gas 3). • Spread the hazelnuts on a large baking sheet. Toast until lightly golden, about 7 minutes. • Transfer to a food processor or blender with 1/4 cup (50 g) of sugar and process until very finely chopped. • Increase the oven temperature to 375°F (190°C/gas 5). • Set out three baking sheets. • Melt the butter with the honey, cream, and remaining sugar in a small saucepan over low heat until the sugar has dissolved completely. • Bring to a boil and simmer for 2 minutes. • Remove from the heat and stir in the nut mixture and salt. • Drop teaspoons of the mixture 3 inches (7 cm) apart on the baking sheets. • Bake, one sheet at a time, until golden brown, 8–10 minutes. • Cool on the sheets until the cookies firm slightly, about 5 minutes. Transfer to wire racks to cool completely. • Melt the two types of chocolate separately in a double boiler over barely simmering water. • Use a pastry brush to paint one side of half of the cookies with the dark chocolate and the rest with the white chocolate. Let stand for 30 minutes until the chocolate is set.

1   lb (500 g) hazelnuts

1   cup (200 g) granulated sugar

1   cup (250 g) butter, softened

½   cup (125 g) honey

½   cup (125 ml) heavy (double) cream

⅛   teaspoon salt

6   oz (180 g) white chocolate, coarsely chopped

6   oz (180 g) semisweet (dark) chocolate, coarsely chopped

Makes: about 35
Preparation: 40 minutes
   + 30 minutes to set
Cooking: 8–10 minutes
Level: 3

CHOCOLATE BANANA CHIP COOKIES

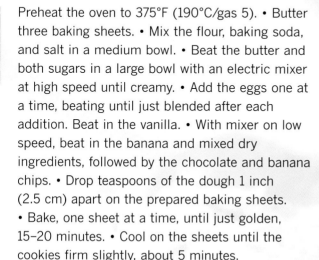

Preheat the oven to 375°F (190°C/gas 5). • Butter three baking sheets. • Mix the flour, baking soda, and salt in a medium bowl. • Beat the butter and both sugars in a large bowl with an electric mixer at high speed until creamy. • Add the eggs one at a time, beating until just blended after each addition. Beat in the vanilla. • With mixer on low speed, beat in the banana and mixed dry ingredients, followed by the chocolate and banana chips. • Drop teaspoons of the dough 1 inch (2.5 cm) apart on the prepared baking sheets. • Bake, one sheet at a time, until just golden, 15–20 minutes. • Cool on the sheets until the cookies firm slightly, about 5 minutes. Transfer to racks and let cool completely.

2⅓ cups (350 g) all-purpose (plain) flour

1 teaspoon baking soda (bicarbonate of soda)

⅛ teaspoon salt

1 cup (250 g) butter, softened

¾ cup (150 g) firmly packed dark brown sugar

½ cup (100 g) granulated sugar

1 teaspoon vanilla extract (essence)

2 large eggs

1 large banana, peeled and mashed

½ cup (125 g) semisweet (dark) chocolate chips

½ cup (50 g) coarsely chopped dried banana chips

Makes: about 36
Preparation: 20 minutes
Cooking: 15–20 minutes
Level: 1

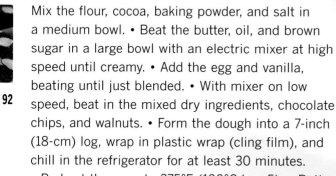

WHITE CHOCOLATE CHIP REFRIGERATOR COOKIES

Mix the flour, cocoa, baking powder, and salt in a medium bowl. • Beat the butter, oil, and brown sugar in a large bowl with an electric mixer at high speed until creamy. • Add the egg and vanilla, beating until just blended. • With mixer on low speed, beat in the mixed dry ingredients, chocolate chips, and walnuts. • Form the dough into a 7-inch (18-cm) log, wrap in plastic wrap (cling film), and chill in the refrigerator for at least 30 minutes. • Preheat the oven to 375°F (190°C/gas 5). • Butter two baking sheets. • Slice the dough 1/4 inch (5-mm) thick and place each slice 2 inches (5 cm) apart on the prepared baking sheets. • Bake until just golden at the edges, 8–10 minutes. • Let cool slightly on the baking sheets, about 5 minutes. Transfer to wire racks to cool completely.

1½ cups (250 g) all-purpose (plain) flour

¼ cup (30 g) unsweetened cocoa powder

1½ teaspoons baking powder

¼ teaspoon salt

½ cup (125 g) butter, softened

¼ cup (60 ml) sunflower or peanut oil

¾ cup (150 g) firmly packed light brown sugar

1 large egg

½ teaspoon vanilla extract (essence)

1 cup (180 g) white chocolate chips

1 cup (100 g) chopped walnuts

Makes: about 28
Preparation: 40 minutes
+ 30 minutes to chill
Cooking: 8–10 minutes
Level: 1

BLACK AND WHITE REFRIGERATOR COOKIES

Light Dough: Mix the flour, baking powder, and salt in a medium bowl. • Beat the butter and shortening with an electric mixer at medium speed. Add both sugars and beat until fluffy. Add the vanilla and egg yolk and beat until just combined. • With mixer on low speed, beat in the dry ingredients.

Chocolate Dough: Mix the flour, cocoa, baking soda, and salt in a medium bowl. • Beat the butter and shortening with an electric mixer at medium speed. Add both sugars and beat until fluffy. • Add the egg and beat until just combined. • With mixer on low speed, beat in the dry ingredients.

Make some or all of the following cookie designs from the doughs.

Checkerboard Cookies: Transfer the light dough to a large sheet of plastic wrap (cling film). Shape into a 2 x 9 inch (5 x 23 cm) log. Wrap tightly and chill in the refrigerator until firm, about 2 hours. • Repeat the shaping and chilling with the chocolate dough. • Slice both doughs lengthways into halves or thirds. Place the strips side by side to form 2 logs, alternating the 2 colors. Wrap each log tightly in plastic wrap. Chill in the refrigerator overnight. • Preheat the oven to 350°F (180°C/ gas 4). • Butter two baking sheets. • Slice the logs into 1/4-inch (5-mm) thick cookies. Arrange on the baking sheets, 1 inch (2.5 cm) apart. Bake until firm to the touch, 8 minutes. Cool on wire racks.

Light Dough

1 1/3 cups (200 g) all-purpose (plain) flour

1/2 teaspoon baking powder

1/4 teaspoon salt

1/2 cup (125 g) butter, softened

1/4 cup (60 g) vegetable shortening

1/2 cup (100 g) granulated sugar

1/2 cup (100 g) firmly packed brown sugar

1/2 teaspoon vanilla extract (essence)

1 large egg yolk

Chocolate Dough

1 cup (150 g) all-purpose (plain) flour

1/4 cup (30 g) unsweetened cocoa powder

1/2 teaspoon baking soda (bicarbonate of soda)

1/4 teaspoon salt

1/2 cup (125 g) butter, softened

1/4 cup (60 g) vegetable shortening

1/2 cup (100 g) granulated sugar

1/2 cup (100 g) firmly packed brown sugar

1 large egg

Pinwheels: Transfer the light dough to a large sheet of plastic wrap (cling film). Shape into a rectangle 1 inch (2.5 cm) thick. Wrap tightly and chill in the refrigerator until firm, about 2 hours. • Repeat the same shaping and wrapping for the chocolate dough. • Place the light dough between two sheets of plastic wrap and roll into a 12 x 16 inch (20 x 40 cm) rectangle. Remove the plastic wrap from the top. • Repeat for the chocolate dough. • Place the sheet of light dough, uncovered side down, over the chocolate dough. Remove the top layer of plastic. Using the bottom layer of plastic wrap, roll the two sheets of dough together jelly-roll fashion. Cut the roll in half to make two 8-inch (20-cm) long rolls. Wrap in plastic wrap and chill in the refrigerator overnight. • Slice and bake as for Checkerboards.

Mosaic Hearts: Divide the light dough in two equal portions. Place each half on a sheet of plastic wrap. Shape into a 2-inch (5-cm) round log. Wrap tightly and chill in the refrigerator until firm, about 2 hours. • Repeat with the chocolate dough. • Cut each log into $1/4$-inch (5-mm) thick slices. Use a small cookie cutter to remove a heart-shape from the center of each cookie. Place light centers in the dark cookies, and vice versa. Bake as for Checkerboards.

Makes: about 70
Preparation: 45 minutes
  + overnight to chill
Cooking: 10–12 minutes
Level: 2

ALMOND CHOCOLATE CHIP COOKIES

Preheat the oven to 325°F (170°C/gas 3).
• Butter two baking sheets. • Mix the flour and confectioners' sugar in a large bowl. • With an electric mixer at medium speed, beat in the butter and egg yolk until well blended. • Mix in the almond extract, almonds, and chocolate chips. • Form the dough into balls the size of walnuts and place 1 inch (2.5 cm) apart on the prepared baking sheets. • Bake until just golden, 15–20 minutes.
• Cool on the sheets until the cookies firm slightly, about 5 minutes. Transfer to wire racks to cool completely.

1²/₃ cups (250 g) all-purpose (plain) flour

³/₄ cup (125 g) confectioners' (icing) sugar

1 cup (250 g) butter, softened

1 large egg yolk

½ teaspoon almond extract (essence)

1 cup (100 g) finely chopped almonds

½ cup (90 g) semisweet (dark) chocolate chips

Makes: about 30
Preparation: 25 minutes
Cooking: 15–20 minutes
Level: 1

CHOCOLATE AND BUTTER WHEEL COOKIES

Mix the flour, baking powder, and salt in a large bowl. • Cut in the butter until the mixture resembles fine crumbs. • Mix in the brown sugar, egg, and rum and vanilla extracts. Divide the dough in half. Wrap each piece in plastic wrap (cling film) and chill in the refrigerator for 30 minutes. • Melt the chocolate in a double boiler over simmering water. Mix in the vanilla sugar, cocoa, and milk. • Take one half of the dough and knead in the chocolate mixture. • Form the chocolate dough into a 9-inch (23-cm) log. Chill in the refrigerator for 30 minutes. • Roll out the plain dough on a work surface to fit around the chocolate roll. Wrap the plain dough around the chilled chocolate dough to form a larger roll. • Chill in the refrigerator for 20 minutes. • Preheat the oven to 350°F (180°C/gas 4). • Butter two baking sheets. • Cut into the log $1/4$-inch (5-mm) thick slices and place 1 inch (2.5 cm) apart on the prepared baking sheets. • Bake until lightly browned, 12–15 minutes. • Let cool on the baking sheets until slightly firm, about 5 minutes. Transfer to wire racks to cool completely.

$1^2/_3$ cups (250 g) all-purpose (plain) flour

1 teaspoon baking powder

$1/_8$ teaspoon salt

$2/_3$ cup (150 g) butter

$3/_4$ cup (150 g) firmly packed light brown sugar

1 large egg, lightly beaten

2 teaspoons rum extract (essence)

1 teaspoon vanilla extract (essence)

2 oz (60 g) semisweet (dark) chocolate, coarsely chopped

2 tablespoons vanilla sugar

4 tablespoons unsweetened cocoa powder

$1^1/_2$ tablespoons milk

Makes: about 36
Preparation: 45 minutes
   + 1 hour 20 minutes
   to chill
Cooking: 12–15 minutes
Level: 2

CHOCOLATE ARCHES

Mix the flour, cornmeal, cornstarch, and salt in a large bowl. • Stir in the sugar and vanilla. • Add the eggs one at a time, beating until just blended after each addition. • Stir in the butter to form a stiff dough. • Cover with a clean kitchen towel and let stand for 30 minutes. • Preheat the oven to 400°F (200°C/gas 6). • Butter two baking sheets. • Fit a pastry bag with a 1/2-inch (1-cm) star tip. Fill the pastry bag, twist the opening tightly closed, and squeeze out 4-inch (10-cm) long arches (horseshoes) spacing them 2 inches (5 cm) apart on the prepared baking sheets. • Bake until just golden, 10–15 minutes. • Cool the cookies completely on the baking sheets. • Melt the chocolate in a double boiler over barely simmering water. • Dip the cookies into the chocolate and let stand until set, about 30 minutes.

- ³/₄ cup (125 g) all-purpose (plain) flour
- ³/₄ cup (125 g) finely ground yellow cornmeal
- ¹/₃ cup (50 g) cornstarch (cornflour)
- ¹/₈ teaspoon salt
- ¹/₃ cup (70 g) granulated sugar
- ¹/₂ teaspoon vanilla extract (essence)
- 2 large eggs
- ²/₃ cup (150 g) butter, softened
- 8 oz (250 g) semisweet (dark) chocolate, coarsely chopped

Makes: about 22
Preparation: 30 minutes
  + 30 minutes to set
Cooking: 10–15 minutes
Level: 2

CHOCOLATE COCONUT SPRITZ COOKIES

Preheat the oven to 325°F (170°C/gas 3). • Butter four baking sheets. • Mix the flour and salt in a medium bowl. • Beat the butter and sugar in a large bowl with an electric mixer at high speed until pale and creamy. • Add the egg and vanilla, beating until just blended. • With mixer at low speed, beat in the dry ingredients and lemon zest to form a stiff dough. • Insert the chosen design plate into a cookie press by sliding it into the head and locking in place. Press out the cookies, spacing about 1 inch (2.5 cm) apart on the prepared baking sheets. • Bake, one sheet at a time, until golden brown, 10–15 minutes. • Transfer to racks to cool. • Melt the chocolate in a double boiler over barely simmering water. • Spread the melted chocolate over the tops of the cookies and sprinkle with the coconut. Let stand for 30 minutes until set.

$3\frac{1}{3}$ cups (500 g) all-purpose (plain) flour

$\frac{1}{8}$ teaspoon salt

1 cup (250 g) butter, softened

$1\frac{1}{4}$ cups (250 g) granulated sugar

1 large egg

$\frac{1}{2}$ teaspoon vanilla extract (essence)

Grated zest of 1 lemon

8 oz (250 g) semisweet (dark) chocolate, coarsely chopped

$\frac{3}{4}$ cup (90 g) shredded (desiccated) coconut

Makes: about 60
Preparation: 40 minutes
 + 30 minutes to set
Cooking: 10–15 minutes
Level: 2

■■■ *You will need a cookie press—also known as a cookie gun—to make these cookies.*

GLAZED COOKIE STICKS

Preheat the oven to 350°F (180°C/gas 4). • Line two baking sheets with parchment paper. • Mix the flour, cornstarch, and salt in a medium bowl. • Beat the butter, confectioners' sugar, and vanilla in a large bowl with an electric mixer at high speed until creamy. • With mixer on low speed, beat in the mixed dry ingredients. • Fit a pastry bag with a 1/2-inch (1-cm) tip. Fill the pastry bag, twist opening tightly closed, and squeeze out 3-inch (7-cm) logs, spacing 2 inches (5 cm) apart on the prepared baking sheets. • Bake until just golden at and firm to the touch, 12–15 minutes. • Transfer to racks to cool. • Melt the semisweet and white chocolate separately in double boilers over barely simmering water. • Spoon the chocolates into separate small freezer bags and cut off tiny corners. • Drizzle over the cookies in a decorative manner. • Let stand for 30 minutes until set.

1 cup (150 g) all-purpose (plain) flour

1/2 cup (75 g) cornstarch (cornflour)

1/8 teaspoon salt

3/4 cup (180 g) butter, softened

1/3 cup (50 g) confectioners' (icing) sugar

1/2 teaspoon vanilla extract (essence)

2 oz (60 g) semisweet (dark) chocolate, coarsely chopped

2 oz (60 g) white chocolate, coarsely chopped

Makes: about 20
Preparation: 30 minutes
  + 30 minutes to set
Cooking: 12–15 minutes
Level: 3

CARAMEL COOKIES

Mix the flour, baking powder, baking soda, and salt in a medium bowl. • Beat the butter and both brown sugars in a large bowl with an electric mixer at high speed until creamy. • Add the eggs one at a time, beating until just blended. • With mixer on low speed, beat in the mixed dry ingredients, chocolates, banana chips, and milk. • Divide the dough in two. Form into two 8-inch (20-cm) logs, wrap in plastic wrap (cling film), and chill in the refrigerator for at least 2 hours. • Preheat the oven to 350°F (180°C/gas 4). • Line two baking sheets with parchment paper. • Slice the dough $1/2$ inch (1 cm) thick and place 1 inch (2.5 cm) apart on the prepared baking sheets. • Bake until the edges are firm and the centers are still slightly soft, 15–18 minutes. • Cool on the sheets until the cookies firm slightly, about 5 minutes. Transfer to wire racks to cool completely.

$2^2/_3$ cups (400 g) all-purpose (plain) flour

1 teaspoon baking powder

$1/2$ teaspoon baking soda (bicarbonate of soda)

$1/4$ teaspoon salt

$3/4$ cup (180 g) butter, softened

$3/4$ cup (150 g) firmly packed light brown sugar

2 tablespoons firmly packed dark brown sugar

2 large eggs

8 oz (250 g) caramel-filled chocolates, such as Rolos, chopped

3 oz (90 g) dried banana chips, coarsely chopped

2 tablespoons milk

Makes: about 35
Preparation: 1 hour
    + 2 hours to chill
Cooking: 15–18 minutes
Level: 1

CHOCOLATE CHIP PECAN SHORTBREAD

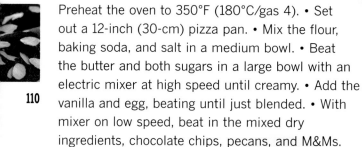

110

Preheat the oven to 350°F (180°C/gas 4). • Set out a 12-inch (30-cm) pizza pan. • Mix the flour, baking soda, and salt in a medium bowl. • Beat the butter and both sugars in a large bowl with an electric mixer at high speed until creamy. • Add the vanilla and egg, beating until just blended. • With mixer on low speed, beat in the mixed dry ingredients, chocolate chips, pecans, and M&Ms. • Spread the mixture in the pan. • Bake until lightly browned, 12–15 minutes. • Cool completely in the pan. • Cut into wedges.

2 cups (300 g) all-purpose (plain) flour

1 teaspoon baking soda (bicarbonate of soda)

⅛ teaspoon salt

½ cup (125 g) butter, softened

⅓ cup (80 g) granulated sugar

½ cup (100 g) firmly packed light brown sugar

½ teaspoon vanilla extract (essence)

1 large egg

¾ cup (125 g) semisweet (dark) chocolate chips

½ cup (50 g) finely chopped pecans

½ cup (50 g) M&Ms

Makes: about 16
Preparation: 20 minutes
Cooking: 12–15 minutes
Level: 1

SHORTBREAD WITH PASSION FRUIT DRIZZLE

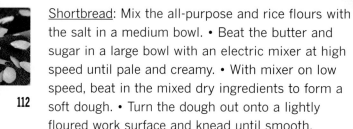

Shortbread: Mix the all-purpose and rice flours with the salt in a medium bowl. • Beat the butter and sugar in a large bowl with an electric mixer at high speed until pale and creamy. • With mixer on low speed, beat in the mixed dry ingredients to form a soft dough. • Turn the dough out onto a lightly floured work surface and knead until smooth. • Press the dough into a disk, wrap in plastic wrap (cling film), and chill in the refrigerator for 30 minutes. • Preheat the oven to 300°F (150°C/gas 2). • Butter four baking sheets. • Roll out the dough on a lightly floured work surface to $1/4$ inch (5 mm) thick. • Cut into $1^1/_2$-inch (4-cm) diamond shapes. • Use a spatula to transfer the cookies to the prepared baking sheets, placing them 1 inch (2.5 cm) apart. • Bake until just golden at the edges, 12–15 minutes. • Transfer to racks to cool.
Passion Fruit Drizzle: Mix the confectioners' sugar, passionfruit pulp, butter, and water in a double boiler over barely simmering water until smooth. • Cover the tops of the cookies with the icing. • Let stand for 30 minutes until set. • Melt the white chocolate in a double boiler over barely simmering water and drizzle over the cookies. Let stand for 30 minutes.

Shortbread

2   cups (300 g) all-purpose flour
$1/3$ cup (75 g) rice flour
$1/8$ teaspoon salt
1   cup (250 g) butter, softened
$1/3$ cup (75 g) granulated sugar

Passion Fruit Drizzle

1   cup (150 g) confectioners' (icing) sugar
2   tablespoons strained passion fruit pulp
1   tablespoon butter, softened
1   tablespoon cold water
2   oz (60 g) white chocolate, coarsely chopped

Makes: about 35
Preparation: 40 minutes
    + 1 hour 30 minutes
    to chill and set
Cooking: 12–15 minutes
Level: 2

GLAZED MOCHA COOKIES

Cookies: Melt the chocolate in a double boiler over barely simmering water. • Mix the flour, cocoa, espresso powder, baking soda, and salt in a medium bowl. • Beat the butter and brown sugar in a large bowl with an electric mixer at high speed until creamy. • Add the egg and vanilla and beat for 1 minute. With mixer on low speed, beat in the mixed dry ingredients and chocolate. • Divide the dough in two. Form into two 9 x 2-inch (23 x 5-cm) logs, wrap in plastic wrap (cling film), and chill in the refrigerator for at least 2 hours. • Preheat the oven to 350°F (180°C/gas 4). • Butter two baking sheets. • Slice the dough $2/3$ inch (1.5 cm) thick and place 1 inch (2.5 cm) apart on the prepared baking sheets. • Bake until the edges are firm and the bottoms lightly browned, 12–15 minutes. • Cool on the baking sheets until the cookies firm slightly, about 5 minutes. Transfer to wire racks to cool completely. • Glaze: Mix the confectioners' sugar and coffee in a small bowl. Stir in enough hot water to obtain a drizzling consistency. • Drizzle over the cookies and let set.

Cookies

3   oz (90 g) semisweet (dark) chocolate, coarsely chopped

1   cup (150 g) all-purpose (plain) flour

2   tablespoons unsweetened cocoa powder

1   teaspoon espresso coffee powder

1   teaspoon baking soda (bicarbonate of soda)

¼   teaspoon salt

⅔   cup (150 g) butter, softened

½   cup (100 g) firmly packed light brown sugar

1   large egg, lightly beaten

1   teaspoon vanilla extract (essence)

Glaze

1⅓ cups (200 g) confectioners' (icing) sugar

1   teaspoon espresso coffee powder

2   tablespoons hot water

Makes: about 22
Preparation: 45 minutes
   + 2 hours to chill
Cooking: 12–15 minutes
Level: 2

STRIPED COOKIES

Line an 8$\frac{1}{2}$ x 4$\frac{1}{2}$-inch (21 x 11-cm) loaf pan with parchment paper. • Mix the flour, baking powder, and salt in a medium bowl. • Beat the butter and sugar in a large bowl with an electric mixer at high speed until pale and creamy. • Add the vanilla and egg yolk, beating until just combined. • With mixer on low speed, beat in the mixed dry ingredients. • Divide the dough evenly among three bowls. • Melt the chocolate in a double boiler over barely simmering water. • Add the almond extract to the first bowl, the chocolate to the second bowl, and the walnuts to the third bowl. • Spread the almond mixture in the pan, followed by the chocolate mixture. Finish with the walnut mixture. • Cover with plastic wrap (cling film) and chill in the refrigerator for 4 hours. • Preheat the oven to 350°F (180°C/gas 4). • Butter four baking sheets. • Cut the dough into $\frac{1}{4}$-inch (5-mm) thick slices. • Place 1 inch (2.5 cm) apart on the sheets. • Bake until lightly browned, 10–12 minutes. • Let cool on the baking sheets for 5 minutes. Transfer to wire racks to cool completely.

1$\frac{1}{3}$ cups (200 g) all-purpose (plain) flour

1 teaspoon baking powder

$\frac{1}{8}$ teaspoon salt

$\frac{1}{2}$ cup (125 g) butter, softened

$\frac{1}{2}$ cup (100 g) granulated sugar

1 teaspoon vanilla extract (essence)

1 large egg yolk

1 oz (30 g) semisweet (dark) chocolate, coarsely chopped

$\frac{1}{2}$ teaspoon almond extract (essence)

$\frac{2}{3}$ cup (70 g) finely chopped walnuts

Makes: about 40
Preparation: 40 minutes
+ 4 hours to chill
Cooking: 10–12 minutes
Level: 2

CHOCOLATE DRIZZLERS

Melt the chocolate in a double boiler over barely simmering water. • Mix the flour, cocoa, baking powder, baking soda, and salt in a medium bowl. • Beat the butter and sugar in a large bowl until pale and creamy. • Add the egg, beating until just blended. • With mixer on low speed, beat in 5 oz (150 g) of the melted chocolate and the vanilla. • Beat in the mixed dry ingredients. • Divide the dough in two. Form into two logs 2 inches (5 cm) in diameter, wrap in parchment paper, and freeze for at least 4 hours. • Preheat the oven to 350°F (180°C/gas 4). • Line two baking sheets with parchment paper. • Slice the dough 1/4 inch (5 mm) thick and place 1 inch (2.5 cm) apart on the prepared baking sheets. • Bake until lightly browned, 10–12 minutes. • Transfer the cookies to wire racks to cool. • Melt the white chocolate in a double boiler over barely simmering water. • Drizzle the remaining semisweet and white chocolate over the cookies.

8 oz (250 g) semisweet (dark) chocolate

2¼ cups (330 g) all-purpose (plain) flour

⅓ cup (50 g) unsweetened cocoa powder

½ teaspoon baking powder

½ teaspoon baking soda (bicarbonate of soda)

⅛ teaspoon salt

¾ cup (180 g) butter, softened

1 cup (200 g) granulated sugar

1 large egg

1 teaspoon vanilla extract (essence)

3 oz (90 g) white chocolate, melted

Makes: about 30
Preparation: 40 minutes
  + 4 hours to freeze
Cooking: 10–12 minutes
Level: 1

CHOCOLATE OAT COOKIES

Preheat the oven to 350°F (180°C/gas 4). • Set out two baking sheets. • Stir together the oats, both sugars, flour, and salt in a large bowl. • Make a well in the center and stir in the butter, egg, and vanilla. • Stir in the chocolate chips, mixing until well combined. • Drop teaspoons of the dough 3 inches (7 cm) apart onto the baking sheets. • Bake until lightly browned, 8–10 minutes. • Let cool on the baking sheets until the cookies firm slightly, about 5 minutes. Transfer to wire racks and let cool completely.

2¼ cups (330 g) old-fashioned rolled oats

1 cup (200 g) firmly packed dark brown sugar

½ cup (100 g) granulated sugar

2 cups (300 g) all-purpose (plain) flour

¼ teaspoon salt

1⅓ cups (330 g) butter, melted

1 large egg, lightly beaten

1 teaspoon vanilla extract (essence)

½ cup (90 g) semisweet (dark) chocolate chips

Makes: about 30
Preparation: 20 minutes
Cooking: 8–10 minutes
Level: 1

CHOCOLATE ALMOND MERINGUES

Preheat the oven to 250°F (130°C/gas 1). • Line two baking sheets with parchment paper. • Beat the egg whites and salt in a large bowl with an electric mixer at medium-high speed until soft peaks form, about 3 minutes. • Reduce speed to medium and gradually add the sugar. Beat until the sugar has dissolved and stiff peaks form, about 3 minutes. • Use a rubber spatula to fold in the chocolate, almonds, and orange zest. • Drop walnut-sized portions of batter onto the prepared baking sheets about 1 inch (2.5 cm) apart. • Bake until the meringues seem set and are just beginning to turn pale gold, 45–50 minutes. Turn the oven off, leaving the meringues inside until they are completely dry (break one to test).

4 large egg whites, at room temperature

1/8 teaspoon salt

3/4 cup (150 g) granulated sugar

4 oz (125 g) bittersweet (dark) chocolate, finely chopped or grated

1 cup (100 g) toasted almonds, flaked

2 teaspoons finely grated orange zest

Makes: about 36
Preparation: 30 minutes
Cooking: 45–50 minutes
Level: 1

CHOCOLATE MERINGUES

Preheat the oven to 250°F (130°C/gas 1/2). • Line two baking sheets with parchment paper. • Beat the egg whites and salt in a large bowl with an electric mixer at medium speed until frothy. • With mixer at high speed, gradually add the sugar, beating until stiff, glossy peaks form. • Fold in the cocoa, cinnamon, and almond extract. • Fit a pastry bag with a 1 1/2-inch (4-cm) star tip. Fill the pastry bag, twist the opening tightly closed, and squeeze out generous rosettes spacing 1 inch (2.5 cm) apart on the prepared baking sheets. • Bake until crisp and dry to the touch, 50–60 minutes. • Turn the oven off, leaving the meringues inside until they are completely dry (break one to test).

2 **large egg whites**

1/8 **teaspoon salt**

3/4 **cup (150 g) superfine (caster) sugar**

1/3 **cup (50 g) unsweetened cocoa powder**

1/2 **teaspoon ground cinnamon**

1/2 **teaspoon almond extract (essence)**

Makes: about 28
Preparation: 25 minutes
Cooking: 50–60 minutes
Level: 2

CHOCOLATE MARSHMALLOW COOKIES

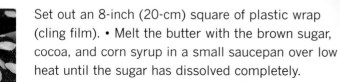

Set out an 8-inch (20-cm) square of plastic wrap (cling film). • Melt the butter with the brown sugar, cocoa, and corn syrup in a small saucepan over low heat until the sugar has dissolved completely.
• Melt the chocolate in a double boiler over barely simmering water. Stir the chocolate into the butter mixture. Mix in the marshmallows and raisins.
• Spoon the mixture onto the center of the plastic wrap. Roll the mixture to form a cylinder. • Chill in the refrigerator until firm, at least 4 hours. • Cut into rounds and place in mini paper cups to serve.

½ cup (125 g) butter, cut up

1 tablespoon dark brown sugar

⅓ cup (50 g) unsweetened cocoa powder

2 tablespoons light corn syrup (golden syrup)

8 oz (250 g) semisweet (dark) chocolate, coarsely chopped

2 cups (250 g) marshmallows, mixed colors, chopped

1 cup (180 g) raisins

Makes: about 20
Preparation: 25 minutes
    + 4 hours to chill
Level: 1

CHOCOLATE ALMOND MICE

Melt the chocolate with the cream in a double boiler over barely simmering water. • Remove from the heat and stir in the chocolate wafer crumbs. • Cover with plastic wrap (cling film) and refrigerate until firm, 1 hour. • Form the dough into balls the size of golf balls, tapering one end to resemble the nose. • Roll the large back half of each ball in the confectioners' sugar until well coated. • Decorate all with the silver balls to resemble the eyes, almonds for ears, and a small length of licorice for the tail. • Chill in the refrigerator for 2 hours.

5 oz (150 g) semisweet (dark) chocolate, coarsely chopped

⅓ cup (90 ml) heavy (double) cream

1 cup (125 g) chocolate wafer crumbs (plain chocolate biscuit crumbs)

⅓ cup (50 g) confectioners' (icing) sugar

24 silver balls, to decorate

24 flaked almonds, to decorate

Red licorice whips, to decorate

Makes: about 12
Preparation: 20 minutes + 3 hours to chill
Level: 1

CHOCOLATE FRUIT SALAMI

130

Stir together the graham cracker crumbs, almonds, apricots, candied cherries, and chocolate chips in a large bowl. • Melt the semisweet chocolate with the butter in a double boiler over barely simmering water. Remove from the heat and let cool for 5 minutes. • Pour the chocolate mixture into the graham cracker mixture and mix well. • Turn the mixture onto a sheet of plastic wrap (cling film) and form into a 10-inch (25-cm) long log. • Wrap in the plastic wrap and chill in the refrigerator for 12 hours. • Slice the log 1/2-inch (1-cm) thick. • Melt the white chocolate in a double boiler over barely simmering water and drizzle over the cookies.

2/3 cup (80 g) graham cracker crumbs (crushed digestive biscuits)

1/2 cup (50 g) coarsely chopped toasted almonds

1/2 cup (50 g) finely chopped dried apricots

1/2 cup (50 g) coarsely chopped candied cherries

1/3 cup (70 g) white chocolate chips

5 oz (150 g) semisweet (dark) chocolate, coarsely chopped

1/4 cup (60 g) butter, cut up

2 oz (60 g) white chocolate, coarsely chopped

Makes: about 20
Preparation: 20 minutes
  + 12 hours to chill
Level: 1

FROSTED NO-BAKE CHOCOLATE COOKIES

132

Line four baking sheets with parchment paper.
• Melt the semisweet chocolate in a double boiler
over barely simmering water. • Mix the vanilla wafer
crumbs, pecans, condensed milk, and melted
semisweet chocolate in a large bowl until well
blended. • Form the mixture into balls the size of
walnuts and place 1 inch (2.5 cm) apart on the
prepared baking sheets, flattening them slightly.
• Chill in the refrigerator until firm, about 30
minutes. • Melt the white chocolate in a double
boiler over barely simmering water. • Spread the
white chocolate over the tops of the cookies.
Decorate with the grated chocolate. • Let stand
for 30 minutes until set.

2　oz (60 g) semisweet
　(dark) chocolate,
　coarsely chopped

1¼ cups (150 g) vanilla
　wafer crumbs (plain
　vanilla biscuit crumbs)

½　cup (50 g) finely
　chopped pecans

1　can (14 oz/400 g)
　sweetened condensed
　milk

10 oz (300 g) white
　chocolate, coarsely
　chopped

½　cup (90 g) semisweet
　(dark) chocolate, grated

Makes: about 45
Preparation: 25 minutes
　+ 1 hour to chill and set
Level: 1

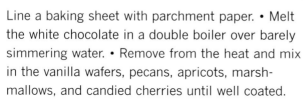

CHOCOLATE MARSHMALLOW COOKIES

Line a baking sheet with parchment paper. • Melt the white chocolate in a double boiler over barely simmering water. • Remove from the heat and mix in the vanilla wafers, pecans, apricots, marsh-mallows, and candied cherries until well coated. • Drop heaped teaspoons onto the baking sheet. • Chill in the refrigerator until set, about 1 hour. • Melt the semisweet chocolate in a double boiler over barely simmering water. Remove from the heat and dip the cookies halfway into the chocolate. • Decorate with the silver balls or sprinkle with sugar strands. • Let stand until set, about 30 minutes.

5 oz (150 g) white chocolate, coarsely chopped

2 tablespoons lightly crushed vanilla wafers (plain vanilla biscuits)

½ cup (50 g) coarsely chopped pecans

½ cup (50 g) coarsely chopped dried apricots

½ cup (50 g) marshmallows, chopped

4 candied cherries, coarsely chopped

3 oz (90 g) semisweet (dark) chocolate, coarsely chopped

Silver balls or sugar strands, jimmies, sprills, or sprinkles, to decorate

Makes: about 20
Preparation: 20 minutes
   + 1 hour 30 minutes
   to chill and set
Level: 1

BARS AND BROWNIES

BROWN SUGAR HAZELNUT BROWNIES

Preheat the oven to 350°F (180°C/gas 4). • Butter and flour an 8-inch (20-cm) square baking pan. Line with parchment paper. • Mix the flour, baking powder, and salt in a medium bowl. • Place the butter in a medium saucepan over medium heat until it begins to turn brown, 3–5 minutes. Let cool a little. • Add the egg, sugar, vanilla, and mixed dry ingredients and beat until just combined. Stir in half the chocolate and half the nuts. • Spoon the batter into the prepared pan. Sprinkle with the remaining nuts and chocolate. • Bake until the brownies are set in the middle, 25–30 minutes. A toothpick inserted into the center will come out slightly gooey. • Cool the brownies in the pan on a wire rack for at least an hour before serving.

1 **cup (150 g) all-purpose (plain) flour**

1 **teaspoon baking powder**

¼ **teaspoon salt**

¼ **cup (60 g) butter**

1 **cup (200 g) firmly packed dark brown sugar**

1 **large egg**

1 **teaspoon vanilla extract (essence)**

1 **cup (180 g) semisweet (dark) chocolate chips**

¾ **cup (100 g) coarsely chopped hazelnuts**

Makes: about 12 brownies
Preparation: 30 minutes
Cooking: 25–30 minutes
Level: 1

DOUBLE CHOCOLATE BROWNIES

Preheat the oven to 350°F (180°C/gas 4). • Butter and flour a 9 x 13-inch (33 x 23-cm) baking pan. Line with aluminum foil, leaving pieces of foil overhanging the sides. • Place the butter and bittersweet chocolate in a double boiler and stir over barely simmering water until melted. Remove from the heat and set aside to cool. • Beat the eggs and both sugars in a large bowl with an electric mixer at high speed until creamy. • With mixer on low speed, beat in the salt and chocolate mixture, followed by the vanilla. Gradually beat in the flour. Stir in the milk chocolate. • Spoon the batter into the prepared pan. • Bake until the brownies are set in the middle, 25–30 minutes. A toothpick inserted into the center will come out slightly gooey. • Cool in the pan on a wire rack for 30 minutes. • Use the overhanging foil to lift the brownies out of the pan. Remove the foil and place on a cutting board. Chill in the refrigerator for 15 minutes before cutting.

½ cup (125 g) unsalted butter

8 oz (250 g) bittersweet (dark) chocolate, coarsely chopped

4 large eggs

1¼ cups (250 g) granulated sugar

½ cup (100 g) firmly packed light brown sugar

¼ teaspoon salt

1½ teaspoons vanilla extract (essence)

1 cup (150 g) all-purpose (plain) flour

8 oz (250 g) milk chocolate, coarsely chopped

Makes: about 24 brownies
Preparation: 30 minutes
Cooking: 25–30 minutes
Level: 1

RICH CHOCOLATE LIQUEUR BARS

142

Base: Preheat the oven to 350°F (180°C/gas 4).
• Butter and flour an 8-inch (20-cm) square baking pan. Line with aluminum foil leaving it overhang the sides. • Mix the flour, cocoa, baking powder, and salt in a medium bowl. • Beat the butter and sugar in a medium bowl at high speed until pale and creamy. • Add the egg, beating until just combined. • With mixer at low speed, beat in the mixed dry ingredients. • Turn the dough out onto a lightly floured work surface and shape into a square about $^1/_2$-inch (1 cm) thick. Wrap in plastic wrap (cling film) and chill in the refrigerator for 30 minutes. • Roll the dough out into an 8-inch (20-cm) square on a work surface lightly dusted with a mixture of flour and cocoa. Place in the prepared pan and bake until puffed and firm, about 20 minutes. • Filling: Place the butter, corn syrup, milk, chocolate, sugar, and cocoa in a medium saucepan over low heat. Stir constantly until melted and smooth, about 15 minutes. • Place the cornstarch in a medium bowl and beat in the eggs. • Stir in about one-third of the chocolate mixture, whisking quickly. Add the remaining chocolate and stir until well combined. • Add the sour cream, chocolate liqueur, and vanilla. • Spoon the filling over the baked crust. Bake until set, 30–35 minutes. The top will be bubbly and slightly puffed. • Let cool on a wire rack, about 45 minutes. • Frosting: Place the chocolate in a small bowl. • Heat the white chocolate liqueur until just bubbling. Pour over the chocolate and stir until

Base

$^2/_3$ cup (100 g) all-purpose (plain) flour

3 tablespoons unsweetened cocoa powder

$^1/_2$ teaspoon baking powder

$^1/_8$ teaspoon salt

$^1/_3$ cup (90 g) butter, softened

4 tablespoons granulated sugar

1 large egg

Filling

$^2/_3$ cup (180 g) butter

3 tablespoons light corn (golden) syrup

3 tablespoons milk

2 oz (60 g) semisweet (dark) chocolate, finely chopped

1 cup (200 g) granulated sugar

1 cup (150 g) unsweetened cocoa powder

1 tablespoon cornstarch (cornflour)

4 large eggs

smooth. • Add the confectioners' sugar and beat until smooth. Add enough milk to obtain a smooth frosting that can be spread. • Remove the bars from the pan while still warm using the foil overhanging as handles. Spread with the frosting. Let set, then cut into bars.

2 **tablespoons sour cream**

2 **tablespoons chocolate liqueur**

1 **teaspoon vanilla extract (essence)**

Frosting

¼ **cup (60 ml) white chocolate liqueur**

2 **oz (60 g) white chocolate, very finely chopped**

⅔ **cup (100 g) confectioners' (icing) sugar**

1 **tablespoon milk, or more, as required**

Makes: about 16 bars
Preparation: 45 minutes
Cooking: 30–35 minutes
Level: 2

FROSTED BOURBON BROWNIES

Brownies: Preheat the oven to 325°F (170°C/gas 3). • Butter and flour a 9-inch (23-cm) square baking pan. Line with aluminum foil leaving it overhang the sides. • Mix the flour, baking soda, and salt in a small bowl. • Place the butter and sugar in a medium saucepan over low heat and stir until melted. • Remove from the heat and add the water, chocolate, and vanilla, stirring until smooth. • Add the eggs, one at a time, beating until just combined after each addition. • Stir in the mixed dry ingredients and the walnuts. • Spoon the batter into the prepared pan. • Bake until the brownies are set in the middle, 25–30 minutes. A toothpick inserted into the center will come out slightly gooey. • Place the pan on a wire rack and drizzle with the bourbon. Cool completely in the pan. • Frosting: Melt the chocolate in a double boiler over barely simmering water. • Gradually beat in the milk. Simmer, stirring constantly, until thickened. Remove from the heat and let cool completely. • Beat the butter, sugar, and vanilla in a large bowl with an electric mixer at high speed until creamy. • With mixer at medium speed, gradually beat in the cooled chocolate mixture. • Spread the brownies with the frosting. Let set before serving.

Brownies

1 cup (150 g) all-purpose (plain) flour

½ teaspoon baking soda (bicarbonate of soda)

¼ teaspoon salt

¾ cup (150 g) granulated sugar

⅓ cup (90 g) butter

2 tablespoons water

1 cup (180 g) semisweet (dark) chocolate chips

1 teaspoon vanilla extract (essence)

2 large eggs

1½ cups (150 g) coarsely chopped walnuts

¼ cup (60 ml) bourbon

Frosting

8 oz (250 g) semisweet (dark) chocolate, coarsely chopped

1 cup (250 ml) milk

1 cup (200 g) granulated sugar

1 cup (250 g) butter

1 teaspoon vanilla extract (essence)

Makes: about 16 brownies
Preparation: 15 minutes
Cooking: 30–35 minutes
Level: 1

148

CAPPUCCINO SQUARES

Preheat the oven to 325°F (170°C/gas 3). • Butter and flour a 9-inch (23-cm) square baking pan. Line with aluminum foil and butter the foil. • Melt the chocolate in a double boiler over barely simmering water. Remove from heat and let cool a little. • Beat the butter, sugar, and vanilla in a medium bowl at high speed until pale and creamy. • Add the eggs, one at a time, beating until just combined after each addition. • With mixer on low speed, beat in the flour, coffee, and salt. • Stir in the nuts and chocolate by hand. • Spoon the batter into the prepared pan. • Bake until the squares are set in the middle, 25–30 minutes. A toothpick inserted into the center will come out slightly gooey. • Place the pan on a wire rack and let cool for 15 minutes. • Heat the apricot preserves and drizzle over the cake in the pan. Let cool completely in the pan. Frosting: Beat the butter, confectioners' sugar, and vanilla in a medium bowl with an electric mixer at high speed until pale and creamy. Spread over the cooled cake. • Cut into 16–20 squares, topping each one with a coffee bean.

8 oz (250 g) bittersweet (dark) chocolate

¼ cup (60 g) butter

½ cup (100 g) firmly packed dark brown sugar

1 teaspoon vanilla extract (essence)

2 large eggs

⅔ cup (100 g) all-purpose (plain) flour

1 tablespoon dry instant coffee granules

¼ teaspoon salt

1 cup (100 g) coarsely chopped macadamia nuts

2 tablespoons apricot preserves (jam)

Frosting

8 oz (250 g) butter

2 cups (300 g) confectioners' (icing) sugar

2 teaspoons vanilla extract (essence)

16–20 coffee beans, to decorate

Makes: 16–20 squares
Preparation: 15 minutes
+ 30 minutes to cool
Cooking: 30–35 minutes
Level: 1

SPICY CHOCOLATE PUMPKIN BARS

Preheat the oven to 325°F (170°C/gas 3). • Butter and flour a 9 x 13-inch (33 x 23-cm) baking pan. Line with aluminum foil leaving it overhang the sides. • Mix the flour, cinnamon, ginger, baking soda, nutmeg, allspice, cloves, and salt in a medium bowl. • Beat the butter and sugar in a large bowl with an electric mixer at high speed until pale and creamy. • Add the egg, beating until just combined after each addition. • With mixer at low speed, beat in the pumpkin, followed by the mixed dry ingredients. • Fold in the chocolate chips by hand. • Spoon the batter into the prepared pan. • Bake until the edges begin to pull away from the sides of the pan and a toothpick inserted into the center comes out clean, 35–40 minutes. • Place the pan on a wire rack and let cool completely. • Lift out of the pan using the overhanging foil as handles and cut into bars.

2 cups (300 g) all-purpose (plain) flour

1 teaspoon ground cinnamon

1 teaspoon ground ginger,

1 teaspoon baking soda (bicarbonate of soda)

½ teaspoon nutmeg

½ teaspoon allspice

¼ teaspoon cloves

¼ teaspoon salt

1 cup (250 g) butter

1¼ cups (250 g) granulated sugar

1 large egg

2 teaspoons vanilla extract (essence)

1 cup (200 g) canned pumpkin purée

1½ cups (270 g) semisweet (dark) chocolate chips

Makes: about 24 bars
Preparation: 30 minutes
Cooking: 35–40 minutes
Level: 1

BANANA BROWNIES

Preheat the oven to 325°F (170°C/gas 3). • Butter an 11 x 7-inch (28 x 18-cm) baking pan. • Mix the flour, cocoa, baking powder, and salt in a medium bowl. • Melt the chocolate with the butter and brown sugar in a double boiler over barely simmering water. • Remove from the heat and stir in the pecans, eggs, and bananas. • Stir in the mixed dry ingredients. • Spoon the mixture into the prepared pan in an even layer. • Bake until dry on top and almost firm to the touch, 25–35 minutes. • Let cool completely before cutting.

1½ cups (225 g) all-purpose (plain) flour

2 tablespoons unsweetened cocoa powder

1 teaspoon baking powder

⅛ teaspoon salt

6 oz (180 g) semisweet (dark) chocolate, coarsely chopped

¾ cup (180 g) butter

1¼ cups (250 g) firmly packed dark brown sugar

1 cup (100 g) coarsely chopped pecans

3 large eggs, lightly beaten

2 firm-ripe bananas, mashed

Makes: about 24 brownies
Preparation: 20 minutes
Cooking: 25–35 minutes
Level: 1

CHOCOLATE ORANGE SQUARES

Base: Preheat the oven to 325°F (170°C/gas 3).
• Line an 8-inch (20-cm) square baking pan with aluminum foil, letting the edges overhang. • Mix the flour, cocoa, and salt in a medium bowl. • Beat the butter, granulated sugar, and confectioners' sugar in a large bowl with an electric mixer at high speed until pale and creamy. • With mixer on low speed, beat in the mixed dry ingredients. • Firmly press the mixture into the prepared pan in a smooth, even layer. Prick all over with a fork. • Bake until firm to the touch, 25–30 minutes. • Let cool for 10 minutes.
Filling: Mix the orange zest and juice, water, cornstarch, and lemon juice in a small saucepan over medium heat. • Bring to a boil and simmer, stirring constantly, until thickened, about 1 minute.
• Remove from the heat and stir in the butter and marmalade. • Pour the filling over the base in an even layer. • Bake for 5 minutes. • Cool completely in the pan. • Chill in the refrigerator until set, about 1 hour. • Glaze: Bring the cream to a boil with the corn syrup in a small saucepan. • Remove from the heat and stir in the chocolate until melted and smooth. • Spread over the filling in an even layer. Chill in the refrigerator for 30 minutes. • Using the foil as handles, transfer to a cutting board.
• Cut into squares.

Base

1 cup (150 g) all-purpose (plain) flour

2 tablespoons unsweetened cocoa powder

¼ teaspoon salt

1 cup (250 g) butter

⅓ cup (70 g) sugar

⅓ cup (50 g) confectioners' (icing) sugar

Filling

Finely grated zest of 1 orange

½ cup (125 ml) freshly squeezed orange juice

½ cup (125 ml) water

⅓ cup (50 g) cornstarch (cornflour)

1 teaspoon lemon juice

1 tablespoon butter

½ cup (160 g) marmalade

Glaze

3 tablespoons cream

1½ teaspoons corn syrup (golden syrup)

3 oz (90 g) semisweet (dark) chocolate, grated

Makes: about 20 squares
Preparation: 40 minutes + 1 hour 30 minutes to chill
Cooking: 35–40 minutes
Level: 2

CHOCOLATE MINT SQUARES

Base: Preheat the oven to 350°F (180°C/gas 4).
• Butter an 8-inch (20-cm) square baking pan.
• Mix the flour, cocoa, baking powder, and salt in a medium bowl. Stir in the sugar. • Cut in the butter until the mixture resembles fine crumbs. • Stir in the egg mixture. • Spoon the mixture into the prepared pan to form a smooth layer. • Bake until firm to the touch, 15–20 minutes. Let cool completely in the pan. • Filling: Place the confectioners' sugar and mint liqueur in a medium bowl and stir until well blended. • Stir in enough milk to make a creamy mixture that can be spread. • Spread the peppermint mixture over the base.
Frosting: Melt the chocolate and butter over barely simmering water. • Pour the frosting over the peppermint layer. Make a swirling pattern with a fork. • Let stand until set, about 30 minutes.
• Cut into squares.

Base

1 cup (150 g) all-purpose (plain) flour

2 tablespoons unsweetened cocoa powder

1 teaspoon baking powder

¼ teaspoon salt

⅓ cup (70 g) granulated sugar

2 tablespoons butter

1 large egg, lightly beaten with ⅓ cup (90 ml) water

Filling

2¼ cups (350 g) confectioners' (icing) sugar

1 tablespoon mint liqueur

2 tablespoons milk

Frosting

4 oz (125 g) semisweet (dark) chocolate, coarsely chopped

⅓ cup (90 g) butter

Makes: 16–20 squares
Preparation: 20 minutes
  + 30 minutes to set
Cooking: 15–20 minutes
Level: 1

RICH CHOCOLATE BROWNIES

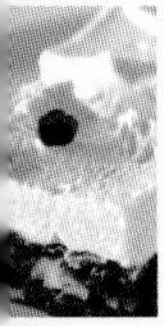

Preheat the oven to 325°F (170°C/gas 3). • Butter and flour a 13 x 9-inch (33 x 23-cm) baking pan. • Mix the flour, baking powder, and salt in a small bowl. • Melt the chocolate and butter in a double boiler over barely simmering water. Remove from the heat and let cool. • Beat the eggs, brown sugar, and vanilla in a large bowl with an electric mixer at high speed until creamy. • Use a large rubber spatula to fold in the chocolate mixture, followed by the mixed dry ingredients. • Spoon the batter into the prepared pan. • Bake until dry on top and almost firm to the touch, 35–40 minutes. Do not overbake. • Let cool completely before cutting into squares.

½ cup (75 g) all-purpose (plain) flour
½ teaspoon baking powder
⅛ teaspoon salt
6 oz (180 g) bittersweet (dark) chocolate, coarsely chopped
1 cup (250 g) butter, cut up
5 large eggs
2¼ cups (450 g) firmly packed light brown sugar
1 teaspoon vanilla extract (essence)

Makes: about 20 brownies
Preparation: 30 minutes
Cooking: 35–40 minutes
Level: 1

NUTTY CHOCOLATE SQUARES

Preheat the oven to 325°F (170°C/gas 3). • Butter an 11 x 7-inch (28 x 18-cm) baking pan. Line with parchment paper, letting the edges overhang. • Mix the flour, baking powder, cinnamon, cloves, cardamom, and salt in a medium bowl. • Bring the dark raisins, golden raisins, and rum mixture to a boil in a small saucepan. Remove from the heat and set aside for 15 minutes to allow the raisins to soak up the liquid. • Coarsely chop the walnuts and almonds. Stir the raisin mixture, cherries, walnuts, and almonds in a large bowl. Fold in 1 tablespoon of the dry ingredients. • Melt the chocolate in a double boiler over barely simmering water. • Beat the butter and brown sugar in a large bowl with an electric mixer at high speed until creamy. • Add the orange zest and melted chocolate. • Add the eggs one at a time, beating until just blended after each addition. • Use a large rubber spatula to fold in the remaining mixed dry ingredients, followed by the raisin mixture and orange juice. • Spoon the batter into the prepared pan, smoothing the top. • Bake until a toothpick inserted into the center comes out clean, 60–75 minutes. • Let cool completely before cutting.

1½ cups (225 g) all-purpose (plain) flour

1 teaspoon baking powder

½ teaspoon ground cinnamon

½ teaspoon ground cloves

¼ teaspoon ground cardamom

¼ teaspoon salt

½ cup (90 g) dark raisins

½ cup (90 g) golden raisins (sultanas)

½ cup (125 m) dark rum mixed with 1 tablespoon cold water

¾ cup (75 g) candied cherries, halved

1 cup (100 g) walnuts

1 cup (100 g) almonds

½ cup (90 g) semisweet (dark) chocolate, chopped

½ cup (90 g) white chocolate, chopped

¾ cup (180 g) butter

1 cup (200 g) firmly packed light brown sugar

Grated zest of 1 orange

3 large eggs

3 tablespoons orange juice

Makes: about 30 squares
Preparation: 45 minutes
Cooking: 60–75 minutes
Level: 2

COCOA SQUARES
WITH MINT FROSTING

162

Base: Preheat the oven to 350°F (180°C/gas 4).
• Set out a 9-inch (23-cm) square baking pan.
• Mix the flour, coconut, sugar, cocoa, baking
powder, and salt in a large bowl. • Use a pastry
blender to cut in the butter until the mixture
resembles fine crumbs. • Press the mixture into the
pan in an even layer. • Bake until lightly browned,
25–30 minutes. • Cool completely in the pan on a
rack. • Mint Frosting: Mix the confectioners' sugar
and mint extract in a small bowl. Add enough water
to make a spreadable frosting. • Spread over the
base. • Let set before cutting into squares.

Base

1   cup (150 g) all-purpose
    (plain) flour

1   cup (125 g) shredded
    (desiccated) coconut

½   cup (100 g) granulated
    sugar

3   tablespoons
    unsweetened cocoa
    powder

½   teaspoon baking powder

⅛   teaspoon salt

¾   cup (180 g) butter,
    cut up

Mint Frosting

1⅔ cups (250 g)
    confectioners' (icing)
    sugar

½   teaspoon mint extract
    (essence)

¼   cup (60 ml) boiling
    water

Makes: about 16 squares
Preparation: 25 minutes
Cooking: 25–30 minutes
Level: 1

NO-BAKE CHOCOLATE SQUARES

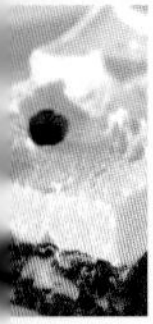

Base: Butter an 8-inch (20-cm) square baking pan.
• Melt the butter in a small saucepan over low heat.
Stir in the cocoa, brown sugar, and corn syrup.
Bring to a boil and let boil for 1 minute. • Remove
from the heat and stir in the crumbs. • Spoon the
mixture into the prepared pan, pressing down
lightly. • Frosting: Melt the chocolate in a double
boiler over barely simmering water. Pour the melted
chocolate over the cookie base. • Chill in the
refrigerator until set, at least 2 hours.
• Cut into squares.

Base

1　cup (250 g) butter

4　tablespoons
　　unsweetened cocoa
　　powder

1　tablespoon firmly
　　packed light brown
　　sugar

2　tablespoons light corn
　　syrup (golden syrup)

2　cups (250 g) graham
　　cracker crumbs
　　(crushed digestive
　　biscuits)

Frosting

4　oz (125 g) semisweet
　　(dark) chocolate,
　　coarsely chopped

Makes: about 20 squares
Preparation: 15 minutes
　　+ 2 hours to chill
Level: 1

CHOCOLATE CARAMEL DELIGHT

Base: Preheat the oven to 325°F (170°C/gas 3).
• Line an 8-inch (20-cm) square baking pan with aluminum foil. • Mix the flour, baking powder, and salt in a medium bowl. • Beat the butter and sugar in a large bowl with an electric mixer at high speed until pale and creamy. • With mixer on low speed, beat in the vanilla and mixed dry ingredients.
• Spread the mixture evenly in the prepared pan.
• Bake until golden brown, 10–15 minutes. •
Topping: Melt the butter with the sugar, corn syrup, and condensed milk in a medium saucepan over low heat, stirring constantly. Bring to a boil and simmer for 5 minutes. Remove from the heat and let cool slightly. • Spread the topping evenly over the cookie base. • Frosting: Melt the chocolate in a double boiler over barely simmering water. Pour the chocolate over the topping and let stand for 30 minutes until set. • Cut into squares.

Base

1½ cups (225 g) all-purpose (plain) flour
1 teaspoon baking powder
⅛ teaspoon salt
¾ cup (180 g) butter, melted
¼ cup (50 g) granulated sugar
1 teaspoon vanilla extract (essence)

Topping

½ cup (125 g) butter
½ cup (100 g) granulated sugar
2 tablespoons light corn syrup (golden syrup)
1 can (14 oz/400 g) sweetened condensed milk

Frosting

8 oz (250 g) semisweet (dark) chocolate, coarsely chopped

Makes: about 20 squares
Preparation: 20 minutes + 30 minutes to set
Cooking: 10 minutes
Level: 2

HONEY WALNUT BROWNIES

Preheat the oven to 350°F (180°C/gas 4). • Butter a 13 x 9-inch (33 x 23-cm) baking pan. • Mix the flour, baking powder, and salt in a medium bowl. • Melt the chocolate and butter in a double boiler over barely simmering water. Transfer the chocolate mixture to a large bowl and let cool for 5 minutes. • Beat in the sugar and honey. • Add the eggs one at a time, beating until just blended after each addition. • Mix in the mixed dry ingredients and walnuts. • Spoon the batter into the prepared pan in an even layer. • Bake until dry on top and almost firm to the touch, 30–35 minutes. • Let cool completely before cutting.

1   cup (150 g) all-purpose (plain) flour

½   teaspoon baking powder

⅛   teaspoon salt

6   oz (180 g) semisweet (dark) chocolate, coarsely chopped

½   cup (125 g) butter

½   cup (100 g) granulated sugar

½   cup (125 ml) honey

2   large eggs

1   cup (100 g) finely chopped walnuts

Makes: about 24 brownies
Preparation: 20 minutes
Cooking: 30–35 minutes
Level: 1

CHOCOLATE FRUIT CHEWIES

<u>Base</u>: Set out a 10½ x 15½-inch (26 x 36-cm) jelly-roll pan. • Melt the butter and sugar in a large saucepan over medium heat. • Remove from the heat and stir in the dates, cherries, raisins, and rice crispies. • Spoon the mixture into the pan in an even layer, pressing down firmly. • Chill in the refrigerator until set, about 2 hours. • <u>Frosting</u>: Melt the chocolate in a double boiler over barely simmering water. Pour the chocolate over the base and let stand until set, about 20 minutes. • Use a sharp knife to cut into squares.

Base

- ½ **cup (125 g) butter**
- ½ **cup (100 g) granulated sugar**
- 1¾ **cups (175 g) finely chopped pitted dates**
- ⅔ **cup (70 g) finely chopped candied cherries**
- ⅓ **cup (45 g) golden raisins (sultanas)**
- 2 **cups (200 g) rice crispies**

Frosting

- 8 **oz (250 g) semisweet (dark) chocolate, coarsely chopped**

Makes: about 20 squares
Preparation: 40 minutes
+ 2 hours 20 minutes
to chill and set
Level: 1

TRIPLE CHOCOLATE PECAN BARS

Preheat the oven to 350°F (180°C/gas 4). • Butter an 8-inch (20-cm) square baking pan. • Mix the flour and salt in a medium bowl. • Melt the semisweet chocolate with the butter in a double boiler over barely simmering water. • Transfer the chocolate mixture to a medium bowl and let cool for 5 minutes. • Stir in the white and milk chocolate chips and half the pecans. • Add the eggs, beating until just blended. • Stir in the mixed dry ingredients. • Spoon the batter into the prepared pan in an even layer. Sprinkle with the remaining pecans. • Bake until firm to the touch, 35–40 minutes. • Let cool completely before cutting into bars.

1½ cups (225 g) all-purpose (plain) flour

⅛ teaspoon salt

8 oz (250 g) semisweet (dark) chocolate, coarsely chopped

½ cup (125 g) butter, cut up

1 cup (180 g) white chocolate chips

1 cup (180 g) milk chocolate chips

2 cups (200 g) coarsely chopped pecans

2 large eggs

Makes: about 20 bars
Preparation: 20 minutes
Cooking: 35–40 minutes
Level: 1

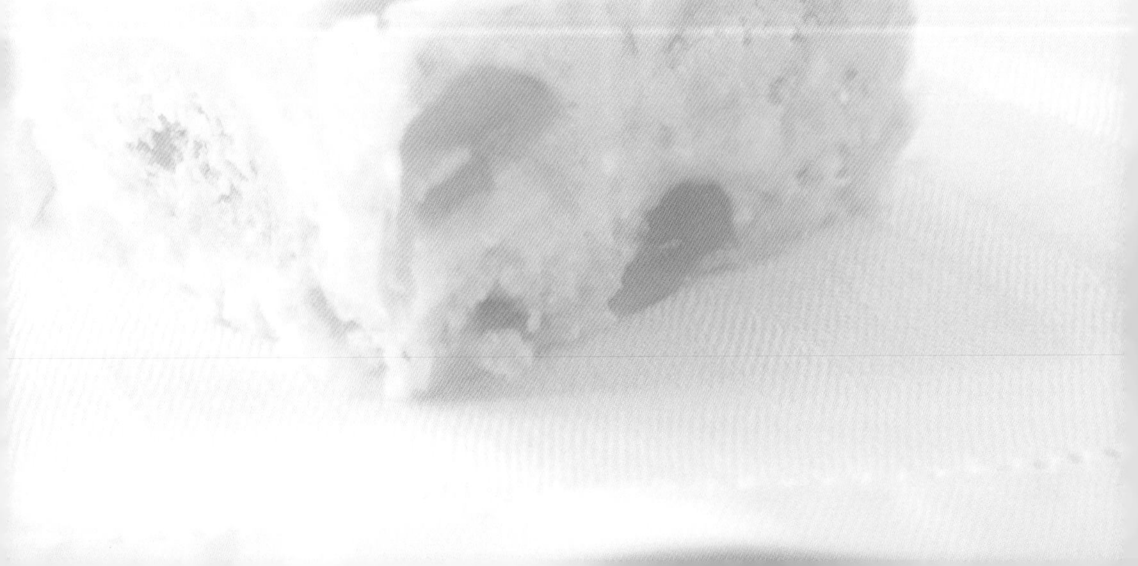

WHITE CHOCOLATE AMARETTI SQUARES

Line an 8-inch (20-cm) square baking pan with parchment paper. • Melt the white chocolate with the butter and cream in a double boiler over barely simmering water. • Remove from the heat and add the amaretti cookies, coconut, cherries, and almonds stirring until well mixed. • Spoon the batter into the prepared pan, spreading it evenly.
• Chill in the refrigerator until set, at least 4 hours.
• Use a knife dipped in hot water to cut into squares.

10 oz (300 g) white chocolate, coarsely chopped

²/₃ cup (150 g) butter,

¼ cup (60 ml) heavy (double) cream

3 oz (90 g) amaretti cookies, crushed

2 tablespoons shredded (desiccated) coconut

1 cup (100 g) coarsely chopped candied cherries

½ cup (50 g) flaked almonds, toasted

Makes: about 16 squares
Preparation: 30 minutes
  + 4 hours to chill
Level: 1

RICE CRISPIE SQUARES

176

Grease an 11 x 7-inch (28 x 18-cm) baking pan with sunflower oil. • Heat the condensed milk in a medium saucepan over low heat for 3 minutes, stirring constantly. • Stir in the chocolate and butter and stir until smooth. • Remove from the heat and stir in the rice crispies. • Spoon the mixture into the prepared pan in an even layer. • Let cool for 5 minutes. Use a sharp knife to score the mixture into bars. • When set, cut into squares.

3/4 **cup (180 ml) sweetened condensed milk**

12 **oz (350 g) semisweet (dark) chocolate, coarsely grated**

2 **tablespoons butter, softened**

2 **cups (200 g) rice crispies**

Makes: about 20 squares
Preparation: 25 minutes
Level: 1

OAT SQUARES WITH WHITE CHOCOLATE FROSTING

Base: Preheat the oven to 325°F (170°C/gas 3).
• Butter a 9-inch (23-cm) square baking pan.
• Melt the butter with the corn syrup and brown sugar in a small saucepan until smooth. • Mix the oats, flour, salt, and currants in a large bowl.
• Stir in the butter mixture. • Spoon the mixture into the prepared pan, pressing down firmly.
• Bake until lightly browned, 25–30 minutes.
• Let cool completely in the pan. • Frosting: Melt the white chocolate in a double boiler over barely simmering water. Use a thin metal spatula to spread the chocolate over the base. Let set then cut into squares.

Base

1   cup (250 g) butter
¾ cup (180 g) light corn syrup (golden syrup)
½ cup (100 g) firmly packed light brown sugar
1   cup (150 g) old-fashioned rolled oats
⅔ cup (100 g) all-purpose (plain) flour
⅛ teaspoon salt
½ cup (90 g) currants

Frosting

5   oz (150 g) white chocolate, coarsely chopped

Makes: about 20 squares
Preparation: 20 minutes
Cooking: 25–30 minutes
Level: 1

MARBLED CREAM CHEESE SQUARES

180

Preheat the oven to 350°F (180°C/gas 4). • Butter a 9-inch (23-cm) square baking pan and line with parchment paper. • <u>Cream Cheese Mixture</u>: Beat the cream cheese and sugar in a large bowl with an electric mixer at high speed until creamy. • Beat in the orange zest and juice and cornstarch. • Add the egg, beating until just blended. • <u>Chocolate Mixture</u>: Melt the chocolate and butter in a double boiler over barely simmering water. Set aside to cool. • Stir in the sugar and vanilla. • Add the beaten eggs, followed by the flour. • Pour the chocolate mixture into the prepared pan. • Drop tablespoons of the cream cheese mixture over the chocolate base. • Use a thin metal spatula to swirl the mixtures together to create a marbled effect. • Bake until slightly risen around the edges and set in the center, 25–30 minutes. • Cool completely in the pan. Cut into bars.

Cream Cheese Mixture

1 cup (250 g) cream cheese, softened

¼ cup (50 g) granulated sugar

2 tablespoons finely grated orange zest

3 tablespoons freshly squeezed orange juice

1 teaspoon cornstarch (cornflour)

1 large egg

Chocolate Mixture

8 oz (250 g) semisweet (dark) chocolate, coarsely chopped

¼ cup (60 g) butter

¾ cup (150 g) granulated sugar

2 teaspoons vanilla extract (essence)

2 large eggs, lightly beaten with 2 tablespoons cold water

½ cup (75 g) all-purpose (plain) flour

Makes: about 16 squares
Preparation: 35 minutes
Cooking: 25–30 minutes
Level: 1

CLASSIC WALNUT BROWNIES

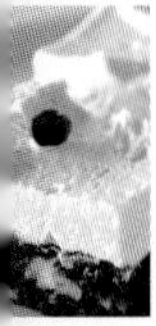

Preheat the oven to 350°F (180°C/gas 4). • Butter and flour an 8-inch (20-cm) square baking pan. Line with parchment paper. • Mix the flour, baking powder, and salt in a medium bowl. • Melt the chocolate and butter in a double boiler over barely simmering water. Remove from the heat and let cool a little. • Gradually add the sugar to the chocolate mixture. Stir in the vanilla. • Stir the eggs into the mixture one at a time. • Fold the mixed dry ingredients into the mixture until just lightly blended. Gently fold in the walnuts. • Spoon the batter into the prepared pan. • Bake until a toothpick inserted into the center comes out clean, 25–30 minutes. • Cool the brownies in the pan on a wire rack for at least one hour before cutting.

1	cup (150 g) all-purpose (plain) flour
1	teaspoon baking powder
¼	teaspoon salt
5	oz (150 g) bittersweet (dark) chocolate
¾	cup (180 g) butter
1½	cups (300 g) granulated sugar
1	teaspoon vanilla extract (essence)
3	large eggs
1	cup (100 g) walnuts, coarsely chopped

Makes: about 16 brownies
Preparation: 15 minutes
    + 1 hour to cool
Cooking: 25–30 minutes
Level: 1

CHEWY CHOCOLATE CHIP BROWNIES

Preheat the oven to 350°F (180°C/gas 4). • Butter and flour an 8-inch (20-cm) square baking pan. Line with parchment paper. • Mix the flour, baking powder, and salt in a medium bowl. • Melt the chocolate and butter in a double boiler over barely simmering water. Remove from the heat and let cool a little. • Beat the eggs and sugar with the vanilla in a medium bowl with an electric mixer at high speed until creamy. • Stir the cooled chocolate mixture into the eggs. • Fold in the mixed dry ingredients, followed by the pecans and chocolate chips. • Spoon the batter into the prepared pan. • Bake until a toothpick inserted into the center comes out clean, 25–30 minutes. • Cool the brownies in the pan on a wire rack for at least one hour before cutting.

$2/3$ cup (100 g) all-purpose (plain) flour

$1/2$ teaspoon baking powder

$1/4$ teaspoon salt

5 oz (150 g) bittersweet (dark) chocolate

$1/2$ cup (125 g) butter

1 cup (200 g) firmly packed dark brown sugar

1 teaspoon vanilla extract (essence)

2 large eggs

1 cup (100 g) pecans, coarsely chopped

1 cup (180 g) semisweet chocolate chips

Makes: about 16 brownies
Preparation: 15 minutes
Cooking: 25–30 minutes
Level: 1

WHITE CHOCOLATE BROWNIES

Preheat the oven to 350°F (180°C/gas 4). • Butter and flour an 8-inch (20-cm) square baking pan. Line with parchment paper. • Mix the flour, baking powder, and salt in a medium bowl. • Melt the chocolate and butter in a double boiler over barely simmering water. Remove from the heat and let cool a little. • Gradually add the sugar to the chocolate mixture. Stir in the vanilla and orange zest. • Stir the eggs into the mixture one at a time. • Fold the mixed dry ingredients into the mixture until just lightly blended. Gently fold in the macadamias. • Spoon the batter into the pan. • Bake until a toothpick inserted into the center comes out clean, 30–35 minutes. • Cool the brownies in the pan on a wire rack for at least one hour before cutting.

1   cup (150 g) all-purpose (plain) flour

1   teaspoon baking powder

¼   teaspoon salt

5   oz (150 g) white chocolate

½   cup (125 g) butter

1   cup (200 g) granulated sugar

1   teaspoon vanilla extract (essence)

2   teaspoons finely grated orange zest

2   large eggs

1   cup (100 g) macadamia nuts, coarsely chopped

Makes: about 16 brownies
Preparation: 15 minutes
Cooking: 30–35 minutes
Level: 1

FRUITY WHITE CHOCOLATE SQUARES

Preheat the oven to 325°F (170°C/gas 3). • Butter and flour an 8 x 12-inch (20 x 30-cm) baking pan. Line with parchment paper. • Melt the chocolate and butter in a double boiler over barely simmering water. • Heat the honey and apricot preserves in a small saucepan over low heat just enough to make them liquid. • Mix the almonds, macadamias, coconut, dried apricots, golden raisins, flour, and ginger in a large bowl. • Add the chocolate mixture and the honey and apricot mixture. Stir until well mixed. • Spoon the batter into the prepared pan, smoothing the top with the back of a spoon.
• Bake until pale golden brown, 40–45 minutes.
• Cool in the pan on a wire rack for at least one hour before cutting.

8 oz (250 g) white chocolate

¼ cup (60 g) butter

½ cup (125 g) apricot preserves (jam)

½ cup (125 g) honey

⅔ cup (80 g) almonds, coarsely chopped

1 cup (100 g) macadamia nuts, coarsely chopped

1½ cups (150 g) shredded (desiccated) coconut

1 cup (100 g) dried apricots, coarsely chopped

1 cup (100 g) golden raisins (sultanas)

⅓ cup (50 g) all-purpose (plain) flour

1 teaspoon ground ginger

Makes: about 20 squares
Preparation: 15 minutes
Cooking: 40–45 minutes
Level: 1

CHOCOLATE CHEESECAKE BARS

Base: Preheat the oven to 350°F (180°C/gas 4).
• Butter and flour an 8 x 12-inch (20 x 30-cm) baking pan. Line with aluminum foil, leaving the edges hanging over. • Place the chocolate, butter, and sugar in a double boiler over barely simmering water. Stir until melted and smooth. • Remove from heat and beat in the eggs, flour, almonds, baking powder, salt, and almond extract. • Spoon the batter into the prepared pan, smoothing the top with the back of a spoon. • Bake until a toothpick inserted into the center comes out clean, about 30 minutes. • Place the pan on a wire rack and let cool completely. • Cheesecake: Beat the cream cheese, condensed milk, sour cream, and vanilla in an electric mixer on low speed until smooth and creamy. Spread over the cooled cake in the pan. • Chill in the refrigerator until set, at least 2 hours. Frosting: Melt the chocolate and butter in a double boiler over barely simmering water. • Let cool a little then spread evenly over the cheesecake layer. • Chill in the refrigerator for at least 30 minutes before serving.

8 oz (250 g) semisweet (dark) chocolate
1/4 cup (60 g) butter
1/2 cup (100 g) granulated sugar
2 large eggs
2/3 cup (100 g) all-purpose (plain) flour
1/3 cup (50 g) finely ground almonds
1/2 teaspoon baking powder
1/8 teaspoon salt
1/3 teaspoon almond extract

Cheesecake

2 cups (500 g) cream cheese
1 cup (250 g) sweet and condensed milk
1/4 cup (60 ml) sour cream
2 teaspoons vanilla extract (essence)

Frosting

4 oz (125 g) semisweet (dark) chocolate
2 tablespoons butter

Makes: about 20 bars
Preparation: 30 minutes
    + 2 hours 30 minutes
    to set and chill
Cooking: 30 minutes
Level: 1

MUFFINS AND CUPCAKES

CHOCOLATE CUPCAKES WITH HAZELNUT TOPPING

194

Cupcakes: Preheat the oven to 350°F (180°C/gas 4).
• Set out 15 foil or paper baking cups. • Mix the
flour, baking powder, and salt in a medium bowl.
• Melt the chocolate in a double boiler over barely
simmering water. Let cool a little. • Beat the butter,
sugar, and corn syrup in a medium bowl with an
electric mixer on high speed until pale and creamy.
• Add the eggs one at a time, beating until just
combined after each addition. • Beat in the
chocolate and vanilla. • With mixer on low speed,
gradually beat in the mixed dry ingredients,
alternating with the sour cream. • Divide the batter
evenly among the muffin cups, filling each one
about two-thirds full. • Bake until a toothpick
inserted into the center comes out clean, 15–20
minutes. • Cool the cupcakes on a wire rack for 5
minutes then invert them onto the rack. Turn right
side up and let cool completely. • Topping: Spread
each cupcake with a generous amount of hazelnut
topping. Top each one with a couple of toasted
hazelnuts or a walnut half and a fresh raspberry.

■ ■ ■ *These cupcakes have a delicious brownie-like texture.*

Cupcakes

3 oz (90 g) bittersweet (dark) chocolate, finely chopped

1½ cups (225 g) all-purpose (plain) flour

1 teaspoon baking powder

⅛ teaspoon salt

½ cup (125 g) butter, softened

1 cup (200 g) granulated sugar

2 tablespoons light corn syrup (golden syrup)

2 large eggs

1 teaspoon vanilla extract (essence)

½ cup (125 ml) sour cream

Topping

1 cup (250 g) chocolate hazelnut spread (Nutella or other), at room temperature

About 15 fresh raspberries

Toasted hazelnuts or walnut halves

Makes: about 15 cupcakes
Preparation: 30 minutes
Cooking: 15–20 minutes
Level: 1

CHOCOLATE SOUR CREAM CUPCAKES

Cupcakes: Preheat the oven to 350°F (180°C/gas 4).
• Line a 12-cup muffin pan with paper liners.
• Mix the flour, cocoa, baking powder, and salt in a medium bowl. • Beat the butter, sugar, and vanilla in a medium bowl with an electric mixer at high speed until pale and creamy. • With mixer on medium speed, add the eggs one at a time, beating until just combined after each addition. • With mixer on low speed, gradually add the flour, alternating with the sour cream. • Spoon the batter into the prepared cups, filling each one about three-quarters full. • Bake until a toothpick inserted into the center comes out clean, 20–25 minutes. • Cool the cupcakes in the pan for 5 minutes. Transfer to a wire rack and let cool completely. • Chocolate Frosting: Place the confectioners' sugar and cocoa in a medium bowl and stir in the butter and vanilla extract. Beat until smooth. If the frosting is too thick, stir in 1–2 tablespoons of sour cream.
• Spread the cupcakes with the frosting and top each one with a walnut half.

Cupcakes

- 1 cup (150 g) all-purpose (plain) flour
- ½ cup (100 g) unsweetened cocoa powder
- 1 teaspoon baking powder
- ¼ teaspoon salt
- ¾ cup (185 g) butter, softened
- 1 cup (200 g) granulated sugar
- 1 teaspoon vanilla extract (essence)
- 3 large eggs
- ½ cup (125 g) sour cream

Chocolate Frosting

- 2 cups (300 g) confectioners' (icing) sugar
- ½ cup (75 g) unsweetened cocoa powder
- ½ cup (125 g) butter, melted
- ½ teaspoon vanilla extract (essence)
- 12 walnut halves, lightly toasted

■ ■ ■ *For a slightly different look, omit the cocoa from the icing and top each cupcake with a candied cherry.*

Makes: about 12 cupcakes
Preparation: 30 minutes
Cooking: 20–25 minutes
Level: 1

CHOCOLATE BANANA CUPCAKES

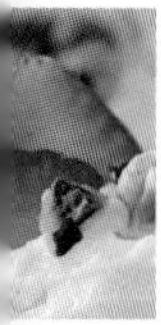

198

Preheat the oven to 375°F (190°C/gas 5). • Arrange 20 foil baking cups on baking sheets. • Mix both flours, baking powder, baking soda, and salt in a large bowl. • Beat the butter and sugar in a large bowl with an electric mixer at high speed until creamy. • Add the eggs one at a time, beating until just combined after each addition. • With mixer at low speed, beat in the bananas, followed by the mixed dry ingredients, alternating with the milk.
• Stir in the chocolate chips and walnuts by hand.
• Spoon the batter into the cups, filling each about two-thirds full. • Bake until a toothpick inserted into the center comes out clean, 20–25 minutes.
• Cool the cupcakes on wire racks.

1 cup (150 g) whole-wheat (wholemeal) flour

1 cup (150 g) all-purpose (plain) flour

2 teaspoons baking powder

½ teaspoon baking soda (bicarbonate of soda)

¼ teaspoon salt

½ cup (125 g) unsalted butter, softened

1 cup (200 g) granulated sugar

3 large eggs

2 large very ripe bananas, mashed

¼ cup (60 ml) milk

1 cup (120 g) bittersweet (dark) chocolate chips

1 cup (120 g) walnuts, chopped

Makes: about 20 cupcakes
Preparation: 20 minutes
Cooking: 20–25 minutes
Level: 1

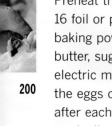

CHOCOLATE CHIP CUPCAKES

Preheat the oven to 350°F (180°C/gas 4). • Set out 16 foil or paper baking cups. • Mix the flour, cocoa, baking powder, and salt in a large bowl. • Beat the butter, sugar, and honey in a large bowl with an electric mixer at high speed until creamy. • Add the eggs one at a time, beating until just combined after each addition. • With mixer at low speed, gradually beat in the mixed dry ingredients, alternating with the milk. • Stir in the chocolate chips by hand. • Spoon the batter into the prepared cups, filling each one about two-thirds full. • Bake until a toothpick inserted into the centers comes out clean, 20–25 minutes. • Cool the cupcakes on wire racks.

2 cups (300 g) all-purpose (plain) flour

½ cup (75 g) unsweetened cocoa powder

2 teaspoons baking powder

¼ teaspoon salt

¾ cup (180 ml) milk

½ cup (125 g) butter, softened

1¼ cups (250 g) granulated sugar

1 tablespoon honey

2 large eggs

2 oz (60 g) semisweet (dark) chocolate chips

Makes: about 16 cupcakes
Preparation: 15 minutes
Cooking: 20–25 minutes
Level: 1

CHOCOLATE CHERRY MUFFINS

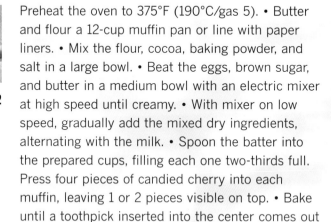

Preheat the oven to 375°F (190°C/gas 5). • Butter and flour a 12-cup muffin pan or line with paper liners. • Mix the flour, cocoa, baking powder, and salt in a large bowl. • Beat the eggs, brown sugar, and butter in a medium bowl with an electric mixer at high speed until creamy. • With mixer on low speed, gradually add the mixed dry ingredients, alternating with the milk. • Spoon the batter into the prepared cups, filling each one two-thirds full. Press four pieces of candied cherry into each muffin, leaving 1 or 2 pieces visible on top. • Bake until a toothpick inserted into the center comes out clean, 20–25 minutes. • Cool the muffins on racks.

1½ cups (225 g) all-purpose (plain) flour

⅓ cup (50 g) unsweetened cocoa powder

2 teaspoons baking powder

¼ teaspoon salt

2 large eggs

½ cup (100 g) firmly packed brown sugar

½ cup (125 g) butter, softened

¾ cup (180 ml) milk

24 candied cherries, halved

Makes: about 12 muffins
Preparation: 15 minutes
Cooking: 20–25 minutes
Level: 1

CHOCOLATE SURPRISE MUFFINS

Preheat the oven to 350°F (180°C/gas 4). • Butter and flour a 12-cup muffin pan or line with paper liners. • Beat the flour, sugar, cocoa, eggs, butter, vanilla, baking powder, and milk in a large bowl with an electric mixer at medium speed until well blended. • Spoon half the batter into the cups. Place a chocolate in each one. Cover with the remaining batter. • Sprinkle each muffin with a few chocolate chips. • Bake until a toothpick inserted into the center comes out clean, 20–25 minutes. • Cool the muffins on racks.

1½ cups (225 g) all-purpose (plain) flour

½ cup (100 g) granulated sugar

½ cup (75 g) unsweetened cocoa powder

2 large eggs

⅓ cup (90 g) butter, melted

2 teaspoons vanilla extract (essence)

2 teaspoons baking powder

½ cup (125 ml) milk

12 small milk chocolates

4 tablespoons semisweet (dark) chocolate chips

Makes: about 12 muffins
Preparation: 10 minutes
Cooking: 20–25 minutes
Level: 1

FROSTED CHOCOLATE MUFFINS

Preheat the oven to 350°F (180°C/gas 4). • Line 20 muffin-pan cups with foil or paper liners. • Melt the chocolate with the cream in a double boiler over barely simmering water. Set aside to cool. • Mix the flour, baking powder, and salt in a large bowl. • Beat the butter and sugar in a large bowl with an electric mixer at high speed until pale and creamy. • Add the eggs, one at a time, beating until just blended after each addition. • With mixer at low speed, gradually beat in the chocolate, followed by the mixed dry ingredients, alternating with the milk and vanilla. • Spoon the batter into the prepared pans, filling each one two-thirds full. • Bake until a toothpick inserted into the center comes out clean, 20–25 minutes. • Cool the muffins on racks. • Spread the cooled muffins with the frosting.

4 oz (125 g) semisweet (dark) chocolate, coarsely chopped

1 tablespoon heavy (double) cream

2 cups (300 g) all-purpose (plain) flour

2 teaspoons baking powder

¼ teaspoon salt

¾ cup (180 g) butter, softened

1½ cups (150 g) granulated sugar

3 large eggs

⅔ cup (150 ml) milk

2 teaspoons vanilla extract (essence)

1 recipe chocolate frosting (see page 688)

Makes: about 20 muffins
Preparation: 20 minutes
Cooking: 20–25 minutes
Level: 1

WHITE CHOCOLATE MUFFINS WITH GINGER FROSTING

<u>Muffins</u>: Preheat the oven to 400°F (200°C/gas 6).
• Arrange 20 foil or paper baking cups on baking
sheets. • Mix the flour, baking powder, and salt
in a large bowl. Stir in the sugar and chocolate
chips. • Make a well in the center. Stir in the milk,
butter, egg, honey, and vanilla. • Spoon the batter
into the cups, filling each one two-thirds full. • Bake
until a toothpick inserted into the center comes out
clean, 15–20 minutes. Cool the muffins on racks.

<u>Ginger Frosting</u>: Beat the cream cheese, butter,
vanilla, and ginger in a large bowl with an electric
mixer at medium speed until smooth and creamy.
With mixer at low speed, gradually beat in the
confectioners' sugar. • Spread each cooled muffin
with plenty of frosting. Top each one with a piece
of candied ginger.

Muffins

2 cups (300 g) all-
   purpose (plain) flour

2 teaspoons baking
   powder

¼ teaspoon salt

¼ cup (50 g) granulated
   sugar

1½ cups (180 g) white
   chocolate chips

1 cup (250 ml) milk

¼ cup (60 g) butter,
   melted

1 large egg, lightly beaten

2 tablespoons honey

2 teaspoons vanilla extract
   (essence)

Ginger Frosting

3 oz (90 g) cream cheese

¼ cup (60 g) butter

1 teaspoon vanilla extract
   (essence)

1 teaspoon ground ginger

2 cups (300 g)
   confectioners' (icing)
   sugar

20 small pieces candied
   ginger

Makes: about 20 muffins
Preparation: 10 minutes
Cooking: 15–20 minutes
Level: 1

WHITE CHOCOLATE HAZELNUT CUPCAKES

Cupcakes: Preheat the oven to 350°F (180°C/gas 4). • Line a 12-cup muffin pan with paper liners. • Mix the flour, baking powder, and salt in a medium bowl. • Beat the butter and sugar in a medium bowl with an electric mixer at high speed until pale and creamy. • Add the egg and beat until just combined. • With mixer at low speed, gradually beat in the mixed dry ingredients, alternating with the pear liqueur and milk. Stir in the hazelnuts by hand. • Divide the batter evenly among the muffin cups, filling each one about two-thirds full. If there is a little extra batter, fill one or two extra paper liners, rather than over-filling the cups. • Bake until a toothpick inserted into the center comes out clean, 15–20 minutes. • Cool the cupcakes on a wire rack for 5 minutes, then invert onto the rack. Turn right side up and let cool completely. • Cream Cheese Frosting: Melt the white chocolate in a double boiler over barely simmering water. Let cool a little. • Place the white chocolate, butter, cream cheese, lemon zest, liqueur, and confectioners' sugar in a medium bowl and beat until smooth and creamy. • Spread the frosting on the cooled cupcakes. • Top each one with a couple of toasted hazelnuts and a slice or two of strawberry.

Cupcakes

- 1⅓ cups all-purpose (plain) flour
- 1 teaspoon baking powder
- ¼ teaspoon salt
- ⅓ cup (90 g) butter
- 1 cup (200 g) granulated sugar
- 1 large egg
- 2 tablespoons pear liqueur
- 1 teaspoon vanilla extract (essence)
- ⅔ cup (150 ml) milk
- ½ cup (60 g) finely chopped toasted hazelnuts

Cream Cheese Frosting

- 4 oz (125 g) white chocolate
- ¼ cup (60 g) butter
- 3 oz (90 g) cream cheese
- 1 tablespoon finely grated lemon zest
- 1 tablespoon pear liqueur
- 1½ cups (225 g) confectioners' (icing) sugar
- 24 toasted hazelnuts
- 6 strawberries, sliced

Makes: about 12 cupcakes
Preparation: 20 minutes
Cooking: 15–20 minutes
Level: 1

WHITE CHOCOLATE STRAWBERRY MUFFINS

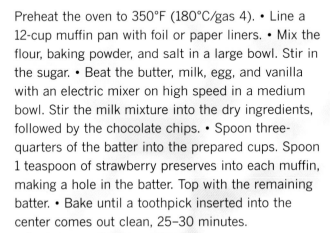

Preheat the oven to 350°F (180°C/gas 4). • Line a 12-cup muffin pan with foil or paper liners. • Mix the flour, baking powder, and salt in a large bowl. Stir in the sugar. • Beat the butter, milk, egg, and vanilla with an electric mixer on high speed in a medium bowl. Stir the milk mixture into the dry ingredients, followed by the chocolate chips. • Spoon three-quarters of the batter into the prepared cups. Spoon 1 teaspoon of strawberry preserves into each muffin, making a hole in the batter. Top with the remaining batter. • Bake until a toothpick inserted into the center comes out clean, 25–30 minutes.
• Cool the muffins on racks.

$1\frac{1}{2}$ cups (225 g) all-purpose (plain) flour

2 teaspoons baking powder

$\frac{1}{4}$ teaspoon salt

$\frac{1}{2}$ cup (100 g) granulated sugar

$\frac{1}{2}$ cup (125 g) butter, melted

$\frac{1}{2}$ cup (125 ml) milk

1 large egg

$\frac{1}{2}$ teaspoon vanilla extract (essence)

$1\frac{1}{2}$ cups (180 g) white chocolate chips

$\frac{1}{2}$ cup (125 g) strawberry preserves (jam)

Makes: 12 muffins
Preparation: 15 minutes
Cooking: 25–30 minutes
Level: 1

JAFFA MUFFINS

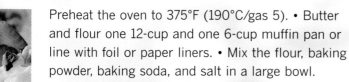

214

Preheat the oven to 375°F (190°C/gas 5). • Butter and flour one 12-cup and one 6-cup muffin pan or line with foil or paper liners. • Mix the flour, baking powder, baking soda, and salt in a large bowl. • Beat the sugar, egg, milk, oil, orange zest, and vanilla with an electric mixer on high speed until well mixed. Stir the orange mixture into the dry ingredients. • Stir in the chocolate chips by hand. • Spoon the batter into the prepared cups, filling each one two-thirds full. • Bake until a toothpick inserted into the center comes out clean, 20–25 minutes. • Cool the muffins on racks.

2 cups (300 g) all-purpose (plain) flour

2 teaspoons baking powder

½ teaspoon baking soda (bicarbonate of soda)

¼ teaspoon salt

1 cup (200 g) granulated sugar

1 large egg

¾ cup (180 ml) milk

½ cup (125 ml) vegetable oil

2 tablespoons finely grated orange zest

2 teaspoons vanilla extract (essence)

1 cup (180 g) semisweet (dark) chocolate chips

Makes: about 18 muffins
Preparation: 15 minutes
Cooking: 20–25 minutes
Level: 1

CHOCOLATE RUM-RAISIN MUFFINS

Plump the raisins in the rum in a small bowl for 30 minutes. • Preheat the oven to 400°F (200°C/gas 6). • Butter and flour two 12-cup muffin pans or line with foil or paper liners. • Mix the flour, cocoa, baking powder, and salt in a large bowl. Stir in the sugar and make a well in the center. • Stir in the raisin mixture, cream, eggs, and butter. Stir in the chocolate chips. • Spoon the batter into the prepared cups, filling each one two-thirds full. • Bake until a toothpick inserted into the center comes out clean, 20–25 minutes. • Cool the muffins on wire racks.

1½ cups (150 g) raisins

⅓ cup (90 ml) rum

2½ cups (375 g) all-purpose (plain) flour

½ cup (75 g) unsweetened cocoa powder

2 teaspoons baking powder

¼ teaspoon salt

1 cup (200 g) granulated sugar

1½ cups (375 ml) light (single) cream or half-and-half

2 eggs, lightly beaten

⅓ cup (90 g) butter, melted

1 cup (180 g) semisweet (dark) chocolate chips

Makes: about 24 muffins
Preparation: 10 minutes
+ 30 minutes to soak
Cooking: 20–25 minutes
Level: 1

CHOCOLATE NUT CUPCAKES

Cupcakes: Preheat the oven to 350°F (180°C/gas 4). • Set out about 16 foil or paper baking cups. • Mix the flour, baking powder, baking soda, and salt in a medium bowl. • Beat the butter, sugar, and rum or butterscotch extract in a large bowl with an electric mixer at high speed until creamy. • Add the eggs, one at a time, beating until just blended after each addition. • With mixer at low speed, gradually beat in the mixed dry ingredients, alternating with the cream. • Stir in the nut chocolate by hand. • Spoon the batter into the prepared cups, filling each one two-thirds full. • Bake until a toothpick inserted into the center comes out clean, 20–25 minutes. • Cool the cupcakes on racks. • Frosting: Melt the milk chocolate in a double boiler over barely simmering water. Set aside to cool. Spread over the cupcakes and top each one with a pecan.

Cupcakes

2 cups (300 g) all-purpose (plain) flour

2 teaspoons baking powder

½ teaspoon baking soda (bicarbonate of soda)

¼ teaspoon salt

½ cup (125 g) butter, softened

½ cup (100 g) granulated sugar

1 teaspoon rum or butterscotch extract

2 large eggs

1 cup (250 ml) heavy (double) cream

4 oz (125 g) nut chocolate, coarsely chopped

Frosting

6 oz (180 g) milk chocolate, coarsely chopped

16 pecan halves

Makes: about 16 cupcakes
Preparation: 20 minutes
Cooking: 20–25 minutes
Level: 1

WHITE CHOCOLATE PEANUT BUTTER CUPCAKES

220

Preheat the oven to 350°F (180°C/gas 4). • Set out about 16 foil or paper baking cups. • Mix both flours, the baking powder, baking soda, and salt in a medium bowl. • Beat the butter, peanut butter, brown sugar, and vanilla in a large bowl with an electric mixer at high speed until creamy. • Add the egg, beating until just blended. • With mixer at low speed, gradually beat in the mixed dry ingredients, alternating with the milk. • Stir in the white chocolate chips by hand. • Spoon the batter into the prepared cups, filling each one two-thirds full. • Bake until a toothpick inserted into the center comes out clean, 20–25 minutes. • Cool the cupcakes on wire racks.

1   cup (150 g) whole-wheat (wholemeal) flour

1/3 cup (50 g) all-purpose (plain) flour

1   teaspoon baking powder

1/2 teaspoon baking soda (bicarbonate of soda)

1/4 teaspoon salt

1/4 cup (60 g) butter, softened

1/2 cup (125 g) crunchy peanut butter

1/2 cup (100 g) firmly packed dark brown sugar

1   teaspoon vanilla extract (essence)

1   large egg

1/2 cup (125 ml) milk

1   cup (180 g) white chocolate chips

Makes: about 16 cupcakes
Preparation: 20 minutes
Cooking: 20–25 minutes
Level: 1

CHOCOLATE MINT CUPCAKES

222

Cupcakes: Preheat the oven to 350°F (180°C/gas 4).
• Line 18 muffin-pan cups with foil or paper liners.
• Mix the flour, cocoa, baking powder, baking soda,
and salt in a large bowl. • Beat the butter and sugar
in a large bowl with an electric mixer at high speed
until creamy. • Add the eggs one at a time, beating
until just blended after each addition. • With mixer
at low speed, beat in the mixed dry ingredients,
alternating with the milk and peppermint extract.
Stir in the chopped chocolate mints. • Spoon the
batter into the prepared cups, filling each one two-
thirds full. • Bake until a toothpick inserted into the
center comes out clean, 20–25 minutes. • Cool the
cupcakes on wire racks. Chocolate Glaze: Melt the
chocolate and butter in a double boiler over barely
simmering water. Stir in the peppermint extract.
Drizzle the glaze over the cupcakes.

Cupcakes

2 cups (300 g) all-purpose (plain) flour

½ cup (75 g) unsweetened cocoa powder

1 teaspoon baking powder

½ teaspoon baking soda (bicarbonate of soda)

¼ teaspoon salt

⅔ cup (165 g) butter, softened

1½ cups (300 g) granulated sugar

3 large eggs

¾ cup (200 ml) milk

1 teaspoon peppermint extract

15 chocolate cream after-dinner mints, chopped

Chocolate Glaze

6 oz (180 g) semisweet (dark) chocolate, coarsely chopped

½ cup (125 g) butter

1 teaspoon peppermint extract

■ ■ ■ *These divine little cakes taste like chocolatey
after-dinner mints. Refreshing and addictive!*

Makes: about 18 cupcakes
Preparation: 20 minutes
Cooking: 20–30 minutes
Level: 1

CHOCOLATE ZUCCHINI MUFFINS

Muffins: Preheat the oven to 350°F (180°C/gas 4).
• Set out about 16 foil or paper baking cups. • Mix both flours and the baking soda in a medium bowl. Stir in the rolled oats. • Beat the butter, brown sugar, and vanilla in a large bowl with an electric mixer at high speed until creamy. • Add the eggs one at a time, beating until just blended after each addition. • With mixer at low speed, gradually beat in the dry ingredients, alternating with the yogurt. • Stir in the chocolate, zucchini, and macadamia nuts by hand. • Spoon the batter into the prepared cups, filling each one two-thirds full. • Bake until a toothpick inserted into the center comes out clean, 15–20 minutes. • Cool the muffins on wire racks.
Chocolate Frosting: Mix the confectioners' sugar and cocoa in a medium bowl. Add the butter and vanilla and beat until smooth and creamy. Spread a little frosting on each muffin and top with a walnut.

Muffins

1 cup (150 g) all-purpose (plain) flour

½ cup (75 g) whole-wheat (wholemeal) flour

1 teaspoon baking soda

⅓ cup (50 g) rolled oats

½ cup (125 g) butter

½ cup (100 g) firmly packed dark brown sugar

1 teaspoon vanilla extract

2 large eggs

2 tablespoons plain yogurt

5 oz (150 g) bittersweet (dark) chocolate, coarsely grated

1 medium zucchini, grated

½ cup (60 g) chopped macadamia nuts

Chocolate Frosting

2 cups (300 g) confectioners' (icing) sugar

½ cup (75 g) unsweetened cocoa powder

½ cup (125 g) butter, melted

½ teaspoon vanilla extract (essence)

16 walnut halves

Makes: about 16 muffins
Preparation: 20 minutes
Cooking: 15–20 minutes
Level: 1

CHOCOLATE FAIRY CUPCAKES

Preheat the oven to 350°F (180°C/gas 4). • Set out about 20 foil or paper baking cups. • Mix the flour, cocoa, baking powder, and salt in a medium bowl. • Beat the butter and sugar in a large bowl with an electric mixer at high speed until creamy. • Add the eggs one at a time, beating until just blended after each addition. • With mixer at low speed, gradually beat in the dry ingredients, alternating with the milk. • Spoon the batter into the prepared cups, filling each one two-thirds full. • Bake until a toothpick inserted into the center comes out clean, 15–20 minutes. • Cool the cakes on wire racks. • With mixer at high speed, beat the cream in a medium bowl until stiff. • Cut a small circle about 1/2-inch (1-cm) deep from the top of each cake. Fill with 1 teaspoon of preserves and top with cream and 1–2 fresh raspberries. Cut the cake tops in two and arrange on the top of each cake like wings.

1¹⁄₃ cups (200 g) all-purpose (plain) flour

²⁄₃ cup (100 g) unsweetened cocoa powder

2 teaspoons baking powder

¼ teaspoon salt

²⁄₃ cup (150 g) butter, softened

1 cup (200 g) granulated sugar

2 large eggs

½ cup (125 ml) milk

1 tablespoon orange liqueur

½ cup (125 g) raspberry preserves (jam)

1 cup (250 ml) heavy (double) cream

Fresh raspberries, to decorate

Makes: about 20 cupcakes
Preparation: 20 minutes
Cooking: 15–20 minutes
Level: 1

PASTRIES

CHOCOLATE CHIP BRIOCHES

Place the yeast, milk, sugar, and salt in a small bowl and stir gently. Set aside for 10 minutes. • Place the flour in a large bowl and pour in the yeast mixture. Beating slowly, gradually add the eggs. Knead (by hand or with a mixer) until soft and smooth, about 5 minutes. Slowly add the butter a little at a time. Continue until all the butter has been added, then knead for 5 more minutes. • Add the chocolate and knead until well combined within the dough.
• Cover the bowl with a clean cloth and leave in a warm place until it has doubled in volume, about 90 minutes. • Gently remove the risen dough from the bowl and on a floured work surface knock it back. This is done by flipping the dough over with your fingers. Place on a tray and refrigerate for up to 2 hours. • Grease 16 small brioche molds with melted butter. • Preheat the oven to 400°F (200°C/ gas 6). • Weigh off sixteen 1-oz (30-g) pieces of dough for the base of the brioches and sixteen $1/3$-oz (10-g) pieces for the tops. • Shape the larger pieces of dough into tight balls and place in the bottoms of the molds. Shape the smaller pieces of dough into tight balls and pull the dough to make one end elongated, like a teardrop. Using your finger make a hole in the larger balls and poke the teardrop into the holes. • Using a pastry brush, lightly glaze with the egg mixture. Cover with a cloth and set aside in a warm place to double in volume, about 30 minutes. • Brush with the glaze again. • Bake until golden brown, about 10 minutes.

½ oz (15 g) fresh yeast or 1 (¼-oz/7-g) package active dry yeast

⅓ cup (90 ml) warm milk

2 tablespoons superfine (caster) sugar

1 teaspoon salt

3⅓ cups (500 g) all-purpose (plain) flour

4 large eggs

1⅓ cups (335 g) butter, softened

2 oz (60 g) semisweet (dark) chocolate chips

1 egg yolk, lightly beaten with 1 teaspoon of milk, to glaze

Makes: 16 brioches
Preparation: 30 minutes
  + 4 hours to rise
Cooking: 10 minutes
Level: 2

CHOCOLATE PITHIVIER

Filling: Stir the butter and sugar in a pan over medium heat until the sugar has dissolved but not caramelized. • Add the chocolate and stir until smooth. • Mix the cocoa, almonds, and cornstarch in a medium bowl. Stir in the chocolate mixture. Finally, stir in the eggs. Beat the mixture briefly until well combined. Set aside, but do not refrigerate. • Place the pastry on a floured work surface. Dust the top with flour and roll out into a rectangle about $1/8$-inch (3-mm) thick. Using a plain 3-inch (9-cm) cutter, cut out 16 rounds of pastry. • Spoon 2 tablespoons of the filling into the center of 8 of the pastry rounds. Brush the egg around the edges of the pastry and place the remaining pastry rounds over the filling, pressing down gently to seal. Using the back of a pastry cutter 2 sizes smaller, carefully center it over the top and press down firmly. This will leave a mark and prevents the pithivier from opening during the baking. • Preheat the oven to 400°F (200°C/gas 6). • Line two baking sheets with parchment paper. • Place the pithiviers on the baking sheet about 1 inch (2.5 cm) apart. Chill in the refrigerator for 15 minutes. • Brush the tops with egg and use the back of a knife to mark curved lines from the center to the edge of the pastry all the way around. Mark each pithivier.
• Bake until golden brown, 25–30 minutes.
• Transfer to a wire rack and let cool.

Filling

- ½ cup (125 g) butter
- ½ cup (100 g) superfine (caster) sugar
- 2 oz (60 g) semisweet (dark) chocolate, chopped and melted
- ¼ cup (30 g) unsweetened cocoa powder
- 1 cup (120 g) finely ground almonds
- ¼ cup (30 g) cornstarch (cornflour)

- 12 oz (350 g) frozen puff pastry, thawed
- 2 large eggs, beaten

Serves: 8
Preparation: 45 minutes
Cooking: 25–30 minutes
Level: 2

CHOCOLATE PALMIERS

234

Preheat the oven to 400°F (200°C/gas 6). • Line a baking sheet with parchment paper. • Melt the butter in a small saucepan over low heat. Add the chocolate and stir until smooth. Set aside to cool. • Dust a work surface with confectioners' sugar and place the pastry on top. Roll out into a 12 x 10-inch (30 x 25-cm) rectangle. Trim the pastry so that the edges are straight. Fold the pastry in half lengthways to mark the center and unfold it again, leaving a mark down the middle. • When the chocolate mixture is thick and cool, pour it onto the pastry, working quickly so that it doesn't set. Use a spatula to spread the chocolate evenly over the pastry. It is important that the chocolate mix is not too thick as it will run out during cooking. Sift the cocoa over the top. Begin to roll the sides of the pastry rectangle to the middle, where the mark is. Repeat for the other end, until it meets the already rolled half. • Roll carefully in the remaining confectioners' sugar and transfer to a plate. Refrigerate for 15 minutes. • When firm, cut across the rolls in $1/4$-inch (5-mm) thick slices. Place on the prepared baking sheet, spacing them 1 inch (2.5 cm) apart. • Bake until golden, 8–10 minutes. • Place on wire racks and let cool completely.

2 teaspoons butter

2 oz (60 g) semisweet (dark) chocolate, chopped

$1/2$ cup (75 g) confectioners' (icing) sugar

5 oz (150 g) frozen puff pastry, thawed

$1/4$ cup (30 g) unsweetened cocoa powder

Serves: 8–10
Preparation: 30 minutes
Cooking: 8–10 minutes
Level: 1

CHOCOLATE AND RICOTTA TURNOVERS

Preheat the oven to 400°F (200°C/gas 6). • Line two baking sheets with parchment paper. • <u>Filling</u>: Process the ricotta in a food processor fitted with a steel blade for a few seconds until smooth. Transfer to a bowl and mix in the sugar, egg yolks, and vanilla. • Combine the flour and cocoa and fold into the mixture. Stir in the raisins and chocolate. Cover and chill in the refrigerator for 30 minutes. • Place the pastry on a floured work surface. Dust the top with flour and roll out into a 20 x 15-inch (38 x 50-cm) rectangle about $1/4$ inch (5 mm) thick. Trim the edges to straighten. • Cut the pastry into twelve 5-inch (13-cm) squares. • Spoon 2 tablespoons of the filling onto the center of each pastry square. Brush the egg around the edges of the pastry and fold one corner diagonally over to meet the opposite corner. Press down on the pastry, joining the 2 layers. • Place on the prepared baking sheets 1 inch (2.5 cm) apart. Refrigerate for 15 minutes. • Brush the tops with egg and sprinkle with demerara sugar. • Bake until golden brown, 25–30 minutes. • Transfer to a wire rack and let cool.

Filling

- 1 cup (250 g) ricotta cheese, drained
- $1/3$ cup (85 g) granulated sugar
- 2 large egg yolks
- 1 tablespoon vanilla extract (essence)
- 2 tablespoons all-purpose (plain) flour
- 1 tablespoon unsweetened cocoa powder
- $1/3$ cup (75 g) raisins
- 2 oz (60 g) semisweet (dark) chocolate, chopped

- 12 oz (350 g) frozen puff pastry, thawed
- 1 large egg, lightly beaten, to glaze
- $1/4$ cup (50 g) demerara sugar

Makes: 12 turnovers
Preparation: 45 minutes
Cooking: 25–30 minutes
Level: 1

CHOCOLATE AND CHERRY DANISH

Pastry: Warm the milk with a pinch of sugar.
• Dissolve the yeast in the milk and set aside until it begins to foam, 10–15 minutes. • Place the flour, remaining sugar, salt, and 2 tablespoons of butter in an electric mixer fitted with a dough hook. On low speed, start to mix the ingredients together, gradually pouring in the yeast mixture. Mix the dough until it comes together. Transfer to an oiled bowl, cover with a clean cloth, and set aside in a warm place. Let rise to double its original volume.
• Beat the remaining butter and margarine together until well combined. Shape the mixture into a rectangle. Place on a lightly floured plate and let cool until firm but not hard. It needs to be about the same temperature as the dough. • Turn the dough out onto a floured work surface, and pat it down gently. Roll out into a square about 1/2-inch (1-cm) thick. • Place the butter mixture in the middle of the square. Flatten the butter mixture so that it covers one-third of the center of the pastry. Take the left side of the dough and fold into the middle over the butter. Tuck it in. Take the right side of the rectangle and fold it over the left. Repeat for the top and the bottom of the pastry. You will have a square parcel now with the butter in the middle.
• Roll the pastry into a 16 x 24-inch (40 x 60-cm) rectangle. Make one turn to the left so that the rectangle is horizontal and fold the left side into the middle and the right side over the left. Repeat the process by rolling the dough out again and folding

Pastry

1 cup (250 ml) milk

¼ cup (50 g) granulated sugar

1 oz (30 g) fresh yeast or 2 (¼-oz/7-g) packages active dry yeast

3 cups (450 g) cups all-purpose (plain) flour

1½ teaspoons salt

¾ cup (125 g) butter, softened

1 large egg

½ cup (125 g) margarine, softened

Filling

1 recipe chocolate pastry cream (see page 678)

1 lb (500 g) jar morello cherries

1 egg, beaten, to glaze

1 cup (250 g) apricot preserves (jam), to glaze

Makes: 18–20 pastries
Preparation: 4 hours
Cooking: 10–15 minutes
Level: 3

in the same way. Make a mark on the left-hand side of the dough. Cover and refrigerate for 30 minutes. • With the mark at the left side repeat the rolling and folding. Turn the pastry once to the left and make a mark on the top left hand corner.
• Refrigerate again and repeat the rolling, folding, and turning once more. Allow the pastry to sit for 30 minutes before using. • Line two baking sheets with parchment paper. • Preheat the oven to 400°F (200°C/gas 6). • Roll the pastry into a $1/2$-inch (1-cm) thick rectangle. Trim the edges and cut into 3-inch (9-cm) squares. Cut a $1^1/_2$-inch (3-cm) line from the tip of each corner to the center of the square leaving a 1-inch (2.5-cm) square in the center uncut. Fold each left point of the cut into the middle and press down. It should look like a wind mill. • Filling: Pipe a little of the pastry cream in the center and arrange a cluster of the cherries on top. • Place on the prepared baking sheets. Space 1-inch (2.5 cm) apart to allow for rising. Cover with a cloth and set aside in a warm place until doubled in volume, about 30 minutes. Brush with the beaten egg. • Bake until golden and crisp, 10–15 minutes. Transfer to a wire rack to cool.
• Bring the apricot preserves to a boil with a little water. Brush over the pastries while still warm.

CHOCOLATE AND BANANA SLICE

Preheat the oven to 400°F (200°C/gas 6). • Line a baking sheet with parchment paper. • Cut off one-third of the pastry. Cover the larger piece of pastry and place in the refrigerator. • Roll out the smaller piece of pastry on a floured work surface into a 5 x 9-inch (13 x 23-cm) rectangle. • Transfer to the prepared baking sheet. Brush with egg. • Cut the banana into quarters lengthways and place down each side of the pastry leaving a space in the middle for the frangipan. Overlap the bananas slightly, if necessary, to make them fit. Leave a border of 1 inch (2.5 cm) all around the pastry. • Spoon the frangipan into a piping bag fitted with a plain nozzle and pipe in between the bananas. Sprinkle with the chocolate and set aside. • Roll out the remaining pastry into a rectangle the same length as the base but an extra 2 inches (5 cm) in width, to accommodate the filling. Fold the rectangle in half lengthways and cut incisions along the fold, about half the width of the pastry. Very carefully transfer the pastry, still folded, onto the prepared base. Ensure that the fold is down the middle of the prepared base. Line up the edges of the uncut side with the edge of the base. Gently unfold the pastry and line up the other edge with the base. Press firmly around the edges and trim off any overlapping pastry. Brush the top with the egg. • Bake until golden, about 20 minutes, then lower the oven to 350°F (180°C/gas 4) and bake for 15 more minutes to cook the base. • Let cool completely on a wire rack.

5 oz (150 g) frozen puff pastry, thawed

1 large egg, lightly beaten

½ recipe chocolate frangipan (see page 684)

1 banana

2 oz (60 g) semisweet (dark) chocolate, chopped

Serves: 6–8
Preparation: 1 hour
Cooking: 35–40 minutes
Level: 2

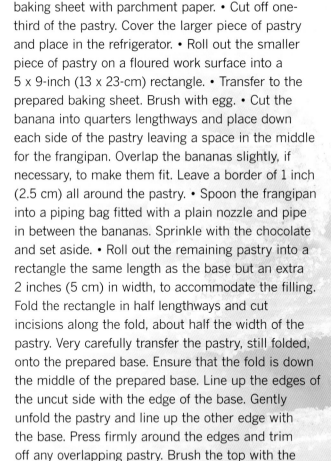

CHOCOLATE DOUGHNUTS

Place the yeast, 1 tablespoon of sugar, the water, and milk in a medium bowl. Set aside in a warm place until it begins to foam, 10–15 minutes. • With an electric mixer fitted with a dough hook, beat the flour, 2 tablespoons of sugar, the eggs, and yeast mixture on medium speed mix until the dough comes together. Turn out onto a floured work surface and knead until smooth, about 5 minutes. • Place the dough in an oiled bowl and cover with a clean cloth. Place the bowl in a warm place until the dough has doubled in volume, about 1 hour. • Line two baking sheets with parchment paper. • Turn the dough out onto a floured work surface and knock back, turning it over with your fingertips. Roll out to $1/2$ inch (1 cm) thick. Using a 2-inch (5 cm) round cutter, cut out the doughnuts and place them on the prepared baking sheet. Cover with a slightly damp cloth and set aside in a warm place until doubled in volume, about 20 minutes. • Place the oil in a deep-fryer over medium-high heat. When the oil is very hot, fry the doughnuts in 3–4 batches until golden brown, turning with a slotted spoon. Remove each doughnut and drain on paper towels for a few minutes before rolling in the remaining sugar. • Spoon the ganache into a piping bag fitted with a plain nozzle. • When cool enough to handle, take a doughnut and gently pipe some of the ganache into it by pushing the nozzle through the crust into the middle. Repeat for each doughnut. • Serve hot or warm.

$1\frac{1}{2}$ oz (45 g) fresh yeast or 3 ($1/4$-oz/7-g) packages active dry yeast

1   cup (200 g) superfine (caster) sugar

$1/4$ cup (60 ml) warm water

1   cup (250 ml) warm milk

4   cups (600 g) all-purpose (plain) flour

3   large eggs

2   cups (500 ml) vegetable oil, to fry

1   recipe chocolate ganache (see page 686)

Makes: 25–30 doughnuts
Preparation: 2 hours
Cooking: 30 minutes
Level: 2

CHURROS WITH HOT CHOCOLATE SAUCE

<u>Dough</u>: Place the water, extra-virgin olive oil, and salt in a heavy-based pan and bring to a boil. • Turn the heat down and add the flour. Beat until the mixture forms a ball then remove from the heat. • Heat the oil in a deep fryer over medium-high heat until very hot. • Place the sugar and cinnamon in a large, low-sided dish. • Using a piping bag with a star nozzle, pipe thick strips of dough into the oil and fry until golden brown. • Remove the churros with a slotted spoon and place in the dish with the sugar and cinnamon. Shake the dish until the churros are lightly coated with the sugar mixture. <u>Chocolate Sauce</u>: Melt the chocolate with half the milk in a double boiler over barely simmering heat. • Dissolve the cornstarch in the rest of the milk and mix into the chocolate together with the sugar. Stir constantly until thickened. Remove from the heat and whisk until really smooth. • Dip the churros in the sauce while still hot and enjoy.

Dough

1   cup (250 ml) water

1   tablespoon extra-virgin olive oil

    Pinch of salt

1   cup (150 g) all-purpose (plain) flour

2   cups (500 ml) vegetable oil, to fry

½   cup (100 g) superfine (caster) sugar

1   tablespoon ground cinnamon

Chocolate Sauce

5   oz (150 g) semisweet (dark) chocolate

2   cups (500 ml) milk

1   tablespoon cornstarch (cornflour)

4   tablespoons granulated sugar

Serves: 4–6
Preparation: 15 minutes
Cooking: 15 minutes
Level: 1

CHOCOLATE HAZELNUT TWISTS

Pastry: Mix the flour, cocoa, and salt in a large bowl.
Roughly break the butter into pieces the size of
hazelnuts and mix into the flour, without rubbing in.
• Make a well in the center of the flour mixture and
add half the water. Use your hands to mix together.
Add the rest of the water and mix with your hands
to form a soft dough. The butter will be firm and
visible throughout the dough. • Roll out on a floured
surface into a 6 x 12-inch (15 x 30-cm) rectangle.
Take the left side of the rectangle and fold into the
center of the dough. Take the right side of the
rectangle and fold over the left. You will have a
3 layered vertical rectangle now. Make one turn to
the left so that the rectangle is now horizontal and
repeat the process by rolling the dough out again,
and folding in the same way. Make a mark on the
left-hand side of the dough. Cover and refrigerate
for 20 minutes. Remove the dough and, with the
mark at the left side, repeat the rolling and folding.
Refrigerate once more and repeat the rolling and
folding one last time. You will see the butter layers
through the pastry. Allow the pastry to sit for 20
minutes before using. • Filling: Place the hazelnuts,
cake crumbs, sugar, honey, and butter in a medium
bowl and mix together until thoroughly combined.
• Roll the pastry out into 10 x 14-inch (25 x 35-cm)
rectangle about $1/2$ inch (1 cm) thick. With the
pastry rectangle facing you vertically, fold the pastry
in half toward you and mark the fold. Unfold the
pastry and carefully spread the nut mixture along

Pastry

3 cups (450 g) all-purpose (plain) flour
$1/2$ cup (75 g) unsweetened cocoa powder
$1/2$ teaspoon salt
$1 1/2$ cups (375 g) butter
$1 1/2$ cups (300 ml) iced water

Filling

2 cups (250 g) hazelnuts, coarsely chopped
1 cup (125 g) dry cake crumbs, finely processed
$1/4$ cup (50 g) superfine (caster) sugar
2 tablespoons honey
2 tablespoons butter, melted

Makes: 20–25 twists
Preparation: 2 hours
Cooking: 10 minutes
Level: 3

the bottom half of the pastry. Gently bring the top half of the pastry down over the nut mix and line up the edges. Press down on the pastry. • Place on a baking sheet, cover, and refrigerate for 10 minutes. • Transfer the pastry to a floured work surface with the fold at the top. Cut into strips about $3/_4$-inch (2-cm) across. • Oil a baking sheet and line with parchment paper. • Preheat the oven to 400°F (200°C/gas 6). • Take each strip, holding the top and the bottom, and pull and stretch it a little, then twist it. • Place on the baking sheet. Repeat with all the strips, placing them well spaced on the sheet. • Bake until crisp and well puffed, about 10 minutes. • Allow the pastry to cool completely before attempting to move.

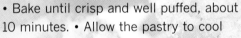

PAIN AU CHOCOLAT

Place the milk, 1 teaspoon of sugar, and yeast in a small bowl. Stir to dissolve then set aside until it begins to foam, 10–15 minutes. • With an electric mixer fitted with a dough hook, beat the flour, remaining sugar, salt, and 2 tablespoons of butter on low, gradually adding the yeast and milk mixture. Mix until the dough comes together. Place in an oiled bowl, cover with a clean cloth, and set aside in a warm place until doubled in volume. • Beat the butter and margarine together until well combined. Shape into a rectangle. Place on a lightly floured plate. Cool until firm, but not hard. It needs to be about the same temperature as the dough. • Turn the dough out onto a floured work surface, and pat down gently. Roll out into a square about 3/4 inch (2 cm) thick. Place the butter mixture in the middle of the square, spreading it so that it covers one-third of the middle of the pastry. Take the left side of the dough and fold into the middle and over the butter. Tuck it in. Take the right side of the rectangle and fold over the left. Repeat for the top and the bottom of the pastry. You will have a square parcel with the butter in the middle. Roll the pastry into a 16 x 24-inch (40 x 60-cm) rectangle. Make one turn to the left so that the rectangle is now horizontal and fold the left side into the middle and the right side over the left. Repeat the process by rolling the dough out again, and folding in the same way. Make a mark on the left-hand side of the dough. Cover and refrigerate for 30 minutes. This is the first turn.

1 cup (250 ml) warm milk

¼ cup (50 g) sugar

1 oz (30 g) fresh yeast or 2 (¼-oz/7-g) packages active dry yeast

3 cups (450 g) cups all-purpose (plain) flour

1 teaspoon salt

½ cup (125 g) butter, softened + 2 tablespoons

½ cup (125 g) margarine, softened

60 squares semisweet (dark) chocolate

1 egg, lightly beaten

Makes: 20 pastries
Preparation: 4 hours
Cooking: 10–15 minutes
Level: 2

Remove the dough and with the mark at the left side repeat the rolling and folding. Turn the pastry once to the left and make a mark on the top left hand corner. This is the second turn. Refrigerate once more and repeat the rolling, folding, and turning once more. You will see the butter layers through the pastry. Let the pastry sit for 30 minutes before using. • Oil two baking sheets and line with parchment paper. • Roll the dough out into a rectangle about $1/2$ inch (1 cm) thick. Trim the edges and cut into $31/2$ x 5-inch (7 x 9-cm) rectangles. • Place 3 pieces of chocolate along the left side of each piece of pastry and roll up to make a flattish cylinder. Transfer to the prepared baking sheets, spacing about 1 inch (2.5 cm) apart to allow for rising. Cover with a clean cloth and set aside in a warm place. Let rise to half their size again, about 30 minutes. • Preheat the oven to 400°F (200°C/ gas 6). • Brush with the beaten egg. • Bake until golden and crisp, 10–15 minutes. • Remove from the oven and place on a wire rack to cool.

PEAR GALLETTES

Mix the flour, cocoa, and salt in a large bowl. Break the butter into pieces the size of hazelnuts and mix into the flour, without rubbing in. • Make a well in the center and add half the water. Use your hands to mix together. Add the rest of the water and mix with your hands to form a soft dough. The butter will be firm and visible throughout the dough. • Roll out on a floured work surface into a 6 x 12-inch (15 x 30-cm) rectangle. Take the left side of the rectangle and fold into the center of the dough. Take the right side of the rectangle and fold over the left. You will have a 3 layered vertical rectangle. Make one turn to the left so that the rectangle is horizontal and repeat the process by rolling the dough out again and folding in the same way. Make a mark on the left-hand side of the dough. Cover and refrigerate for 20 minutes. • With the mark at the left side of the dough, repeat the rolling and folding. Refrigerate once more and repeat the rolling and folding one last time. You will still be able to see the butter layers through the pastry. Let sit for 20 minutes before using. • Line a baking sheet with parchment paper. • Preheat the oven to 400°F (200°C/gas 6). • Roll the pastry into a square about $1/2$-inch (1-cm) thick. Using a plain round $31/2$-inch (10-cm) pastry cutter, cut out disks of pastry. • Transfer to the baking sheet. Top each disk with slices of pear, leaving a $1/4$-inch (5-mm) border. • Bake until crisp and well puffed and the pear begins to brown a little, 10–15 minutes. • Cool on wire racks.

3 cups (450 g) all-purpose (plain) flour

$1/2$ cup (75 g) unsweetened cocoa powder

$1/2$ teaspoon salt

$11/2$ cups (375 g) butter

$11/2$ cups (300 ml) iced water

6 pears, peeled, cored, and sliced thinly lengthways

Makes: 8–10 pastries
Preparation: 2 hours
Cooking: 10–15 minutes
Level: 2

PEAR AND FRANGIPAN TARTLETS

Butter twelve 4-inch (10-cm) tartlet pans. • Roll the pastry out on a floured work surface to $1/4$ inch (5 mm) thick. • Using a plain pastry cutter, cut into twelve 4-inch (10-cm) rounds. Line the pans with the pastry rounds, smoothing the base and pressing into the sides. Trim off any excess pastry. <u>Chocolate Frangipan</u>: Melt the chocolate in a double boiler over barely simmering water. Remove from the heat and let cool for a few minutes. • With an electric beater on high speed, beat the butter and sugar until pale and creamy. • Add the eggs one at a time, beating until just combined after each addition. • With mixer on low, slowly pour in the chocolate. Briefly turn the speed to high, then scrape down the sides of the bowl. • Mix the flour and almonds in a separate bowl. • With mixer on low speed, gradually beat in the flour mixture. Cover and refrigerate for 30 minutes before using. • Preheat the oven to 350°F (180°C/gas 4). • Spoon the mixture into the prepared tart cases. Spread evenly until it reaches two-thirds of the way up the sides of each case. • Place one half pear in the center of each tart. • Bake until the bases are firm, 15–20 minutes. • Bring the apricot preserves to a boil with a little water and carefully brush over the tops of the tartlets.

½ recipe chocolate pastry (see page 682)

Chocolate Frangipan

8 oz (250 g) semisweet (dark) chocolate, chopped

½ cup (125 g) butter

½ cup (100 g) superfine (caster) sugar

3 large eggs

¼ cup (30 g) all-purpose (plain) flour

1 cup (120 g) ground almonds

6 pears, peeled, halved, and cored, with stalks

Warmed apricot preserves (jam), to glaze

Makes: 12 tartlets
Preparation: 40 minutes
Cooking: 15–20 minutes
Level: 2

PLUM TARTLETS

Pastry: Melt the chocolate in a double boiler over barely simmering water. Set aside. • Place the yeast and milk in a large bowl and beat lightly with a wire whisk. Add the salt and sugar. • With an electric mixer fitted with a dough hook and on low speed, add the flour and eggs and beat for 1 minute. Increase the speed to medium and mix until soft and smooth. Gradually add the butter, making sure it has come together between additions. Mix for 5 more minutes. • Add the chocolate and mix until well combined and the dough is an even dark brown. • Cover the bowl with a clean cloth and set aside in a warm place until doubled in volume. • Gently remove the risen dough from the bowl and flatten slightly on a floured work surface. This is done by flipping the dough over several times with your fingers. • Place on a plate and refrigerate for up to 2 hours. • When the pastry has cooled and rested, roll out on a floured work surface to $1/2$-inch (1-cm) thick. • Butter twelve 4-inch (10-cm) tartlet pans. • Using a cutter 2 sizes bigger than the tartlet pans, cut out rounds and line the pan. • Filling: Spoon in the pastry cream and arrange the plums on top, allowing 3 per tart. • Cover the tarts with a clean cloth and leave in a warm place to rise, about 15 minutes. • Preheat the oven to 350°F (180°C/gas 4). • Oil a baking sheet. • Place the tartlets on the prepared baking sheet. • Bake for 15–20 minutes. • Let cool on a wire rack before removing from the tartlet pans.

Pastry

5 oz (150 g) semisweet (dark) chocolate, chopped

1 oz (30 g) fresh yeast or 2 (¼-oz/7-g) packages active dry yeast

$1/3$ cup (90 ml) warm milk

1 teaspoon salt

2 tablespoons superfine (caster) sugar

$3\frac{1}{3}$ cups (500 g) all-purpose (plain) flour

4 large eggs

$1\frac{1}{3}$ cups (335 g) butter, softened

Filling

$1/2$ recipe pastry cream (see page 678. Omit the chocolate in the recipe)

16 plums, pitted and halved

Makes: 12 tartlets
Preparation: 3 hours
Cooking: 15–20 minutes
Level: 2

■ ■ ■ *Any leftover dough can be wrapped and frozen for later use.*

SWEET CHOCOLATE BUNS

Place the raisins in a small bowl. Cover with water and soak for at least 30 minutes. • Drain, reserving 1/4 cup (60 ml) of the soaking liquid. • Place the milk in a small bowl and stir in the yeast. Let stand until it begins to foam, 10–15 minutes. • Add 1/2 cup (75 g) of flour and the reserved soaking liquid and stir until smooth. Cover and let rest in a warm place until double its original volume, about 30 minutes. • Mix the flour, cocoa, sugar, yeast mixture, salt, eggs, egg yolk, grated zests, and vanilla in a large bowl. With an electric mixer on medium speed, beat until well blended, then gradually add the butter, beating well. • Change the beater for the dough hook and mix on medium until soft and glossy. • Place the dough in an oiled bowl, cover with a clean cloth, and set aside in a warm place until double its original volume, about 1 hour. • Turn the dough out onto a floured work surface and flatten by patting gently.
• Mix together the soaked raisins and the chocolate.
• Cut the dough into 18–20 equal sized pieces.
• Place a tablespoon of the chocolate raisin mix onto the center of each piece and roll up into a ball.
• Place the buns on an oiled baking sheet, cover with a clean cloth, and let rise to half their size again, about 30 minutes. • Preheat the oven to 400°F (200°C/gas 6). • Bake until the buns sound hollow when lightly tapped on the bottom, 10–15 minutes. • Cool on wire racks. Either dust with confectioners' sugar before serving or brush with the apricot preserves.

1/2 cup (100 g) raisins

Water to cover

1/2 cup (125 ml) warm milk

1 oz (30 g) fresh yeast or 2 (1/4-oz/7-g) packages active dry yeast

3 cups (450 g) all-purpose (plain) flour

1/3 cup (50 g) unsweetened cocoa powder

1/2 cup (100 g) granulated sugar

1 teaspoon salt

2 large eggs + 1 large egg yolk

Grated zest of 1 orange and 1 lemon combined

1 teaspoon vanilla extract (essence)

1/2 cup (125 g) butter, softened

3 oz (90 g) semisweet (dark) chocolate, finely chopped

Confectioners' (icing) sugar, to dust or warmed apricot preserves (jam), to glaze

Makes: 18 buns
Preparation: 2 hours
Cooking: 10–15 minutes
Level: 2

PISTACHIO AND ORANGE FILO ROLL

Preheat the oven to 350°F (180°C/gas 4). • Oil a baking sheet. • Place the pistachio nuts, cake crumbs, and chocolate in a food processor and process until coarsely chopped. • Add the juice and zest of the orange and process again until it just comes together, a few seconds. • Unroll the filo pastry. Lay it out and cover with a slightly damp cloth. • Combine the almonds and sugar in a small bowl. • Lay one piece of pastry out on a work bench. Lightly brush with the melted butter, sprinkle with the sugar mix, and lay the second sheet on top. Repeat with the butter and sugar. Repeat the process until all the pastry, butter, and sugar mix are used up, finishing with a sheet of pastry just brushed with butter. • Leaving a 1-inch (2.5-cm) border, place the chocolate filling on the lower third of the pastry in a sausage shape. Fold in the ends and roll up as tightly as you can into a log shape. • Place on the prepared baking sheet with the seam side down. Give the roll one final brush with butter. • Bake until golden brown, 25–35 minutes. • Transfer the log to a wire rack and let cool to just warm. Dust with confectioners' sugar. Using a serrated knife, slice into servings and serve warm.

1 cup (150 g) unsalted pistachio nuts

½ cup (60 g) dry cake crumbs

8 oz (250 g) semisweet (dark) chocolate, coarsely chopped

Freshly squeezed juice and finely grated zest of 1 orange

6 sheets frozen filo pastry, thawed

½ cup (60 g) ground almonds

3 tablespoons dark brown sugar

½ cup (125 g) butter, melted

Confectioners' (icing) sugar, to dust

Serves: 6–8
Preparation: 30 minutes
Cooking: 35 minutes
Level: 2

ÉCLAIRS

Place the water and butter in a saucepan over medium heat until the butter has melted and the mixture just begins to boil. Add the flour and beat with a wooden spoon until the mixture comes together in a ball and is smooth. Continue to cook over a low heat until it starts to come away from the sides. • Remove from the heat and beat in the eggs one at a time. The mixture will become a little sticky and of dropping consistency. (A spoonful held up will take about 5 seconds to drop). • Spoon into a piping bag fitted with a plain ½ inch (1 cm) nozzle. • Preheat the oven to 400°F (200°C/gas 6). • Oil a baking sheet and line with parchment paper. • Pipe the mixture onto the baking sheet in logs about 3 inches (7 cm) long, spacing them well, so they have room to rise. • Sprinkle with water and bake for 20 minutes. Turn the oven down to 300°F (150°C/gas 2) and bake until golden and hollow sounding when tapped on the bottom, 15–20 minutes. • Cool on wire racks. • When cooled, carefully slice lengthways along the side of each éclair. Slice only three quarters of the way through, leaving the top still joined. • Lift the top of each éclair and pipe in the pastry cream. • Melt the chocolate in a double boiler over barely simmering water. Let cool a little. • Holding the éclairs by their sides, dip the top third of each one in the chocolate. Shake of any excess and let set before serving.

1 cup (250 ml) water

⅓ cup (90 g) + 1 tablespoon butter

⅔ cup (100 g) all-purpose (plain) flour

4 large eggs

1 recipe chocolate pastry cream (see page 678)

5 oz (150 g) semisweet (dark) chocolate, chopped

Makes: 30 éclairs
Preparation: 30 minutes
Cooking: 35–40 minutes
Level: 2

MILLEFEUILLE

Mix the flour, cocoa, and salt in a large bowl.
• Roughly break the butter into pieces the size of hazelnuts and mix into the flour, without rubbing in. Make a well in the center and add half the water. Use your hands to mix together. Add the rest of the water and bring together until it forms a soft dough. The butter should be firm and visible throughout.
• Turn the dough out onto a floured work surface and roll out into a 6 x 12-inch (15 x 30-cm) rectangle. Take the left side and fold into the middle of the dough. Take the right side and fold over the left. You will have a 3 layered vertical rectangle. Make one turn to the left so that the rectangle is horizontal and repeat the process by rolling the dough out again, and folding in the same way. Make a mark on the left-hand side of the dough before covering it and refrigerating for 20 minutes. Remove the dough and with the mark at the left side repeat the rolling and folding. Refrigerate once more and repeat the rolling and folding one last time. You will still be able to see the butter layers through the pastry. Allow the pastry to sit for 20 minutes before using. • Roll the pastry out to a 10 x 12-inch (25 x 30-cm) slab about 1/2-inch (1-cm) thick. Fold the pastry in three to mark equal thirds, and cut along the marks. You should now have 3 strips of pastry. • Preheat the oven to 400°F (200°C/gas 6).
• Oil a baking sheet and place the pastry on it leaving space between the strips. Using a fork "dock" the pastry. This is when you prick the pastry

3 cups (450 g) all-purpose (plain) flour

1/2 cup (75 g) unsweetened cocoa powder

1/2 teaspoon salt

1 1/2 cups (375 g) butter

1 1/4 cups (300 ml) iced water

1 recipe pastry cream (see page 678) made with double the chocolate in the recipe for an extra rich cream

Unsweetened cocoa powder, to dust

Serves: 10–12
Preparation: 2 hours
Cooking: 10–15 minutes
Level: 2

evenly with a fork to prevent it rising too much. •
Bake the pastry until crisp and well puffed, 10–15
minutes.

• Place on wire racks and let cool completely.

• Spread 2 layers of pastry generously with
chocolate pastry cream. Assemble, by placing one
layer on top of the other, and finishing with the
plain layer. Dust with cocoa powder and refrigerate
for 20 minutes. Use a serrated knife to slice.

ELEGANT DESSERTS

AFFOGATO
Chocolate ice cream

Place the chocolate in a large bowl and set aside.
• Beat the egg yolks and sugar with an electric mixer on high speed until pale and creamy. • Place the cream and milk in a saucepan over medium heat and bring to a boil. Remove from the heat. • Add half the cream mixture to the egg mixture, beating constantly. Return this mixture to the saucepan with the remaining milk and cream and return to the heat. Stir constantly with a wooden spoon until the mixture begins to thicken and coats the back of the spoon.
• Remove from the heat and pour over the chocolate. Stir occasionally until the chocolate has melted and the mixture is thick and smooth. Cover and let cool completely. • Place in an ice cream machine and churn according to the manufacturer's instructions.
• Alternatively, if you don't have an ice cream machine, place the mixture in a metal bowl and freeze. When the mixture has just begun to set, beat with an electric beater or by hand, until creamy. Repeat at least 3 or 4 more times. • To serve: Place 3 glasses per person on 6 plates. Pour a shot of Baileys into one glass, a shot of espresso coffee into another, and a scoop of chocolate ice cream in the third glass. Serve immediately. • Your guests will choose how they want to combine the three. Traditionally the Baileys and coffee are poured over the ice cream.

8 oz (250 g) semisweet (dark) chocolate, chopped

6 large egg yolks

½ cup (100 g) superfine (caster) sugar

2 cups (500 ml) heavy (double) cream

1 cup (250 ml) milk

1 shot Baileys Irish Cream per person

1 shot espresso coffee per person

Serves: 6
Preparation: 30 minutes
+ 4 hours to freeze
Level: 1

ICED CAPPUCCINOS

Beat the egg yolks and half the sugar with an electric mixer on high speed until pale and creamy. • Beat the egg whites and remaining sugar on high speed until soft peaks form. Fold the whites into the egg yolk mixture. • Fold in the whipped cream followed by the coffee mixture and chocolate.
• To prepare the molds: Take 12 espresso cups and place them on a tray. Using parchment paper, cut strips long enough to wrap around the cups with an over lap and tall enough to come over the top of the cup about 1 inch (2.5 cm). Wrap the paper tightly around the cup and use a rubber band to keep it in place. • Pour in the coffee mixture to just below the top of the paper and carefully set in the freezer overnight. When completely set, remove the rubber bands and carefully peel off the paper. Dust with cocoa powder just before serving.

4   **large eggs, separated**

½   **cup (100 g) + 1 tablespoon superfine (caster) sugar**

2   **cups (500 ml) double (heavy) cream, firmly whipped**

3   **tablespoons instant coffee dissolved in 1 tablespoon boiling water**

2   **oz (60 g) bittersweet (dark) chocolate, finely grated**

Unsweetened cocoa powder, to dust

Serves: 6–12
Preparation: 45 minutes + overnight to freeze
Level: 1

CHOCOLATE BLANCMANGE

Place the chocolate in a bowl and set aside.
• Place the milk and cream in a medium saucepan over medium and heat to just below simmering point. Pour over the chocolate and stir until the chocolate is completely melted. • Beat the egg yolks, sugar, and cornstarch with an electric mixer on high speed until pale and creamy. • With mixer on low speed, slowly pour the hot chocolate mixture into the egg yolk mixture. Return the custard mixture to the saucepan, place it over low heat and, beat constantly until the mixture has thickened. Remove from the heat. • Place the gelatin in a small bowl, add the boiling water, stir well, and then let sit until all the gelatin has dissolved completely. • Stir into the chocolate custard. Let cool completely. • Oil eight 5-oz (150-ml) ramekins. • Divide the cooled chocolate mixture evenly among the molds, filling them to around three-quarters full. Place on a tray, cover and refrigerate for at least 2 hours. • Using your fingertips, pull the edge of the blancmange from the sides of the ramekins and shake out. Arrange on serving plates and top with whipped cream and shards of chocolate.

8 oz (250 g) bittersweet (dark) chocolate, chopped

1 cup (250 ml) milk

1 cup (250 ml) double (heavy) cream

6 large egg yolks

1 cup (200 g) granulated sugar

2 teaspoons cornstarch (cornflour)

1½ teaspoons powdered gelatin

2 tablespoons boiling water

Whipped cream, to serve

Shards of chocolate, to serve (optional)

Serves: 8
Preparation: 35 minutes
  + 2 hours to chill
Level: 1

CHOCOLATE CHARLOTTE

280

Sponge: Oil an 8 x 12-inch (20 x 30-cm) baking pan. Line with parchment paper. • Preheat the oven to 400°F (200°C/gas 6). • Beat the butter and half the sugar in an electric mixer on high speed until pale and creamy. • Add the egg yolks one at a time, beating until just combined after each addition. • In a separate bowl, combine the egg whites and the remaining sugar. Beat on high speed until the eggs are creamy and glossy and the sugar has completely dissolved. • Combine the cornstarch and ground almonds and fold alternate spoonfuls of the almond mixture and the egg whites into the butter mixture. • Spoon some of the mixture (about 3 large serving spoons) into the prepared pan. Spread to about 1/8-inch (2-mm) thick. Add or remove some of the mix if required. Sift an even layer of cocoa over the top. • Bake until the sponge is cooked and springs back when pressed. Spoon more of the mixture over the first layer and spread to the same thickness. Sift some of the cocoa evenly over the sponge and return to the oven until the sponge layer is cooked. Repeat using all of the sponge mixture and all of the cocoa. • Turn the oven down to 350°F (180°C/gas 4). Cover the cake with foil and bake for 10 more minutes. A skewer inserted should come out clean. • Turn the cake out on a wire rack and let cool completely. • Transfer the cooled cake to a board. Using the base of an 8-inch (20-cm) springform pan as a guide, cut around the base and remove the off cuts. This will leave you with a

Sponge

3/4 cup (200 g) butter

11/4 cups (250 g) granulated sugar

6 large eggs, separated

11/4 cups (175 g) cornstarch (cornflour)

1/2 cup (60 g) ground almonds

1/4 cup (30 g) unsweetened cocoa powder

Mousse

11/2 lb (750 g) bittersweet (dark) chocolate

8 large egg yolks

1/2 cup (100 g) superfine (caster) sugar

4 teaspoons powdered gelatin dissolved in 3 tablespoons boiling water

11/2 cups (375 ml) milk

2 cups (500 ml) heavy (double) cream

Serves: 8–10
Preparation: 1 hour 30 minutes + 2 hours to chill
Cooking: 35 minutes
Level: 2

circular sponge cake. • Line the base and sides of an 8-inch (20-cm) springform pan with parchment paper. • Place the round of sponge in the pan. Set aside until the mouse is ready. • <u>Mousse</u>: Place the chocolate in a large bowl and set aside. • Beat the egg yolks and sugar with an electric beater on high speed until pale and creamy. • Bring the milk to a boil in a saucepan over medium heat. Remove from the heat • Pour half the hot milk into the egg mixture, whisking constantly. Pour back into the saucepan with the remaining milk and return to medium heat. Stir constantly until it begins to thicken and coats the back of a metal spoon. • Remove from the heat and pour over the chocolate. Stir until the chocolate has melted and the mixture is thick and smooth. Stir in the gelatin. Let cool completely. • Beat the cream until thick. Fold into the chocolate mixture. • Pour the mousse into the pan over the sponge. • Refrigerate for at least 2 hours before serving.

WHITE CHOCOLATE AND HAZELNUT SOUFFLÉS

284

Preheat the oven to 400°F (200°C/gas 6). • Melt the butter and use a pastry brush to coat the insides of 6 ramekin molds. Sprinkle the molds with the 1–2 tablespoons of extra sugar. Coat the sides well as this is where the soufflé may stick. Set the ramekins aside. • Place the egg yolks and 1/4 cup (50 g) of the sugar in a bowl and beat with an electric mixer on high speed until pale and creamy. • With mixer on low speed, beat in the flour. • Place 1/4 cup (50 g) of sugar with the milk in a saucepan and bring to a boil. • Pour onto the egg mixture a little at a time, stirring continuously. Pour the mixture back into the pan and simmer over low heat for 2 minutes. • Cover and let cool completely. • Combine the egg whites and remaining sugar in a bowl and beat with mixer on high speed until soft peaks form. • Fold one-third of the egg whites into the cooled cream mixture. Fold in the hazelnuts and chocolate. Fold in the remaining egg whites. • Spoon into the prepared molds. • Place the ramekins on a baking sheet. Bake until puffed but firm, about 20 minutes.
• Dust with the confectioners' sugar and serve immediately with the chocolate sauce on the side.

2 tablespoons butter

3/4 cup (150 g) superfine (caster) sugar + 1–2 tablespoons extra

4 large eggs, separated

1/2 cup (75 g) all-purpose (plain) flour

3/4 cup (200 ml) milk

1/2 cup (125 g) finely ground toasted hazelnuts

1 oz (30 g) white chocolate, finely grated

   Confectioners' (icing) sugar, to dust

1 recipe chocolate sauce (see page 690)

Serves: 6
Preparation: 30–40 minutes
Cooking: 20 minutes
Level: 2

CHOCOLATE ALMOND SOUFFLÉS

Preheat the oven to 400°F (200°C/gas 6). • Melt the butter and use a pastry brush to coat the insides of 6 ramekin molds. Sprinkle the molds with the 1–2 tablespoons extra sugar. Coat the sides well as this is where the soufflé may stick. Set the ramekins aside. • Beat the egg yolks and about one-third of the sugar with an electric mixer on high speed until pale and creamy. • With mixer on low speed, beat in the flour. • Bring the milk and remaining sugar to a boil over medium heat. • Pour onto the egg mixture a little at a time, stirring continuously. Pour the mixture back into the pan and simmer over low heat for 2 minutes. • Remove from the heat and stir in the chocolate until melted and completely smooth. • Cover and let cool completely. • Beat the egg whites until stiff peaks form. • Fold one-third of the whites into the cooled cream, followed by the almonds and then the remaining egg whites. • Pour the batter into the prepared ramekins. • Place the ramekins on a baking sheet. Bake until puffed but firm, about 20 minutes. • Serve immediately with the chocolate sauce on the side.

2 tablespoons butter

4 large eggs, separated

½ cup (100 g) granulated sugar + 1–2 tablespoons extra

½ cup (75 g) all-purpose (plain) flour

¾ cup (200 ml) milk

5 oz (150 g) semisweet (dark) chocolate, grated

1 cup (125 g) finely ground almonds

1 recipe chocolate sauce (see page 690)

Serves: 6
Preparation: 40–50 minutes
Cooking: 20 minutes
Level: 1

WHITE CHOCOLATE AND STRAWBERRY CHEESECAKES

Melt the chocolate in a double boiler over barely simmering water. Set aside. • Brush a 12-cup muffin pan with butter. • Combine the crushed cookies and melted butter to form a paste. Press the mixture into the base and up the sides of the muffin cups. Place in the refrigerator to chill while you prepare the filling. • Beat the cream cheese, sugar, and lemon zest until light and creamy. Beat in the gelatin mixture. • Beat the cream until thick then fold into the cream cheese mixture. • Divide the mixture into two. Fold the melted chocolate into one half and the strawberry pulp into the other. • Remove the prepared muffin pan from the refrigerator and place alternate spoonfuls of the chocolate and strawberry mixture in the cups, swirling them together to create a marbled effect. Smooth the top. • Chill in the refrigerator for 30 minutes. • Carefully remove from the cheesecakes by running a knife around the edges of each cup and gently lifting them out.

5 oz (150 g) white chocolate, grated

⅓ cup (90 g) butter, melted

1¼ cups (170 g) crushed plain chocolate cookies (biscuits)

2 cups (500 g) cream cheese softened

¾ cup (150 g) superfine (caster) sugar

1 teaspoon finely grated lemon zest

3 teaspoons gelatin dissolved in ¼ cup (60 ml) boiling water

1 cup (250 ml) heavy (double) cream

½ cup (75 g) strawberry pulp

Serves: 6–12
Preparation: 20 minutes
   + 30 minutes to chill
Level: 1

WHITE CHOCOLATE AND RASPBERRY TRIFLE

<u>Sponge</u>: Preheat the oven to 350°F (180°C/gas 4).
• Butter and flour a 9-inch (23-cm) square baking pan. Line with parchment paper. Butter the paper.
• Mix the flour, baking powder, and salt in a large bowl. • Beat the butter, sugar, and vanilla in a large bowl with an electric mixer at high speed until creamy. • Add the eggs, one at a time, beating until just blended after each addition. • With mixer at low speed, gradually beat in the dry ingredients, alternating with the milk. • Spoon the batter into the prepared pan. Bake until a toothpick inserted into the center comes out clean, 45–55 minutes.
• Cool the cake in the pan for 10 minutes. Turn out onto a rack. Carefully remove the paper and let cool completely. • Cut the sponge into 1 inch (2.5 cm) cubes. • <u>White Chocolate Mousse</u>: Place the chocolate in a large bowl and set aside. • Beat the egg yolks and sugar with an electric mixer on high speed until pale and creamy. • Bring the milk to a boil in a saucepan over medium heat. • Remove from the heat and pour half the hot milk into the egg mixture, whisking continuously. Pour back into the saucepan and return to the heat. Stir continuously until it begins to thicken and coats the back of a metal spoon. • Remove from the heat and pour over the chocolate. Stir until melted and smooth.
• Stir in the gelatin until completely amalgamated. Let cool completely. • Beat the cream until thick. Fold into the mousse.

Sponge

1½ cups (225 g) all-purpose (plain) flour

1½ teaspoons baking powder

¼ teaspoon salt

1 cup (250 g) butter, softened

1 cup (200 g) granulated sugar

2 teaspoons vanilla extract (essence)

4 large eggs

⅔ cup (180 ml) milk

White Chocolate Mousse

14 oz (400 g) white chocolate, finely chopped

8 large egg yolks

¼ cup (50 g) granulated sugar

4 teaspoons powdered gelatin dissolved in 3 tablespoons boiling water

¾ cup (200 ml) milk

1⅓ cups (325 ml) heavy (double) cream

Syrup: Combine the sugar and water in a heavy-based pan over medium heat and bring to a boil. Boil rapidly for 5 minutes. Remove from the heat and stir in the kirsch. • Raspberry Sauce: Place all the ingredients in a pan over medium heat and bring to a boil. Simmer for 5 minutes. • Remove from the heat chop in a food processor until smooth. • Strain the sauce through a fine sieve to remove the seeds. Let cool completely.

To Assemble: Take a large glass or crystal bowl and add enough sponge cubes to cover the base. Pour enough of the syrup over the top to saturate the sponge. Sprinkle some of the raspberries over the top and drizzle some of the raspberry sauce in. Spoon in one-third of the chocolate mousse. At this stage, gently bang the bowl down onto a cloth to release any air bubbles. Cover with the remaining sponge and saturate with the remaining syrup. Scatter with raspberries, reserving a few for the top, and drizzle with the remaining sauce. Arrange the jelly over the sauce and spread the remaining mousse over the top. Cover and refrigerate for 10 minutes. • Whip the cream and spread over the mousse, smoothing the top. • Top with chocolate curls and fresh raspberries. • Chill in the refrigerator for at least 30 minutes before serving.

Syrup

1 cup (200 g) granulated sugar

2 cups (500 ml) water

¼ cup (60 ml) kirsch

Raspberry Sauce

8 oz (250 g) frozen raspberries, thawed

¼ cup (50 g) granulated sugar

¼ cup (60 ml) water

2 cups (500 g) raspberry jelly made to the manufacturers instructions. Set the jelly in a tray and cut into cubes

3 cups (750 ml) whipped cream

White chocolate curls (see page 694)

Fresh raspberries

Serves: 12
Preparation: 2 hours
  + 30 minutes to chill
Level: 2

MINT CHOCOLATE CHIP ICE CREAM

Beat the egg yolks and sugar with an electric mixer on high speed until pale and creamy. • Bring the cream and milk to a boil in a saucepan over medium heat. • Remove from the heat. Beat half of the hot cream mixture into the egg mixture. Return to the pan with the milk and cream and return to the heat. Stir continuously until it begins to thicken and coats the back of a metal spoon. • Remove from the heat, pour into another bowl, cover, and let cool completely. • Add the chocolate and peppermint extract—be careful not to add too much, as too much peppermint can be overpowering. Add one drop at a time, to taste. • Place in an ice cream machine and churn according to the manufacturers instructions. • Alternatively, if you do not have an ice cream machine, place the mixture in a metal bowl and freeze. When the mixture has just begun to set, whisk with an electric beater or by hand, until creamy. Repeat at least 3 or 4 more times or until thick and smooth.

6 large egg yolks

½ cup (100 g) superfine (caster) sugar

2 cups (500 ml) light (single) cream

1 cup (250 ml) milk

5 oz (150 g) semisweet (dark) chocolate, chopped

⅛ teaspoon mint extract (essence)

Serves: 4–6
Preparation: 30 minutes + 4 hours to freeze
Level: 1

PROFITEROLES

Place the water and butter in a pan over medium heat until the butter has melted and the mixture just begins to boil. Add the flour and beat with a wooden spoon until the mixture comes together in a ball and is smooth. Simmer over low heat until it starts to come away from the sides of the pan. Remove from the heat. • Beat in the eggs one at a time. The mixture will become a little sticky and of dropping consistency. (A spoonful held up will take about 5 seconds to drop). • Spoon into a piping bag fitted with a plain nozzle. • Preheat the oven to 400°F (200°C/gas 6). Oil a baking sheet and line with parchment paper. • Pipe mounds about the size of large walnuts onto the baking sheet, spacing them out so that they have room to spread. Sprinkle with water. • Bake for 20 minutes. Turn the oven down to 300°F (150°C/gas 2) and bake until golden and hollow sounding when tapped on the bottoms, about 15 minutes. Cool on racks. • Fill a piping bag with the whipped cream and push the nozzle through the pastry base and squeeze until you feel the profiterole become heavy and full. • Arrange on serving plates and pour the warm chocolate sauce over the top.

1 cup (250 ml) water

⅓ cup + 1 tablespoon (100 g) butter

⅔ cup (100 g) all-purpose (plain) flour

4 large eggs

2 cups (500 ml) heavy (double) cream whipped to soft peaks

1 recipe chocolate sauce (see page 690)

Serves: 8–10
Preparation: 30 minutes
Cooking: 45 minutes
Level: 1

COFFEE GRANITA WITH CREAM AND CHOCOLATE

298

Place 1¹/₂ cups (375 ml) of boiling water and the sugar in heavy-based saucepan over medium heat until the sugar is dissolved and syrup is boiling. Boil for 1 minute. Remove from the heat and let cool. • Place the remaining boiling water in a medium bowl and mix in the coffee and cocoa to make a smooth paste. • Stir in the sugar syrup. Whisk together then strain. • Pour the mixture into a medium-size metal bowl or tray. Place in the freezer and freeze until solid, about 3 hours.
• Use a fork to break the ice up into large crystals. Return to the freezer; keep frozen until ready to serve. • Spoon the granita into 8 serving glasses. Top with cream and chocolate.

2   cups (500 ml) boiling water

³/₄ cup (150 g) superfine (caster) sugar

4   tablespoons instant coffee granules

2   tablespoons unsweetened cocoa powder

1   cup (250 ml) whipped cream

Grated chocolate, to decorate

Serves: 8
Preparation: 15 minutes
    + 3 hours to freeze
Level: 1

MILK CHOCOLATE AND VANILLA SEMIFREDDO

300

Place the chocolate in a bowl. • Bring one-third of the cream to a boil and pour over the chocolate. Stir until the chocolate is melted and smooth. Let cool completely. • Beat the egg yolks and half the sugar with an electric mixer on high speed until pale and creamy. • Beat the egg whites and remaining sugar with mixer on high speed until soft peaks form. • Fold the whites into the egg yolk mixture. • Whip the remaining cream and fold into the egg mixture. • Divide the mixture between two bowls, placing one-third of the mixture in one, and two-thirds in the other. • Scrape the vanilla pod and mix into the smaller mixture. • Gently fold the chocolate into the larger mixture. • Pour the vanilla mixture into dariole molds or medium sized ramekin molds to about one-third of the way up the mold. Place on a tray and freeze until firm, 20–30 minutes. • Pour the chocolate mixture in on top and freeze overnight. • To turn the semifreddo out, dip each ramekin base into warm water and shake out. Place on a tray and freeze for a few minutes before transferring to serving plates.

3 oz (90 g) milk chocolate, chopped

2⅓ cups (600 ml) heavy (double) cream

2 large eggs, separated

⅔ cup (130 g) superfine (caster) sugar

1 vanilla pod split lengthways

Serves: 4–6
Preparation: 45 minutes + overnight to freeze
Level: 1

RICH CHOCOLATE ICE CREAM CAKE

Line the base and sides of a 9-inch (23-cm) springform pan with parchment paper. The paper needs to stand above the top of the springform by 1 inch (2.5 cm). • Cut the chocolate sponge into three horizontally. • Place a layer of the cake in the prepared pan and top with a 1-inch (2.5-cm) layer of the chocolate ice cream. Place the next layer of cake over the ice cream and press down lightly. Spread a 1-inch (2.5-cm) layer of vanilla ice cream over the cake and top with the last layer of cake. • Spread with a 1-inch (2.5-cm) layer of chocolate ice cream, smoothing the top. Freeze overnight. • Melt the chocolate in a doubler boiler over barely simmering water. • Cut a strip of parchment paper long enough to wrap around the springform pan with a small overlap and tall enough to just come over the top of the cake. • Remove the cake from the freezer and carefully remove from the springform pan. Place on a serving plate. • Spread the melted chocolate onto the strip of parchment paper and let cool for a few minutes, without letting it set. • Carefully take one end of the parchment paper and wrap it, chocolate side in, around the cake. Allow to set completely before carefully removing the parchment paper. • Top the cake with scoops of the remaining vanilla and chocolate ice cream. Refreeze for at least 1 hour before serving.

1 **recipe basic chocolate sponge (see page 696)**

1 **lb (500 g) double chocolate chip ice cream, softened**

8 **oz (250 g) vanilla ice cream, softened**

8 **oz (250 g) semisweet (dark) chocolate**

Serves: 8–10
Preparation: 30 minutes + 4 hours to freeze
Level: 2

CHOCOLATE SOUFFLÉ SURPRISES

304

Preheat the oven to 350°F (180°C/gas 4). • Butter 6 ramekins with the 2 tablespoons of butter. Dust with the cocoa. • Beat the butter and sugar with an electric mixer on high speed until pale and creamy. • Beat in the egg yolks one at a time. • With mixer on low, beat in half the flour, the sour cream, and then the remaining flour. • Beat the egg whites with the mixer on high speed until stiff peaks form. Fold into the batter. • Half fill each ramekin with batter and place 2 small chocolates in each one. Cover with the remaining batter, leveling the surface. • Baked until puffed, 35–45 minutes. • Let cool for 5 minutes before serving. • These little desserts are delicious when served with whipped cream or vanilla ice cream.

½ cup + 2 tablespoons (150 g) butter

2 tablespoons unsweetened cocoa powder

1¼ cups (175) g self-rising white flour

⅔ cup (130 g) granulated sugar

2 large eggs, separated

½ cup (125 ml) sour cream

12 small chocolates

Whipped cream or vanilla ice cream, to serve (optional)

Serves: 6
Preparation: 30 minutes
Cooking: 35–45 minutes
Level: 1

CHOCOLATE ZABAGLIONE

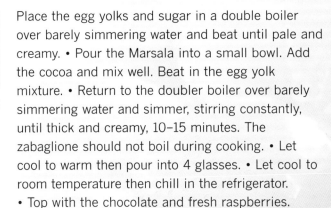

Place the egg yolks and sugar in a double boiler over barely simmering water and beat until pale and creamy. • Pour the Marsala into a small bowl. Add the cocoa and mix well. Beat in the egg yolk mixture. • Return to the doubler boiler over barely simmering water and simmer, stirring constantly, until thick and creamy, 10–15 minutes. The zabaglione should not boil during cooking. • Let cool to warm then pour into 4 glasses. • Let cool to room temperature then chill in the refrigerator. • Top with the chocolate and fresh raspberries.

5 large egg yolks

½ cup (100 g) granulated sugar

½ cup (125 ml) dry Marsala wine

2 tablespoons unsweetened cocoa powder

2 oz (60 g) semisweet (dark) chocolate, grated

Fresh raspberries, to decorate

Serves: 4
Preparation: 20 minutes
    + 1 hour to chill
Cooking: 10–15 minutes
Level: 2

CHOCOLATE AND COINTREAU MOUSSE

Chocolate Mousse: Melt the chocolate in a double boiler over barely simmering water. Stir occasionally until the chocolate has melted. Set aside to cool.
• Beat the egg whites and sugar in a bowl with an electric beater on high speed until soft peaks form.
• Scrape the chocolate into a large bowl. Carefully stir the dissolved gelatin into the melted chocolate and then alternately fold in the whipped cream and the egg whites until well combined. Set aside until ready to use. • Cointreau Mousse: Beat the egg yolks and sugar with an electric mixer on high speed until pale and creamy. • Bring half the orange juice to a boil in a small pan. Remove from the heat and add the gelatin. Stir until completely dissolved. Stir in the remaining orange juice and liqueur. • Gradually whisk the gelatin mixture into the egg yolks and sugar. Fold in the cream. • Spoon the chocolate mousse into a piping bag fitted with a star nozzle.
• Set out 8 long stemmed glasses on a tray. Place some of the orange segments in the base of each glass. Pipe in generous rosettes of the chocolate mousse. Top with more orange segments and chocolate mousse. Finish with a few more segments and a large dollop of the cointreau mousse. Decorate with grated chocolate. Chill in the refrigerator for 30 minutes before serving.

Chocolate Mousse

- **12 oz (350 g) semisweet (dark) chocolate**
- **6 large egg whites**
- **¼ cup (50 g) superfine (caster) sugar**
- **2 teaspoons powdered gelatin dissolved in 2 tablespoons boiling water**
- **2⅓ cups (600 ml) cups heavy (double) cream, softly whipped**

Cointreau Mousse

- **4 large egg yolks**
- **¼ cup (50 g) superfine (caster) sugar**
- **¼ cup (60 ml) freshly squeezed orange juice**
- **2 teaspoons powdered gelatin**
- **¼ cup (60 ml) Cointreau**
- **2 cups (500 ml) heavy (double) cream, softly whipped**
- **4 oranges, in segments**
- **Grated chocolate, to decorate**

Serves: 8
Preparation: 45 minutes
    + 30 minutes to chill
Level: 1

CHOCOLATE CARAMEL TRIFLE

310

Sponge: Preheat the oven to 350°F (180°C/gas 4). • Butter a 9-inch (23-cm) square baking pan. Line with parchment paper. • Melt the chocolate in a double boiler over barely simmering water. Set aside to cool. • Mix the flour, cocoa, baking powder, baking soda, and salt in a large bowl. • Beat the butter and sugar in a large bowl with an electric mixer at medium speed until creamy. • Add the eggs one at a time, beating until just blended after each addition. • With mixer at low speed, gradually beat in the mixed dry ingredients, alternating with the chocolate, milk, and oil. • Spoon the batter into the prepared pan. Bake until a toothpick inserted into the center comes out clean, 50–60 minutes. • Cool the cake in the pan on a rack for 10 minutes. Carefully remove the parchment paper and let cool completely. • Cut the sponge into 1 inch (2.5 cm) cubes.

Syrup: Combine the sugar and water in a heavy-based pan over medium heat and bring to a boil. Boil rapidly for 5 minutes. Remove from the heat and stir in the chocolate liqueur. • Caramel Sauce: Place the sugar and the water in a heavy-based pan. Bring to a boil over medium heat. Occasionally brush down the sides with a wet, clean pastry brush, collecting any crystals that may have formed. When the sugar begins to bubble rapidly reduce the heat and simmer until the sugar starts to caramelize, turning golden brown. Remove from the heat immediately and plunge the base of the pan into a large bowl half filled with cold water. Remove from

12 oz (350 g) bittersweet (dark) chocolate, coarsely chopped

2 cups (300 g) all-purpose (plain) flour

1/3 cup (50 g) unsweetened cocoa powder

2 teaspoons baking powder

1/2 teaspoon baking soda (bicarbonate of soda)

1/4 teaspoon salt

1 cup (250 g) butter, softened

1 1/4 cups (250 g) granulated sugar

4 large eggs

1/2 cup (125 ml) milk

2 tablespoons vegetable oil

Syrup

1 cup (200 g) granulated sugar

2 cups (500 ml) water

1/4 cup (60 ml) chocolate liqueur

Caramel Sauce

1 cup (200 g) granulated sugar

1/2 cup (125 ml) water

the water and very carefully pour in the cream, reserving 1/4 cup (60 ml) to mix with the cornstarch. • Return the pan to the heat and bring back to a boil. Stir in the cornstarch mixture and whisk until thick and bubbly. Remove from the heat and stir in the lemon juice. Cover and let cool completely.

To Assemble: Arrange cubes of sponge in the bases of 6 individual glass bowls or coupes. Pour enough of the syrup over the top to saturate the sponge. Place a few slices of pear on top and pour in some of the caramel sauce. Spoon in some of the pastry cream. Repeat the layers with the sponge, syrup, fruit, pastry cream and sauce until about 1/4 inch (5 mm) from the top. Top with cream and decorate with chocolate curls. • Cover and refrigerate for 30 minutes before serving.

1 cup (250 ml) heavy (double) cream

2 teaspoons cornstarch (cornflour)

1 tablespoon freshly squeezed lemon juice

4 ripe pears, peeled, cored, and sliced lengthways

1/2 recipe chocolate pastry cream (see page 678)

2 cups (500 ml) whipped cream

Chocolate curls, to decorate (see page 694)

Serves: 6
Preparation: 2 hours
   + 30 minutes to chill
Cooking: 1 hour
Level: 1

CHOCOLATE AND SOUR CHERRY CRÊPES

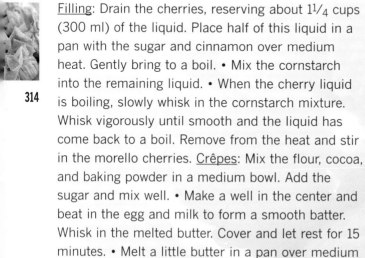

314

<u>Filling</u>: Drain the cherries, reserving about 1¹/₄ cups (300 ml) of the liquid. Place half of this liquid in a pan with the sugar and cinnamon over medium heat. Gently bring to a boil. • Mix the cornstarch into the remaining liquid. • When the cherry liquid is boiling, slowly whisk in the cornstarch mixture. Whisk vigorously until smooth and the liquid has come back to a boil. Remove from the heat and stir in the morello cherries. <u>Crêpes</u>: Mix the flour, cocoa, and baking powder in a medium bowl. Add the sugar and mix well. • Make a well in the center and beat in the egg and milk to form a smooth batter. Whisk in the melted butter. Cover and let rest for 15 minutes. • Melt a little butter in a pan over medium heat. Spoon in enough batter to thinly coat the bottom of the pan. Cook until lightly browned on the bottom. Using a spatula, gently flip the crêpe and cook for 1 more minute. Repeat until all the batter has been used. • Fold the crêpes in half and in half again. • Place 2 crêpes on each plate and spoon the cherry mix into the middle of each. Keep warm in the oven, until all crêpes have been filled. <u>Cinnamon Cream</u>: Beat the cream with the confectioners' sugar and cinnamon until thick. • Serve the crêpes with the chocolate sauce and cinnamon cream.

Filling

1¹/₄ lb (600 g) morello cherries

2 tablespoons superfine (caster) sugar

¹/₂ teaspoon ground cinnamon

3 teaspoons cornstarch (cornflour)

Crêpes

1 cup (150 g) all-purpose (plain) flour

2 tablespoons unsweet-ened cocoa powder

1 teaspoon baking powder

2 tablespoons superfine (caster) sugar

1 large egg, lightly beaten

1 cup (250 ml) milk

2 tablespoons melted butter

Cinnamon Cream

1 cup (250 ml) heavy (double) cream

1 tablespoon confec-tioners' (icing) sugar

1 teaspoon ground cinnamon

1 recipe chocolate sauce (see page 690)

Serves: 6
Preparation: 30 minutes
Cooking: 20 minutes
Level: 1

ICE CREAM CAKE

Line the base and sides of a 9-inch (23-cm) springform pan with parchment paper. The paper needs to stand above the top of the springform pan by 1 inch (2.5 cm). • Spread an even layer of chocolate ice cream in the pan. Place in the freezer until hardened, 15–20 minutes. • Cover with a layer of strawberry ice cream. Place in the freezer until hardened, 15–20 minutes. • Cover with another layer of chocolate ice cream and let harden. Top with the vanilla ice cream, cover, and freeze overnight. • Carefully remove from the springform pan and place on a serving plate. Top with the strawberries. • Bring the apricot preserves to a boil in a small saucepan with the water. Spread over the strawberries and serve at once.

1½ lb (750 g) chocolate ice cream, softened

14 oz (400 g) vanilla ice cream, softened

14 oz (400 g) strawberry ice cream, softened

About 20 fresh strawberries, halved

5 oz (150 g) apricot preserves (jam)

2 tablespoons water

Serves: 10–12
Preparation: 30 minutes
 + 4 hours and overnight
 to freeze
Level: 1

CHOCOLATE SORBET

Place the chocolate in a double boiler over barely simmering water. Stir occasionally until melted. Remove from the heat and let cool slightly. • Place the sugar and water in a saucepan over medium heat and stir until the sugar has dissolved. Stir in the chocolate. Remove from the heat. Let cool to room temperature. Chill in the refrigerator for 30 minutes. • Place the mixture in an ice cream machine and proceed according to the manufacturer's instructions. • If you don't have an ice cream machine, place the chocolate syrup in a metal bowl and freeze. When the mixture has just begun to set whisk it with an electric beater or by hand, until creamy. Repeat at least 3 or 4 more times, or until the sorbet is thick and smooth.

8 oz (250 g) semisweet (dark) chocolate, finely chopped
2 cups (500 ml) water
1 cup (200 g) granulated sugar

Serves: 4
Preparation: 10 minutes + 4 hours to freeze
Level: 1

CHOCOLATE AND STRAWBERRY SHORTBREAD

320

Shortbread: Mix the flour, confectioners' sugar, cocoa, and almonds in a medium bowl. Add the butter and rub in with your fingertips until the mixture resembles fine crumbs. • Make a well in the center and pour the egg in a little at a time mixing with your fingers until the mixture comes together but is not sticky. You may not need all the egg. • Dust with flour and wrap in plastic wrap (cling film). Refrigerate for 30 minutes.
• Bring the apricot preserves to a boil over low heat. Whisk in a little water and remove from the heat.
• Take a strawberry by the stem and dip it in the preserves. Set aside on a plate. Dip each strawberry in the same way. For a very glossy look, double dip each strawberry. • Mousse: Place the chocolate in a large bowl. Bring 1¼ cups (300 ml) of cream to a boil over medium heat. Pour over the chocolate. Stir until melted and smooth. Transfer to a smaller bowl, cover with plastic wrap (cling film) and refrigerate until cool, 30 minutes. • Whip the remaining cream until thick. Fold into the chocolate mixture. Refrigerate until needed. • Preheat the oven to 350°F (180°C/gas 4). • Line 2 baking sheets with parchment paper. • Roll out the pastry to ¼-inch (5-mm) thick. With a fluted 2-inch (5-cm) cookie cutter, cut out 24 disks. Place on the prepared baking sheets. • Bake for 8–10 minutes. Cool on a wire rack. • Spoon the mousse into a piping bag with a star nozzle. Place a shortbread disk on a plate and pipe a spiral of mousse on top. Cover with shortbread and mousse. Top with more shortbread. Dust with confectioners' sugar and top with a strawberry.

Shortbread

- ½ cup (75 g) all-purpose (plain) flour
- ¼ cup (30 g) confectioners' (icing) sugar
- 3 tablespoons unsweetened cocoa powder
- 1 tablespoon ground almonds
- 3 tablespoons butter, diced and cold
- 1 large egg, lightly beaten

- ¼ cup (60 g) apricot preserves (jam)

Mousse

- 12 oz (350 g) semisweet (dark) chocolate, very finely chopped
- 2 cups (500 ml) heavy (double) cream
- 8 strawberries
  Confectioners' (icing) sugar, to dust

Serves: 8
Preparation: 2 hours
Cooking: 8–10 minutes
Level: 2

CHOCOLATE STAR PANCAKES

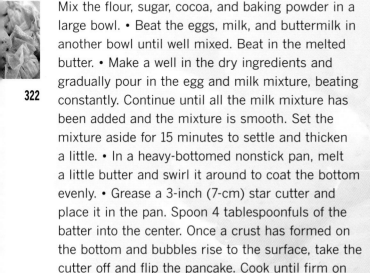

322

Mix the flour, sugar, cocoa, and baking powder in a large bowl. • Beat the eggs, milk, and buttermilk in another bowl until well mixed. Beat in the melted butter. • Make a well in the dry ingredients and gradually pour in the egg and milk mixture, beating constantly. Continue until all the milk mixture has been added and the mixture is smooth. Set the mixture aside for 15 minutes to settle and thicken a little. • In a heavy-bottomed nonstick pan, melt a little butter and swirl it around to coat the bottom evenly. • Grease a 3-inch (7-cm) star cutter and place it in the pan. Spoon 4 tablespoonfuls of the batter into the center. Once a crust has formed on the bottom and bubbles rise to the surface, take the cutter off and flip the pancake. Cook until firm on the second side. Repeat until all the mixture had been used. Keep the cooked pancakes on a plate in the oven to keep warm. • Serve with chocolate sauce and mixed berries for garnish.

$1^2/_3$ cups (250 g) all-purpose (plain) flour

$^1/_2$ cup (100 g) superfine (caster) sugar

$^1/_4$ cup (30 g) unsweetened cocoa powder

3 teaspoons baking powder

2 large eggs

$1^1/_4$ cups (300 ml) milk

$^3/_4$ cup (200 ml) buttermilk

$^1/_4$ cup (60 g) butter, melted

1 recipe chocolate sauce (see page 690)

Serves: 6–8
Preparation: 30 minutes
Cooking: 30 minutes
Level: 1

CHOCOLATE CRÈME BRÛLEÉ

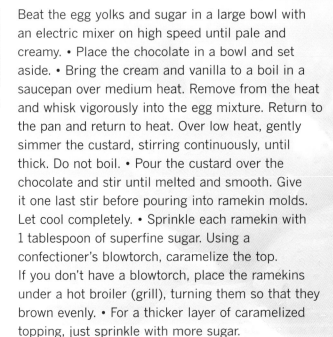

324

Beat the egg yolks and sugar in a large bowl with an electric mixer on high speed until pale and creamy. • Place the chocolate in a bowl and set aside. • Bring the cream and vanilla to a boil in a saucepan over medium heat. Remove from the heat and whisk vigorously into the egg mixture. Return to the pan and return to heat. Over low heat, gently simmer the custard, stirring continuously, until thick. Do not boil. • Pour the custard over the chocolate and stir until melted and smooth. Give it one last stir before pouring into ramekin molds. Let cool completely. • Sprinkle each ramekin with 1 tablespoon of superfine sugar. Using a confectioner's blowtorch, caramelize the top. If you don't have a blowtorch, place the ramekins under a hot broiler (grill), turning them so that they brown evenly. • For a thicker layer of caramelized topping, just sprinkle with more sugar.

8 large egg yolks
½ cup (100 g) granulated sugar
12 oz (350 g) bittersweet (dark) chocolate, chopped
1 teaspoon vanilla extract (essence)
2 cups (500 ml) heavy (double) cream
6 tablespoons superfine (caster) sugar

Serves: 6
Preparation: 40 minutes + 40 minutes to chill
Level: 1

325

CONCORDE

Meringue: Preheat the oven to 250°F (120°C).
• Beat the egg whites and sugar with an electric mixer on high speed until stiff peaks form. • Sift the confectioners' sugar and cocoa together and gently fold into the egg whites. • Spoon into a piping bag fitted with a plain 1/2-inch (1-cm) nozzle. • Grease two baking sheets and line with parchment paper.
• Pipe 18 ovals 2 inches (5 cm) long on one baking sheet. Try to keep them uniform as you will lay them on top of each other when assembling. Pipe the rest into strips the length of the baking sheet.
• Bake for 2 hours. Turn the oven off, leave the door ajar, and let the oven cool and the meringues set.
Mousse: Melt the chocolate in a double boiler over barely simmering water. Set aside. • Beat the butter with an electric mixer on high speed until creamy. Add the egg yolks one at a time, beating until just combined after each addition. • Beat the egg whites and sugar on high speed until stiff peaks form. • Stir the chocolate into the butter mixture then fold in the egg whites. Set aside until the meringues are ready.
• Take one oval of meringue and spread with mousse. Cover with another oval of meringue and repeat. Top with the third and final oval of meringue. Spread all over with mousse. • Take a meringue strip and break it into pieces and stick them over the mousse in a random pattern. Completely cover the top and sides of the mousse. • Dust with a little confectioners' sugar before serving.

Meringue

- 1/2 cup (100 g) granulated sugar
- 4 large egg whites
- 2/3 cup (100 g) confectioners' (icing) sugar
- 2 tablespoons unsweetened cocoa powder

Mousse

- 5 oz (150 g) bittersweet (dark) chocolate
- 1/3 cup (90 g) butter
- 3 large eggs, separated
- 1/3 cup (75 g) granulated sugar

Confectioners' sugar, to dust

Serves: 6
Preparation: 30 minutes
Cooking: 2 hours
Level: 2

CHOCOLATE MARQUISE

Sponge: Preheat the oven to 350°F (180°C/gas 4).
• Oil a 12 x 18-inch (30 x 40-cm) jelly-roll pan. Line with parchment paper. • Mix the flour and cocoa in a medium bowl. • Beat the eggs and egg yolks with an electric mixer on high speed until creamy. • Beat the egg whites and sugar on high speed until soft peaks form. Fold the egg whites into the egg yolk mixture.
• Use a spatula to spread the mixture in the jelly-roll pan in a layer about 2/3-inch (1.5-cm) thick. • Bake until springy to the touch, 10 minutes. Remove from the oven and let cool completely. • Mousse: Beat the egg yolks and sugar with an electric mixer on high speed pale and creamy. • Bring the milk to a boil in a saucepan over medium heat. • Pour half the hot milk into the egg mixture, beating constantly. Pour back into the pan and return to the heat. Stir continuously until it coats the back of a metal spoon. • Place the chocolate in a large bowl and pour the egg custard over the top. Stir occasionally until the chocolate has melted and the mixture is smooth. Cover and refrigerate until cool.
• Gently fold in the whipped cream. Set aside until ready to use. • Line a 9 x 5-inch (23 x 12-cm) loaf pan with parchment paper. Cut the sponge in half, then slice horizontally so that you have 4 strips the same size as the loaf pan. Place one strip of sponge in the pan. Cover with a 1/2-inch (1-cm) layer of mousse. Cover with a layer of sponge and gently press down. Repeat until all the mousse and sponge are in the pan. Cover and refrigerate overnight. Turn out into a plate and dust with cocoa before serving.

Sponge

1 cup (150 g) all-purpose (plain) flour

4 tablespoons teaspoons unsweetened cocoa powder

4 large eggs

3 large eggs, separated

½ cup (100 g) granulated sugar

Mousse

1 cup (250 ml) milk

⅓ cup (75 g) granulated sugar

8 large egg yolks

1¼ lb (600 g) milk chocolate, chopped

5 oz (150 g) semisweet (dark) chocolate, chopped

1 cup (250 ml) whipped cream

Unsweetened cocoa powder, to dust

Serves: 8–10
Preparation: 40 minutes + overnight to chill
Cooking: 10 minutes
Level: 1

CHOCOLATE DISKS WITH MINT MOUSSE

330

Chocolate Disks: Melt the chocolate in a double boiler over barely simmering water. • Pour onto a sheet of parchment paper. Using a stepped palate knife, spread the chocolate out evenly to $1/8$-inch (2-mm) thick. Let the chocolate set but not go brittle. Use a 2.5-inch (5-cm) plain round pastry cutter to cut out 18 disks. Set aside. • Mousse: Beat the eggs and sugar with an electric mixer on high speed until pale and creamy. • With mixer on low, beat in the crème de menthe and dissolved gelatin. Fold in the whipped cream. • Place the mousse in a bowl and chill in the refrigerator. Syrup: Bring the sugar and water to a boil over medium heat. Boil rapidly for 5 minutes. Remove from the heat and stir in the food coloring and mint. • Lay out one of the disks of chocolate. Spoon the mousse into a piping bag fitted with a star nozzle. Pipe the mousse onto the disk in a decorative manner. Place another disk on top and pipe with another layer of mousse. Top with a third disk of chocolate. • Place the chocolate mint dessert on a plate and drizzle with the mint syrup. Repeat with the remaining chocolate disks and mousse.

Chocolate Disks

12 oz (350 g) semisweet (dark) chocolate, chopped

Mousse

4 large eggs

2 tablespoons granulated sugar

3 tablespoons crème de menthe

3 teaspoons gelatin dissolved in $1/4$ cup (60 ml) boiling water

2 cups (500 ml) heavy (double) cream whipped

Syrup

$1/2$ cup (100 g) granulated sugar

1 cup (250 ml) water

1 drop green coloring

8 leaves mint, finely chopped

Serves: 6
Preparation: 40 minutes
Level: 2

CHOCOLATE AND MASCARPONE PARCELS

332

Preheat the oven to 350°F (180°C/gas 4). • Oil a baking sheet. Line with parchment paper. • Beat the mascarpone and sugar with an electric mixer on medium speed until light and creamy. • Add the egg yolk and beat until well combined. • Fold in the chocolate and hazelnuts. • Unroll the filo pastry and take off the 3 sheets. Lay the pastry out and cover with a slightly damp cloth. • Combine the sugar and cinnamon in a small bowl. • Lay one piece of pastry out on a work surface and lightly brush with the melted butter. Sprinkle with the sugar mix, lay the second sheet on top, and repeat with the butter and sugar. Repeat the process, finishing with a sheet of pastry just brushed with butter. • Use the back of a knife to mark squares on the pastry, 3 across and 2 down. You should get 6 out of the pastry sheets. With a sharp knife, press down on the pastry, cutting through. Try to avoid dragging the knife as it will tear the pastry. • Place 2 teaspoons of the mascarpone mixture in the center of each square of pastry and bring the sides of the pastry around it to form a parcel that looks like a money bag. Squeeze tightly where the pastry joins. Tie a piece of string around the top to stop them opening in the oven. • Place on the prepared baking sheet. • Bake until golden, 10–15 minutes. • Using small scissors, cut off and discard the string. Dust with the confectioners' sugar just before serving.

½ cup (125 g) mascarpone cheese

2 tablespoons granulated sugar

1 large egg yolk

2 oz (60 g) semisweet (dark) chocolate, chopped

⅓ cup (40 g) roasted hazelnuts, roughly chopped

4 sheets filo pastry

3 tablespoons superfine (caster) sugar

1 teaspoon cinnamon combined

3 tablespoons melted butter

Confectioners' (icing) sugar, to dust

Serves: 6
Preparation: 30 minutes
Cooking: 10–15 minutes
Level: 2

CHOCOLATE PAVLOVAS

<u>Pavlovas</u>: Preheat the oven to 275°F (140°C).
• Line a baking sheet with parchment paper.
• Beat the egg whites in an electric mixer until foamy. Gradually add the sugar and beat until stiff peaks form. The meringue should feel smooth and look shiny. If it feels gritty the sugar has not fully dissolved; keep beating until it feels smooth.
• Using a large spatula, fold in the vinegar and vanilla extract. • Sift the cocoa powder and cornstarch over the meringue. Gently fold in with the spatula. • Spoon out six dollops of the meringue onto the baking sheet. Shape with a spoon so that the edges of the meringue are slightly higher than the center. • Bake until the outside is dry, 35–45 minutes. • Turn the oven off, leave the door slightly ajar, and let the meringues cool completely in the oven. • <u>Topping</u>: Defrost the berries, strain the liquid, reserving half and discarding the rest. Bring the liquid to a boil in a small sauce pan over a low heat. Add the preserves and bring back to a boil. Boil rapidly for 3 minutes. Remove from the heat and stir in the berries. • Let cool to room temperature then refrigerate until chilled. • Just before serving, gently place the meringues on a serving plate. • Beat the cream until thick. Mound into the center of the meringues. Arrange the berry mixture on top of the cream. Serve immediately.

Pavlovas

6   large egg whites, room temperature

1¼ cups (250 g) superfine (caster) sugar

1   teaspoon white vinegar

1   teaspoon vanilla extract (essence)

1   teaspoon cornstarch (cornflour)

4   tablespoons unsweetened cocoa powder

Topping

1   lb (500 g) frozen berries

¾ cup (200 g) raspberry preserves (jam)

1   cup (250 ml) heavy (double) cream

Serves: 6
Preparation: 30 minutes
Cooking: 40 minutes
Level: 1

CHOCOLATE MERINGUES

Meringues: Preheat the oven to 275°F (140°C).
• Line a baking sheet with parchment paper.
• Beat the egg whites and salt in a large bowl with
an electric mixer at high speed until frothy. • With
mixer at high speed, gradually add the sugar, beating
until stiff glossy peaks form. • Fold in the cinnamon.
• Fill a pastry bag without a nozzle. Twist the opening
tightly closed, and squeeze out generous rounds of
the meringue, spacing 1 inch (2.5 cm) apart on the
prepared baking sheet. • Bake until crisp and dry
to the touch, 1 1/2–2 hours. Cool completely on the
sheets. • Mousse: Place the chocolate in a large
bowl. • Bring 1 1/4 cups (300 ml) of the cream to
a boil over medium heat. • Pour into the chocolate.
Stir until the chocolate has melted and smooth.
• Transfer to a smaller bowl, cover with plastic wrap
(cling film), and refrigerate until cool, about 30
minutes. • Whip the remaining cream until firm.
• Fold the chocolate into the whipped cream and
refrigerate until needed. • Spoon the mousse into a
piping bag fitted with a star nozzle. Place one of the
meringues in a bowl and pipe a spiral of the
mousse on top. Sandwich with another meringue.

Meringues

4   large egg whites
1/4 teaspoon salt
1   cup (200 g) superfine
   (caster) sugar
1/2 teaspoon ground
   cinnamon

Mousse

12 oz (350 g) bittersweet
   (dark) chocolate, finely
   chopped
2   cups (500 ml) heavy
   (double) cream

Serves: 6–8
Preparation: 25 minutes
Cooking: 2 hours
Level: 1

BOMBES ALASKA

Bombes: Preheat the oven to 400°F (200°C/gas 6).
• Toast the hazelnuts until golden. Remove their skins by rubbing in a cloth and chop finely. • Place the nuts on a tray lined with lightly oiled parchment paper.
• Bring the sugar and water to a boil over medium heat, Simmer until pale golden brown. Remove from the heat and pour over the hazelnuts. Let cool and set completely. • Chop into pieces. Fold into the softened vanilla ice cream. Return to the freezer. • Place eight 4-oz (120-g) individual pudding molds in the freezer and chill for 10 minutes. Remove one at a time.
• Spoon the chocolate ice cream into the molds one by one, spreading it to about 3/4-inch (2-cm) thick. This will leave a hole for the praline ice cream. • One by one, fill the molds with the vanilla ice cream. Smooth off the base and return to the freezer. Let the bombes freeze for 30 minutes to 1 hour. • To unmold the bombes, dip the bottom of each mold into hot water and shake out onto your hand. Place back in the freezer while you unmold the rest. • Meringue: Beat the egg whites and sugar with an electric mixer on high speed until stiff peaks form. • Working on one bombe at a time, completely cover the ice cream with the meringue. Repeat with the remaining ice cream molds. • Use a confectioner's blowtorch to gently brown the meringue. Serve immediately.

Bombes

½ **cup (60 g) hazelnuts**

½ **cup (100 g) superfine (caster) sugar**

¼ **cup (60 ml)**

1 **lb (500 g) vanilla ice cream, softened**

1 **lb (500 g) chocolate ice cream, softened**

Meringue

8 **large egg whites**

2 **cups (400 g) superfine (caster) sugar**

Serves: 8
Preparation: 30 minutes
  + 4 hours to freeze
Level: 1

CHOCOLATE CARAMEL PUDDINGS

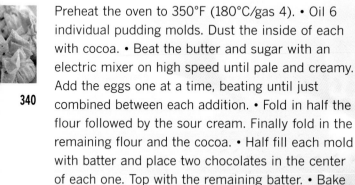

Preheat the oven to 350°F (180°C/gas 4). • Oil 6 individual pudding molds. Dust the inside of each with cocoa. • Beat the butter and sugar with an electric mixer on high speed until pale and creamy. Add the eggs one at a time, beating until just combined between each addition. • Fold in half the flour followed by the sour cream. Finally fold in the remaining flour and the cocoa. • Half fill each mold with batter and place two chocolates in the center of each one. Top with the remaining batter. • Bake until springy to the touch, 30–40 minutes. • Let the puddings cool for a few minutes before inverting. • Dust with cocoa and serve hot with cream or ice cream.

½ cup (125 g) butter

½ cup (100 g) superfine (caster) sugar

2 large eggs

1¼ cups (175 g) self-raising flour

½ cup (125 ml) sour cream

2 tablespoons unsweetened cocoa powder

12 rolos (soft, chewy chocolate flavored caramel candies)

Unsweetened cocoa powder, to dust

Whipped cream or ice cream, to serve

Serves: 6
Preparation: 30 minutes
Cooking: 35 minutes
Level: 1

WHITE CHOCOLATE CHEESECAKES WITH BERRY COMPÔTE

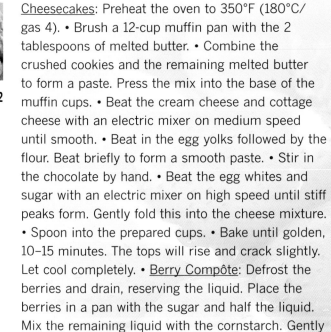

Cheesecakes: Preheat the oven to 350°F (180°C/ gas 4). • Brush a 12-cup muffin pan with the 2 tablespoons of melted butter. • Combine the crushed cookies and the remaining melted butter to form a paste. Press the mix into the base of the muffin cups. • Beat the cream cheese and cottage cheese with an electric mixer on medium speed until smooth. • Beat in the egg yolks followed by the flour. Beat briefly to form a smooth paste. • Stir in the chocolate by hand. • Beat the egg whites and sugar with an electric mixer on high speed until stiff peaks form. Gently fold this into the cheese mixture. • Spoon into the prepared cups. • Bake until golden, 10–15 minutes. The tops will rise and crack slightly. Let cool completely. • Berry Compôte: Defrost the berries and drain, reserving the liquid. Place the berries in a pan with the sugar and half the liquid. Mix the remaining liquid with the cornstarch. Gently bring the berry mixture to a boil. When simmering, stir in the cornstarch mixture. Reduce the heat and simmer for 2 minutes. • Remove from the pan and let cool before serving with the cheesecakes.

Cheesecakes

- ¼ cup (60 g) butter + 2 tablespoons, melted
- 1 cup (135 g) crushed plain chocolate cookies (biscuits)
- 1 cup (250 g) cream cheese
- 1 cup (250 g) cottage cheese
- 4 large eggs, separated
- ¼ cup (30 g) all-purpose (plain) flour
- 3 oz (90 g) white chocolate, chopped
- 4 tablespoons superfine (caster) sugar

Berry Compôte

- 8 oz (250 g) frozen mixed berries
- 2 tablespoons granulated sugar
- 1 teaspoon cornstarch (cornflour)

Serves: 4–6
Preparation: 35–40 minutes
Cooking: 15 minutes
Level: 1

DOUBLE CHOCOLATE CHIP ICE CREAM

344

Place the chocolate in a large bowl and set aside.
• Beat the egg yolks and sugar in an electric mixer
at high speed until pale and creamy. • Bring the
cream and milk to a boil in a saucepan over
medium heat. • Pour half the hot cream mixture
into the egg mixture, beating constantly. Return
to the pan with the remaining cream mixture and
return to medium heat. Stir constantly until it
begins to thicken or coats the back of a metal
spoon. • Remove from the heat and pour over the
chocolate. Stir until the chocolate has melted and
the mixture is thick and smooth. Let cool
completely. • Stir in the chocolate chips.• Place
in an ice cream machine and churn to the
manufacturers instructions. • Alternatively, if you
don't have an ice cream machine, place the mixture
in a metal bowl and freeze. When it has just begun
to set, whisk it with an electric beater or by hand
until creamy. Repeat at least 3 or 4 more times
or until thick, smooth, and scoopable.

8 oz (250 g) semisweet
(dark) chocolate,
chopped

6 large egg yolks

½ cup (100 g) superfine
(caster) sugar

2 cups (500 ml) heavy
(double) cream

1 cup (250 ml) milk

5 oz (150 g) semisweet
(dark) chocolate chips

Serves: 4–6
Preparation: 30 minutes
+ 4 hours to freeze
Level: 1

CHARGRILLED FRUITS WITH CHOCOLATE SYRUP

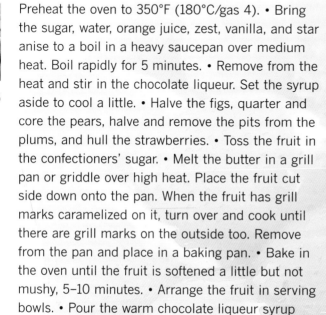

346

Preheat the oven to 350°F (180°C/gas 4). • Bring the sugar, water, orange juice, zest, vanilla, and star anise to a boil in a heavy saucepan over medium heat. Boil rapidly for 5 minutes. • Remove from the heat and stir in the chocolate liqueur. Set the syrup aside to cool a little. • Halve the figs, quarter and core the pears, halve and remove the pits from the plums, and hull the strawberries. • Toss the fruit in the confectioners' sugar. • Melt the butter in a grill pan or griddle over high heat. Place the fruit cut side down onto the pan. When the fruit has grill marks caramelized on it, turn over and cook until there are grill marks on the outside too. Remove from the pan and place in a baking pan. • Bake in the oven until the fruit is softened a little but not mushy, 5–10 minutes. • Arrange the fruit in serving bowls. • Pour the warm chocolate liqueur syrup over the top. Serve with the cream passed separately so that everyone can help themselves.

1   cup (200 g) superfine (caster) sugar

½   cup (125 ml) water

    Juice and zest of 1 orange

1   vanilla pod slit lengthways

2   star anise

¼   cup (60 ml) chocolate liqueur

2   figs

2   pears

2   plums

12 strawberries

2   tablespoons butter

2   tablespoons confectioners' (icing) sugar

1   cup (250 ml) heavy (double) cream, to serve

Serves: 4
Preparation: 15 minutes
Cooking: 20 minutes
Level: 1

CHARLOTTE RUSSE

348

Sponge: Preheat the oven to 350°F (180°C/gas 4).
• Oil a 12 x 14-inch (30 x 35-cm) baking pan. Line
with parchment paper. • Mix the flour and cocoa in
a medium bowl. • Beat the whole eggs and egg
yolks in an electric mixer on high speed until
creamy. • Beat the egg whites and sugar in a
separate bowl on high speed until soft peaks form.
• Alternately fold a quarter of the flour mixture and
a quarter of the egg whites into the egg yolk
mixture until just combined, taking care not to
overbeat the batter. • Pour the batter into the
prepared pan. • Bake until springy to the touch,
10–12 minutes. Let cool on a rack for 10 minutes.
Turn out of the pan and carefully remove the
parchment paper. Let cool completely. • Mock
Cream: Beat the butter and sugar in an electric
mixer on high speed until light and fluffy. • Very
gradually pour in the boiling water, beating on
medium speed, until all the water has been
incorporated. Stir in the vanilla. The cream should
be fairly firm. • Use an 8-inch (20-cm) bowl to cut
out a circle from one end of the sponge. Set aside.
Trim the remaining sponge to form a rectangle and
cut this in half lengthways, so that you have 2
strips. • Spread the mock cream over the sponge.
Leave a 1/2-inch (1-cm) strip at the lower end of
each strip free of cream. Roll up the sponge
beginning from the end with cream. • Chill in the
refrigerator until ready to assemble. • Filling: Place
the chocolate in a large bowl and set aside. • Beat

Sponge

1   cup (150 g) all-purpose
    (plain) flour

1/3 cup (50 g) unsweetened
    cocoa powder

4   large eggs

3   large eggs, separated

1   cup (100 g) granulated
    sugar

Mock Cream

1   cup (250 g) butter

3/4 cup (150 g) superfine
    (caster) sugar

1   cup (250 ml) boiling
    water

1   teaspoon vanilla extract
    (essence)

Filling

14 oz (400 g) white
    chocolate, chopped

8   large egg yolks

1/4 cup (50 g) granulated
    sugar

3/4 cup (200 ml) milk

4   teaspoons powdered
    gelatin dissolved
    in 3 tablespoons
    boiling water

1 1/4 cups (300 ml) heavy
    (double) cream

the egg yolks and sugar with an electric mixer on high speed until pale and creamy. • Bring the milk to a boil in a saucepan over medium heat. Remove from the heat and pour half the hot milk into the egg mixture, beating constantly. • Pour this mixture back into the remaining milk and return to the heat. Stir constantly until it begins to thicken and coats the back of a metal spoon. • Remove from the heat and pour over the chocolate. Stir until the chocolate has melted and the mixture is thick and smooth. • Add the gelatin and stir until completely dissolved. Let cool completely. • Beat the cream until thick and firm. • Fold the whipped cream into the cooled chocolate mixture. • <u>To Assemble</u>: Line a 2-quart (2-liter) pudding mold with plastic wrap (cling film). • Remove the sponge roll from the refrigerator and cut in $1/4$-inch (5-mm) thick slices. • Arrange these in the mold, fitting them snugly together and pressing into the bowl firmly. Fill the spaces with the white chocolate mousse and top with the sponge round for the base. Cover and refrigerate for 2 hours. • Turn onto a plate. Remove the plastic wrap. • Heat the apricot preserves and water over low heat and brush over the dessert to give it a nice shine.

$1/2$ **cup (125 g) apricot preserves (jam)**
$1/4$ **cup (60 ml) water**

Serves: 6–8
Preparation: 2 hours + 2 hours to chill
Cooking: 10–12 minutes
Level: 3

349

PIES AND TARTS

MOCHA TART
WITH ICE CREAM

Ice Cream: Place the egg yolks in a large bowl.
• Fill a large bowl one-third full with ice water.
• Place 1 cup (250 ml) of milk in a medium saucepan over medium heat and bring to a gentle simmer. Pour one-third of the hot milk over the egg yolks, whisking constantly until well combined. Pour in the remaining hot milk. Pour the mixture back into the saucepan and return to low heat. Stir constantly until mixture has thickened enough to coat the back of a wooden spoon. • Remove from the heat and stir in the remaining 1 cup (250 ml) of milk, salt, and condensed milk. Pour into a medium bowl. • Place the bowl in the bowl of ice water until the mixture is cool, about 10 minutes. Place in an ice cream machine and freeze according to the manufacturer's directions. • Crust: Place the almonds and 2 tablespoons of confectioners' sugar in a food processor and chop until the almonds are very finely ground. • With an electric mixer on medium speed, beat the butter, cocoa, ground almonds, and salt until well-combined. • With mixer on low, beat in the remaining confectioners' sugar and flour. • Add the eggs and mix until just incorporated. • Shape the dough into a ball, wrap in plastic wrap (cling film), and chill in the refrigerator for at least 4 hours. • Preheat the oven to 350°F (180°C/gas 4). • Butter and flour an 11-inch (28-cm) tart pan with a removable bottom. • Roll the dough out between two sheets of lightly floured parchment or waxed paper until about 1/8 inch (3 mm) thick

Ice Cream

6   large egg yolks
2   cups (500 ml) milk
1/4 teaspoon salt
1   (15-oz/450-g) can sweetened condensed milk

Crust

1/4 cup (35 g) slivered almonds
1   cup (150 g) confectioners' (icing) sugar
1/2 cup (125 g) butter, softened
1/4 cup (40 g) unsweetened cocoa powder
1/4 teaspoon salt
1½ cups (200 g) all-purpose (plain) flour
2   large eggs

Mocha Filling

1   lb (500 g) bittersweet (dark) chocolate, finely chopped
1/2 cup (70 g) coarsely ground French roast coffee powder
2   cups (500 ml) heavy (double) cream

and 13 inches (32 cm) in diameter. • Line the tart pan with the dough, with the excess dough hanging over the edges. Roll the pin over the top to remove the excess dough. Place a sheet of parchment paper on the dough and fill with dried beans or pie weights. • Bake for 20 minutes, then remove the beans and bake until dry, about 20 more minutes. Remove from the oven and place on wire rack to cool. Leave the oven on. • <u>Mocha Filling</u>: Place the chocolate in a medium bowl. • Place the coffee, cream, condensed milk, and salt in a medium saucepan over low heat and bring to a gentle simmer, whisking constantly. • Strain the mixture though a fine mesh sieve into the bowl with the chocolate. Stir until the chocolate is melted and smooth. • Whisk in the eggs until smooth and shiny. Pour into the baked tart shell. • Bake until filling is just slightly jiggly in the center, 25–30 minutes. • Place the tart on a wire rack and let cool completely. • Slice the tart into 8–10 slices and serve with scoops of the ice cream.

⅓ **cup (90 ml) sweetened condensed milk**

¼ **teaspoon salt**

2 **large eggs**

Serves: 8–10
Preparation: 1 hour
     45 minutes + 4 hours
     to chill
Cooking: 1 hour 15 minutes
Level: 2

355

GRAND MARNIER WALNUT TART

<u>Crust</u>: Preheat the oven to 425°F (210°C/gas 7). • Wash the orange and finely grate the zest. Set the orange aside. • In the bowl of a food processor, pulse to combine 3/4 cup (120 g) of flour, the confectioners' sugar, rolled oats, 1/4 cup (35 g) of cocoa, the cornstarch, 1 teaspoon of orange zest, and the salt. Add the butter and pulse until the mixture resembles coarse breadcrumbs. • Transfer the mixture to a medium bowl. Knead in the Grand Marnier until the dough forms a ball. Shape into a ball and wrap in plastic wrap (cling film). Chill in the refrigerator for 30 minutes. • Combine the remaining flour and cocoa. • Grease a 9-inch (23-cm) tart pan with a removable bottom. Dust a work surface with the flour and cocoa mix. • Roll the dough out into an 11-inch (28-cm) disk. • Place the dough in the tart pan and firmly press into the bottom and sides. Leave about 1/2 inch (1 cm) hanging over the edges of the tart pan. • Bake until firm, 15–20 minutes. Check halfway during baking, if it is puffing in large areas gently press it down. Remove the crust from the oven. Lower the oven temperature to 350°F (180°C/gas 4). • <u>Filling</u>: Using a sharp knife, chop the orange into small cubes. Prepare 1/2 cup of diced orange pieces. • Whisk the egg yolks in a medium bowl then set aside. • Place the corn syrup, brown sugar, salt, and orange pieces in a medium saucepan. Simmer over medium-low heat until the sugar is melted, 5–7 minutes. • Add the butter, cream, and remaining orange zest.

Crust

1   orange

1   cup (150 g) all-purpose (plain) flour

1/3 cup (50 g) confectioners' (icing) sugar

6   tablespoons old-fashioned rolled oats (not quick-cooking variety)

1/3 cup (50 g) unsweetened cocoa powder

2   tablespoons cornstarch (cornflour)

1/4 teaspoon salt

1/2 cup (125 g) butter, chilled and chopped

2   tablespoons Grand Marnier, chilled

Filling:

8   large egg yolks

2/3 cup light corn syrup (golden syrup)

1   cup (200 g) firmly packed dark brown sugar

1/4 teaspoon salt

1/2 cup (125 g) butter

1/3 cup (75 ml) heavy (double) cream

Simmer until the butter is just melted. Remove from the heat and stir in the vanilla and Grand Marnier.
• Slowly add about one-third of the hot syrup to the eggs, whisking constantly. Add almost all the remaining syrup (leave a little to garnish the slices) and whisk until well combined. Set aside. • Place the walnuts in the baked crust, then sprinkle with the chunks of chocolate. Pour the filling over the top. • Bake until the filling is set, 35–40 minutes. • Cool on a wire rack until just warm, about 1 hour.
Orange Cream: In a chilled bowl, beat the cream and sugar until soft peaks form. Add the Grand Marnier and vanilla and beat until thick. • Cut the tart into slices. Top with the orange cream and drizzle with the remaining orange syrup.

359

1   teaspoon vanilla extract (essence)
2   tablespoons Grand Marnier
2   cups (200 g) coarsely chopped walnuts
3 oz (90 g) semisweet (dark) chocolate, coarsely chopped

Orange Cream

1   cup (250 ml) heavy (double) cream
2   tablespoons granulated sugar
1   tablespoon Grand Marnier
1   teaspoon vanilla extract (essence)

Serves: 8–10
Preparation: 45 minutes + 4 hours to chill
Cooking: 1 hour
Level: 2

CHOCOLATE CROSTATA

Shortcrust Pastry: Mix the flour and salt in a large bowl and make a well in the center. Cut in the butter and enough water to form a smooth dough. • Knead the dough on a lightly floured work surface until smooth and elastic, about 5 minutes. • Roll into a rectangle and fold the short sides over. Roll into a rectangle once more, working in the opposite direction. Fold the short sides over once more. Repeat once more. • Shape into a disk, wrap in plastic wrap (cling film), and chill in the refrigerator for at least 30 minutes. • Preheat the oven to 375°F (190°C/gas 5). • Butter a 9-inch (23-cm) springform pan. • Roll the dough out on a lightly floured work surface into a 9-inch (23-cm) disk. Fit into the prepared pan. Chill in the refrigerator for 30 minutes. Chocolate Filling: Melt the butter in a saucepan over low heat. Stir in the sugar, chocolate, cornstarch, and vanilla. Add the milk, cream, and egg yolks and simmer, stirring constantly, until thickened, about 10 minutes. Remove from the heat and set aside to cool. • Beat the egg whites in a large bowl with an electric mixer at medium speed until stiff peaks form. • Use a large rubber spatula to fold the beaten whites into the cooled chocolate filling. • Spoon into the pastry shell. • Bake until set, 50–60 minutes. • Cool completely in the pan on a rack. • Loosen and remove the pan sides. Transfer to a serving plate. Dust with the cocoa just before serving.

Shortcrust Pastry

2   cups (300 g) all-purpose (plain) flour

¼   teaspoon salt

¼   cup (60 g) butter, cut up

⅓   cup (90 ml) iced water

Chocolate Filling

½   cup (125 g) butter

1   cup (100 g) granulated sugar

8   oz (250 g) bittersweet (dark) chocolate, coarsely chopped

¼   cup (35 g) cornstarch (cornflour)

1   teaspoon vanilla extract (essence)

¼   cup (60 ml) milk

1   cup (250 ml) heavy (double) cream

4   large eggs, separated

4   tablespoons unsweetened cocoa powder, to dust

Serves: 6–8
Preparation: 30 minutes + 30 minutes to chill
Cooking: 50–60 minutes
Level: 2

CHOCOLATE RASPBERRY CROSTATA

Mix the crushed cookie crumbs, almonds, and butter in a large bowl. • Press into the bottom and partway up the sides of a 9-inch (23-cm) pie plate. • Chill in the refrigerator until set, about 2 hours. • Spoon the chocolate pastry cream into the crust and chill in the refrigerator for 2 hours. • Top with the raspberries. • If liked, heat the apricot preserves in a small pan until liquid. Brush the preserves over the raspberries.

1½ cups (300 g) finely crushed vanilla cookies (biscuits)

2/3 cup (100 g) almonds, finely ground

3/4 cup (180 g) butter, melted

1 recipe chocolate pastry cream (see page 678)

1½ cups (300 g) fresh raspberries

1/4 cup (60 g) apricot preserves (jam) (optional)

Serves: 8–10
Preparation: 30 minutes + 4 hours to chill
Level: 1

CHOCOLATE ALMOND PIE

Melt the chocolate in a double boiler over barely simmering water. Set aside to cool. • Mix the flour, almonds, sugar, and salt in a large bowl. Beat in the butter and egg yolks with an electric mixer at medium speed. • With mixer at low speed, beat in the chocolate. • Shape the mixture into a smooth ball. Wrap in plastic wrap (cling film) and chill in the refrigerator for 1 hour. • Preheat the oven to 350°F (180°C/gas 4). • Roll the dough out on a lightly floured work surface into a 10-inch (25-cm) disk. Fit into a 9-inch (23-cm) pie plate. Prick all over with a fork. • Bake until firm, 20–30 minutes. • Cool the crust completely in the pan on a wire rack. • Fill with the pastry cream. • With mixer at high speed, beat the cream in a medium bowl until stiff. • Spread the crostata with the cream and top with the slivered almonds.

4 oz (125 g) bittersweet (dark) chocolate, coarsely chopped

1⅓ cups (200 g) all-purpose (plain) flour

1⅓ cups (200 g) finely ground almonds

½ cup (100 g) granulated sugar

¼ teaspoon salt

¾ cup (180 g) butter, softened

3 large egg yolks

1 recipe chocolate pastry cream, chilled (see page 687)

1 cup (250 ml) heavy (double) cream

Slivered almonds, to top

Serves: 8–10
Preparation: 30 minutes
+ 1 hour to chill
Cooking: 20–30 minutes
Level: 2

ITALIAN CHOCOLATE PIE

368

Preheat the oven to 350°F (180°C/gas 4). • Butter and flour a 10 inch (25 cm) pie plate. • Beat the butter and sugar in a medium bowl with an electric mixer on high speed until pale and creamy. • Add the eggs one at a time, beating until just combined after each addition. • Gradually beat in the flour and baking powder. • Divide the dough in half and roll it out on a lightly floured work surface into two disks about 12 inches (30 cm) in diameter. • Place one disk in the prepared pie plate. Cover with the pastry cream, piling it slightly higher in the center. • Cover with the other disk of pastry and seal the edges together. • Bake until the pastry is firm, about 40 minutes. • Sprinkle the pie with the slivered almonds and dust with the cocoa. Serve warm.

½ cup (125 g) butter, softened

⅔ cup (125 g) granulated sugar

2 large eggs

1⅔ cups (250 g) all-purpose (plain) flour, sifted

1 teaspoon baking powder

⅛ teaspoon salt

1 recipe chocolate pastry cream, (see page 687)

2 tablespoons almonds, slivered

2 tablespoons unsweetened cocoa powder, to dust

Serves: 8–10
Preparation: 30 minutes
Cooking: 40 minutes
Level: 2

HAZELNUT CREAM PIE

Preheat the oven to 350°F (180°C/gas 4). • Butter and flour a 10-inch (25-cm) pie plate. • <u>Pastry</u>: Beat the butter and sugar in a large bowl with an electric mixer at high speed until pale and creamy. • With mixer at medium speed, add the eggs one at a time, beating until just combined after each addition. • Stir in the flour, baking powder, and cinnamon. Add all but 2 tablespoons of the yogurt and the lemon zest. Mix until smooth. • Divide the dough in half and roll it out on a lightly floured work surface into two disks about 12 inches (30 cm) in diameter. • Place one disk in the prepared pie dish. Spread with the chocolate hazelnut cream. • Cover with the other disk of pastry and seal the edges together. • Topping: Place the flour, butter, sugar, and nuts in a medium bowl and beat until the mixture resembles coarse bread crumbs. Sprinkle over the pie. • Bake until the pastry is golden brown, 40–50 minutes. • Whip the cream with the remaining yogurt and serve with the pie.

Pastry

- ³/₄ cup (200 g) butter, softened
- ½ cup (100 g) granulated sugar
- 2 large eggs
- 1²/₃ cups (250 g) all-purpose (plain) flour
- 2 teaspoons baking powder
- ½ teaspoon ground cinnamon
- 1 cup (250 ml) plain yogurt
- Grated zest of 1 lemon
- 1 cup (250 g) chocolate hazelnut spread (Nutella or other), at room temperature

Topping

- 2 tablespoons all-purpose (plain) flour
- 2 tablespoons butter
- 3 tablespoons granulated sugar
- 1 cup (100 g) hazelnuts, toasted and coarsely chopped
- ½ cup (125 ml) heavy (double) cream

Serves: 6–8
Preparation: 20 minutes
Cooking: 40–50 minutes
Level: 2

DIVINE MOUSSE PIE

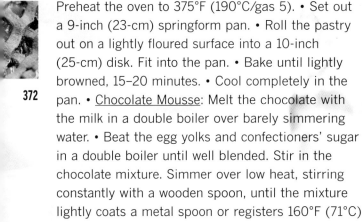

Preheat the oven to 375°F (190°C/gas 5). • Set out a 9-inch (23-cm) springform pan. • Roll the pastry out on a lightly floured surface into a 10-inch (25-cm) disk. Fit into the pan. • Bake until lightly browned, 15–20 minutes. • Cool completely in the pan. • <u>Chocolate Mousse</u>: Melt the chocolate with the milk in a double boiler over barely simmering water. • Beat the egg yolks and confectioners' sugar in a double boiler until well blended. Stir in the chocolate mixture. Simmer over low heat, stirring constantly with a wooden spoon, until the mixture lightly coats a metal spoon or registers 160°F (71°C) on an instant-read thermometer. Immediately plunge the pan into a bowl of ice water and stir until the egg mixture has cooled. • Beat the cream in a large bowl with an electric mixer at high speed until stiff. Fold into the chocolate mixture. • Beat the egg whites, cream of tartar, and sugar at high speed until stiff peaks form. Fold into the chocolate mixture. Chill in the refrigerator for 4 hours.
• Spoon the mousse into the baked pastry case. Refrigerate until set, at least 1 hour. • <u>Topping</u>: Beat the cream, 2 tablespoons of cocoa, the confectioners' sugar, and amaretto in a large bowl with an electric mixer at high speed until stiff.
• Sprinkle the mousse with the remaining cocoa.
• Spoon the cream into a pastry bag fitted with a 3/4-inch (2-cm) star tip. Decorate the top of the pie with a border of cream.

1 recipe chocolate pastry (see page 682)

Chocolate Mousse

12 oz (350 g) bittersweet (dark) chocolate

½ cup (125 ml) milk

6 large eggs, separated

½ cup (75 g) confectioners' (icing) sugar

¾ cup (180 ml) heavy (double) cream

¼ teaspoon cream of tartar

2 tablespoons granulated sugar

Topping

1 cup (250 ml) heavy (double) cream

6 tablespoons unsweetened cocoa powder

2 tablespoons confectioners' (icing) sugar

1 teaspoon amaretto or other almond liqueur

Serves: 8–10
Preparation: 30 minutes
   + 4 hours to chill
Cooking: 30 minutes
Level: 2

WHITE CHOCOLATE LIME PIE

374

White Chocolate Filling: Heat the cream in a medium saucepan until it just comes to a boil. • Place the white chocolate in a large bowl and pour the hot cream over the top. Stir until the chocolate has melted and the mixture is well blended. • Place a sheet of plastic wrap (cling film) on the surface and chill in the refrigerator for at least 2 hours. Pastry: Mix the flour, cocoa, and confectioners' sugar in a large bowl. • Use a pastry blender to cut in the butter until the mixture resembles coarse crumbs. • Add the egg yolk and enough water to bind the mixture into a smooth dough. • Shape the dough into a ball, wrap in plastic wrap (cling film), and chill in the refrigerator for at least 30 minutes. • Preheat the oven to 400°F (200°C/gas 6). • Set out a 10-inch (25-cm) springform pan. • Roll the pastry out on a lightly floured work surface to a 10-inch (25-cm) disk. Fit into the pan. • Bake until firm and lightly browned, 15–20 minutes. Let cool completely in the pan. • Spoon the filling into the pastry case. Top with the sliced limes. Chill in the refrigerator for at least 2 hours.

White Chocolate Filling

2 cups (500 ml) heavy (double) cream

8 oz (250 g) white chocolate, coarsely chopped

Pastry

3/4 cup (125 g) all-purpose (plain) flour

2 tablespoons unsweetened cocoa powder

1 tablespoon confectioners' (icing) sugar

1/4 cup (60 g) butter

1 large egg yolk

2 tablespoons iced water

4 limes, peeled and very thinly sliced, to decorate

Serves: 6–8
Preparation: 40 minutes + 4 hours to chill
Cooking: 20 minutes
Level: 2

COOL CHOCOLATE MACADAMIA TART

Lightly butter a 9-inch (23-cm) springform pan.
• Place the crushed cookies and butter in a bowl and mix well. Firmly press the mixture into the bottom and sides of the prepared pan. • Stir the chocolate in a double boiler over barely simmering water until melted. Remove from the heat and let cool a little. • Place the chocolate, cream cheese, sugar, and vanilla in a large bowl and beat with an electric mixer at medium speed until smooth. • Stir in the macadamia nuts. • Beat the cream at high speed with an electric mixer until thick. Use a large spatula to fold about one-fourth of the cream into the chocolate mixture. Fold in the remaining whipped cream. • Spoon the filling into the pie crust. Cover with foil and freeze for 4–6 hours.
• Carefully loosen and remove the sides of the pan. Let the pie stand at room temperature for 15 minutes before serving.

2 cups (200 g) plain chocolate cookie (biscuit) crumbs

½ cup (125 g) butter, melted

6 oz (180 g) semisweet (dark) chocolate, coarsely chopped

1 cup (250 g) cream cheese, softened

½ cup (100 g) granulated sugar

2 teaspoons vanilla extract (essence)

¾ cup (90 g) macadamia nuts, coarsely chopped

2 cups (500 ml) heavy (double) cream

Serves: 8–10
Preparation: 45 minutes
  + 4–6 hours to freeze
Cooking: 10 minutes
Level: 1

CHOCOLATE PECAN PIE

Crust: Mix the flour, cocoa, baking powder, and salt in a large bowl. Stir in the sugar. • Add the butter and mix gently with your fingertips until the mixture resembles a soft crumble. • Add the egg to the dough and stir until it forms a ball. • Wrap the dough in plastic wrap (cling film) and chill in the refrigerator for at least 30 minutes. • Preheat the oven to 350°F (180°C/gas 4). • Butter a 9-inch (23-cm) pie pan. • Filling: Place the corn syrup and sugar in a medium saucepan over low heat and bring to a boil. Remove from the heat and stir in the chocolate and butter until melted. • Stir in the eggs until the mixture is smooth. • Stir in the pecans. • Roll the dough out on a lightly floured work surface until it is large enough to line the prepared pan. • Place the dough in the pan. Pour the filling over the crust. • Bake until set, 45–55 minutes. • Let cool in the pan on a rack.

Pastry

1 cup (150 g) all-purpose (plain) flour

⅓ cup (50 g) unsweetened cocoa powder

½ teaspoon baking powder

⅛ teaspoon salt

2 tablespoons granulated sugar

⅓ cup (90 g) cold butter

1 large egg, lightly beaten

Filling

1 cup (250 g) light corn syrup (golden syrup)

⅓ cup (85 g) granulated sugar

5 oz (150 g) bittersweet (dark) chocolate

3 tablespoons butter

3 large eggs, lightly beaten

2 cups (225 g) pecans, coarsely chopped

Serves: 8–10
Preparation: 25 minutes
  + 30 minutes to chill
Cooking: 45–55 minutes
Level: 1

WHITE CHOCOLATE COCONUT CREAM PIES

380

Pastry: Mix the flour, cocoa, baking powder, and salt in a large bowl. Stir in the sugar. • Add the butter and mix gently with your fingertips until the mixture resembles a soft crumble. • Stir the egg into the dough until it forms a ball. • Wrap the dough in plastic wrap and chill in the refrigerator for at least 30 minutes. • Preheat the oven to 350°F (180°C/gas 4). • Butter 6–8 fluted tartlet pans. • Roll the dough out on a lightly floured work surface. Cut into 6–8 disks and use them to line the prepared pans. Prick well with a fork. • Bake until the dough is cooked, 15–20 minutes. Let cool on a rack. • Filling: Place the sugar and cornstarch in a medium saucepan. Stir in $1/2$ cup (125 ml) of milk to form a smooth paste. Stir in the remaining milk. • Place the pan over medium-low heat and, stirring constantly, bring to a gentle simmer. Remove from the heat. • Beat the eggs in a small bowl. Pour half the hot milk mixture into the bowl and beat until smooth. • Return the egg and milk mixture to the saucepan and place over medium-low heat. Stirring constantly, bring to a gentle boil. Remove from the heat. • Add the chocolate and vanilla and stir until the chocolate is melted. • Let cool to room temperature then chill in the refrigerator for 2–3 hours. • When ready to serve, beat the cream in a bowl until stiff. • Fold half the cream and half the coconut into the chocolate mixture. • Spoon the filling into the baked pie shells. Top with the remaining cream and coconut.

Pastry

1 cup (150 g) all-purpose (plain) flour
1/3 cup (50 g) unsweetened cocoa powder
1/2 teaspoon baking powder
1/8 teaspoon salt
2 tablespoons granulated sugar
1/3 cup (90 g) cold butter
1 large egg, lightly beaten

Filling

4 tablespoons granulated sugar
5 tablespoons cornstarch (cornflour)
2 cups (500 ml) milk
3 large eggs
10 oz (300 g) white chocolate, coarsely chopped
1 teaspoon vanilla extract (essence)
2 cups (500 ml) heavy (double) cream
1 cup (100 g) shredded coconut

Serves: 6–8
Preparation: 30 minutes
    + 2–3 hours to chill
Cooking: 30 minutes
Level: 1

WICKED WHITE CHOCOLATE AND STRAWBERRY PIES

382

Pastry: Mix the flour, cocoa, baking powder, and salt in a large bowl. Stir in the sugar. • Add the butter and mix gently with your fingertips until the mixture resembles a soft crumble. • Stir enough water into the dough to form a ball. • Wrap the dough in plastic wrap and chill in the refrigerator for at least 30 minutes. • Preheat the oven to 350°F (180°C/gas 4). • Butter 6–8 tartlet pans. • Roll the dough out on a lightly floured work surface. Cut into 6–8 disks and use them to line the prepared pans. Prick well with a fork. • Bake until the dough is cooked, 15–20 minutes. Let cool on a rack. • Filling: Stir the chocolate in a double boiler over barely simmering water until melted. • Remove from heat and pour about 1/2 cup of chocolate into a small bowl. Dip the strawberries into the chocolate, coating them to about half way up. Place on a plate and chill in the refrigerator. • Stir the cream into the remaining melted chocolate. Cool to room temperature then chill in the refrigerator for 2 hours. • Place the egg whites and sugar in a double boiler over barely simmering water and whisk until the sugar is melted. Remove from the heat and beat until the mixture is cool and the whites have thickened. • Stir the Grand Marnier into the filling. Fold the egg white mixture into the filling. • Spoon the filling into the baked pie crusts. • Place a strawberry on each tartlet.

Pastry

- 1 cup (150 g) all-purpose (plain) flour
- 1/3 cup (50 g) unsweetened cocoa powder
- 1/2 teaspoon baking powder
- 1/8 teaspoon salt
- 2 tablespoons granulated sugar
- 1/3 cup (90 g) cold butter
- 3 tablespoons iced water

Filling

- 14 oz (400 g) white chocolate, coarsely chopped
- 6–8 medium-sized strawberries
- 1/2 cup (125 ml) heavy (double) cream
- 2 large egg whites
- 4 tablespoons granulated sugar
- 1 tablespoon Grand Marnier

Serves: 6–8
Preparation: 30 minutes + 2–3 hours to chill
Cooking: 30 minutes
Level: 1

RICH MOCHA PIE

Crust: Preheat the oven to 350°F (180°C/gas 4). Butter a 10-inch (25-cm) pie pan. • Place the cookie crumbs, coffee, and sugar in a large bowl. Stir in the butter and mix well. Press the crust into the base and sides of the prepared pan. • Bake for 10 minutes. Cool on a rack. • Filling: Stir the chocolate in a double boiler over barely simmering water until melted. Remove from the heat and stir in the coffee. Set aside to cool. • Place the cold water in a small bowl. Sprinkle with the gelatin and set aside to soften. • Place the egg yolks and half the sugar in a double boiler over barely simmering water and beat with a wooden spoon until the sugar has melted and the mixture coats the spoon. • Add the gelatin mixture and stir until the gelatin is dissolved. • Remove from the heat and stir in the chocolate. Let cool to room temperature then chill in the refrigerator for 1 hour. • When the chocolate mixture is chilled, beat the cream with 2 tablespoons of the remaining sugar until stiff peaks form. Fold into the chocolate mixture. • Beat the egg whites and remaining sugar with an electric mixer at high speed until stiff peaks form. Gently fold into the chocolate mixture. • Pour the filling into the pie crust and chill in the refrigerator for 6 hours before serving.
• Top with the chocolate curls just before serving.

Crust

- 2 cups (200 g) plain chocolate cookie (biscuit) crumbs
- 1 tablespoon instant coffee granules
- 1/3 cup (70 g) granulated sugar
- 1/3 cup (90 g) butter, melted

Filling

- 5 oz (150 g) bittersweet (dark) chocolate, coarsely chopped
- 1 tablespoon instant coffee granules
- 1/4 cup (60 ml) cold water
- 2 teaspoons unflavored gelatin
- 4 large eggs, separated
- 1/2 cup (100 g) granulated sugar
- 1/2 cup (125 ml) heavy (double) cream

Topping

- 1 recipe milk chocolate curls (see page 694)

Serves: 8–10
Preparation: 30 minutes
+ 7 hours to chill
Cooking: 30 minutes
Level: 1

CHOCOLATE RASPBERRY TARTLETS

Crust: Preheat the oven to 350°F (180°C/gas 4).
• Butter 16–20 small tartlet pans. • Place the flour, cocoa, and salt in a medium bowl. • Place the butter and confectioners' sugar in a large bowl and beat with an electric mixer at high speed until pale and creamy. • With mixer at medium speed, add the egg yolks one at a time, beating until just combined after each addition. • Use a rubber spatula to beat in the mixed dry ingredients. • Shape the dough into a ball, wrap in plastic wrap (cling film), and chill in the refrigerator for at least 30 minutes.
• Break the dough into 4 pieces. Roll out one piece (keep the remaining pieces in the refrigerator) on a lightly floured work surface to about 1/8 inch (3 mm) thick. Cut out disks just slightly larger than the tartlet pans. Place in the pans. Repeat with the remaining dough. • Fill with dried beans and bake until the dough is firm, 12–15 minutes. • Let cool on a rack. • Filling: Stir the chocolate in a double boiler over barely simmering water until melted. Remove from the heat and gradually stir in the cream, butter, and kirsch. Beat until smooth then let cool. • Pipe or spoon some chocolate filling into each tartlet case. Top each one with 5–6 raspberries.

Crust

1⅓ cups (200 g) all-purpose (plain) flour

⅓ cup (50 g) unsweetened cocoa powder

⅛ teaspoon salt

¾ cup (180 g) butter, softened

1 cup (150 g) confectioners' (icing) sugar

2 large egg yolks

Filling

8 oz (250 g) bittersweet (dark) chocolate

½ cup (125 ml) heavy (double) cream

2 tablespoons butter

1 tablespoon kirsch (cherry schnapps)

3 cups fresh raspberries

Serves: 8–10
Preparation: 30 minutes
   + 30 minutes to chill
Cooking: 30 minutes
Level: 1

■ ■ ■ *This recipe is equally good when the filling is made with white chocolate. It can also be made with milk chocolate, in which case top the tartlets with strawberries rather than raspberries,*

APRICOT TART TATIN

Mix the flour, cocoa, and salt in a large bowl.
• Roughly break the butter into pieces the size of
hazelnuts and mix into the flour, without rubbing in.
Make a well in the center of the flour and add half
the water. Use your hands to mix together. Add the
rest of the water and bring the mixture together
until a soft dough forms. The butter will be firm and
visible throughout the dough. • Roll out on a floured
surface into a 12 x 6-inch (30 x 15-cm) rectangle.
Take the left side and fold into the middle of the
dough. Take the right side of the rectangle and fold
over the left. You will now have a 3-layered vertical
rectangle. Make one turn to the left so that the
rectangle is horizontal and repeat the process by
rolling the dough out again, and folding in the same
way. • Make a mark on the left-hand side of the
dough before covering and refrigerating for
20 minutes. • Remove the dough and with the mark
at the left side repeat the rolling and folding.
• Refrigerate once more and repeat the rolling and
folding one last time. You will still be able to see the
butter layers through the pastry. Allow the pastry to
sit for 20 minutes before using. • Roll the pastry out
on a floured work surface into a 10-inch (25-cm)
disk about 1 inch (2.5 cm) thick. Cover and
refrigerate for 30 minutes. • Butter a 10-inch
(25-cm) round pan. It is best not to use a
springform pan for this recipe as the caramel may
leak out at the seam. • Place the sugar and water in
a saucepan and mix to a paste. Place the pan over

3 cups (450 g) all-purpose (plain) flour

⅓ cup (50 g) unsweetened cocoa powder

⅓ teaspoon salt

1½ cups (375 g) cold butter

1¼ cups (300 ml) iced water

12 fresh apricots, pitted and halved, or one (14-oz/400-g) can apricot halves

¾ cup (150 g) granulated sugar

5 tablespoons (75 ml) water

Whipped cream or ice cream, to serve (optional)

Serves: 8–10
Preparation: 3 hours
Cooking: 30–40 minutes
Level: 3

medium heat and bring to a boil. Use a wet, clean pastry brush to occasionally brush down the sides of the pan, collecting any crystals that may have formed. • Boil the sugar until it begins to turn a light brown, caramel color. Mix the sugar with a spoon to ensure the color is even then immediately pour it into the prepared cake pan, covering the base with caramel. Allow to cool and set. • Preheat the oven to 400°F (200°C/gas 6). • Place the apricot halves on top of the caramel cut side up, fitting them in snugly as they will shrink during cooking. • Cover the apricots with the pastry. • Bake until the pastry has risen, about 15 minutes, then reduce the heat to 350°F (180°C/gas 4) and bake for 15–20 minutes more. • Let cool for 10 minutes then place a plate on top of the cake pan. Invert it, turning out the tart. • Serve with whipped cream or ice cream, if liked.

CHOCOLATE TART WITH BERRIES

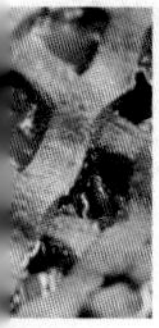

Mix the cookie crumbs, almonds, and butter in a large bowl. • Firmly press into the bottom and up the sides of a 9-inch (23-cm) springform pan. • Chill in the refrigerator until set, at least 2 hours. • Spoon the pastry cream into the prepared base, taking care not to disturb the crumbs. Chill in the refrigerator for 2 hours. • Decorate with the berries. • Heat the apricot preserves in a small pan until liquid and brush over the berries. • Loosen and remove the pan sides to serve.

1½ cups (180 g) finely crushed vanilla cookies (biscuits)

⅔ cup (100 g) finely ground almonds

¾ cup (180 g) butter, melted

1 recipe chocolate pastry cream (see page 678)

1¼ cups (300 g) mixed berries

¼ cup (60 g) apricot preserves (jam)

Serves: 8–10
Preparation: 30 minutes
+ 4 hours to chill
Level: 1

PORTUGUESE TARTS

Roll the pastry out on a lightly floured work surface into an 8 x 11-inch (21 x 28 cm) rectangle. • Mix the sugar and cinnamon together. • Brush the pastry with the egg and scatter the cinnamon mix over the top. Roll the pastry up tightly to make a long sausage shape. Using a sharp knife, cut across the roll to make twelve 1-inch (2.5-cm) thick pieces. • Preheat the oven to 400°F (200°C/gas 6). • Place all the pieces of pastry with the swirl facing up and flatten them slightly. Dust with flour then roll each piece out into a thin circle (about the size of a saucer). • Lightly grease the outside of a standard 12-cup muffin pan. Place a circle of pastry on each cup. Press the pastry around the cups so that it sticks to the mold. • Place the muffin pan on a baking sheet, pastry at the top. Bake until crisp and golden, about 10 minutes. • Remove from the oven and, while still hot, take each case off and place on its base, pushing down gently to make a flat base. Let cool. Leave the oven on. • Filling: Place the cream, sugar, and salt in a saucepan and bring to a boil. Remove from the heat and let cool for 3–4 minutes. • Add the butter, egg yolks, and chocolate and stir until the chocolate has melted. Let cool for 3–4 minutes, then stir in the milk until smooth. • Pour the mixture into the pastry shells. Place each tart on a baking sheet and bake until the mixture is still wobbly in the center but set, 3–5 minutes. • Remove from the oven and let cool completely.

5 oz (150 g) frozen puff pastry, thawed

2 tablespoons granulated sugar

½ teaspoon ground cinnamon

1 large egg, lightly beaten

Filling

⅔ cup (150 ml) heavy (double) cream

2 level tablespoons granulated sugar

¼ cup (60 g) butter, softened

¼ teaspoon salt

6 large egg yolks

8 oz (250 g) bittersweet (dark) chocolate, chopped

¼ cup (60 ml) cold milk

Serves: 6–12
Preparation: 20 minutes
Cooking: 15 minutes
Level: 1

CHOCOLATE PRALINE TARTS

Preheat the oven to 350°F (180°C/gas 4). • Butter twelve 2-inch (5-cm) tartlet pans. • Roll the pastry out to $1/4$ inch (5 mm) thick on a floured work surface. Using the rolling pin, roll up the pastry and gently lay it over each case. Push the pastry into the case smoothing the base and pressing into the sides. Trim off excess pastry. • Line each pan with parchment paper. Fill with dried beans. • Bake for 7 minutes. Remove from the oven and take out the beans and parchment paper. • Place the cases on a baking sheet and bake until the base is firm, 2–3 minutes more. Let cool completely. • Filling: Place the butter, brown sugar, honey, sugar, and cream in a large saucepan over medium-high heat and bring to a boil. Simmer for 3 minutes then remove from the heat. • Place a little of the whole and chopped hazelnuts in each case and pour the sugar mixture over the top. • Return the tarts to the oven and bake until center is bubbling, 5–7 minutes. • Let cool to room temperature before serving.

1 **recipe chocolate pastry (see page 682)**

Filling

1 cup (250 g) butter

1½ cups (300 g) firmly packed dark brown sugar

1 cup (250 g) honey

¼ cup (60 g) granulated sugar

⅓ cup (90 ml) heavy (double) cream

1 cup (100 g) whole toasted hazelnuts

1 cup (100 g) hazelnuts roughly chopped

Serves: 12
Preparation: 30 minutes
Cooking: 15 minutes
Level: 1

CHOCOLATE LINZER TORTE

Crust: Preheat the oven to 350°F (180°C/gas 4).
• Place the flour, ground almonds, sugar, and cocoa in a food processor and blend until well mixed.
• Add butter and process until crumbly. • Add the egg yolks and vanilla and mix well. • Remove one-third of the dough. Wrap in plastic wrap (cling film) and chill in the refrigerator. • Press the remaining dough into the bottom and sides of a 10-inch (25-cm) springform pan. • Bake for 15 minutes.
• Let cool in the pan on a wire rack. • Filling: Place the apricots and orange juice in a small saucepan over medium-high heat, stirring occasionally. Bring to a boil and simmer for 10 minutes. • Stir in the apricot liqueur, 10 oz (300 g) of the apricot preserves, reserving the rest for the glaze. Mix until smooth and allow to cool and thicken slightly before spreading over the bottom of the cooled tart shell.
• Roll out the remaining dough on a floured work surface to about $1/4$ inch (5 mm) thick. Cut into $1/2$-inch (1-cm) cm wide strips and arrange in a cross-hatch pattern on top of the pie. • Bake until the filling is bubbly, 30–35 minutes. Let cool then carefully remove from the pan. • Bring the remaining apricot preserves to a boil and, using a pastry brush, evenly brush the top of the tart with the preserves.

Crust

$1^1/3$ cups (180 g) cups all-purpose (plain) flour

1   cup (110 g) finely ground almonds

$1/2$ cup (100 g) granulated sugar

$1/4$ cup (30 g) unsweetened cocoa powder

$3/4$ cup (180 g) butter

2   large egg yolks

1   teaspoon vanilla extract (essence)

Filling

$2/3$ cup (120 g) chopped dried apricots

$1/4$ cup (60 ml) freshly squeezed orange juice

3   tablespoons apricot liqueur

1   (12-oz/350-g) jar apricot preserves (jam)

Serves: 8–10
Preparation: 20-30 minutes
Cooking: 30-35 minutes
Level 1

PUDDINGS AND CREAMS

RUMMY MUD PUDDING

402

Preheat the oven to 350°F (180°C/gas 4). • Butter a 9-inch (23-cm) springform pan. Wrap the outside of the pan with heavy-duty aluminum foil. • Melt the chocolate in a double boiler over barely simmering water. Set aside and let cool to warm. • Beat the eggs and brown sugar in a large bowl with an electric mixer at high speed until creamy. • With mixer at low speed, gradually beat in the warm chocolate. • Beat the cream in a separate bowl until thick. Use a large rubber spatula to fold the cream and rum into the pudding. • Spoon the batter into the prepared pan. • Place the springform pan in a roasting pan. Pour enough boiling water into the roasting pan to come halfway up the sides of the springform pan. • Bake for 25–30 minutes. Cover the pan with foil and bake until the cake is set but still jiggles slightly, 30–35 minutes. Remove from the water bath and remove the foil cover. Cool the cake completely in the pan on a rack. • Refrigerate for at least 8 hours. Loosen and remove the pan sides. • Dust with the cocoa.

14 oz (400 g) bittersweet (dark) chocolate, coarsely chopped

6 large eggs

½ cup (100 g) firmly packed dark brown sugar

1 cup (250 ml) heavy (double) cream

⅓ cup (90 ml) dark rum

2 tablespoons unsweetened cocoa powder, to dust

Serves: 8–10
Preparation: 30 minutes
+ 8 hours to chill
Cooking: 55–65 minutes
Level: 2

■ ■ ■ *Serve this very rich chilled chocolate cake with fresh fruit, such as raspberries and strawberries or peeled and chopped fresh oranges, soaked in a mixture of sugar and orange liqueur.*

CHOCOLATE MOUSSE WITH PISTACHIO FRANGIPAN COUPE

Preheat the oven to 350°F (180°C/gas 4). • Lightly butter and flour a 9 x 5-inch (23 x 15-cm) loaf pan. Pistachio Frangipan: Process the pistachio nuts and 2 tablespoons of sugar in a food processor until finely ground. Set aside. • Beat the butter and remaining sugar with an electric mixer at high speed until light and creamy. • Add the eggs one at a time, beating until just blended after each addition. • With mixer at low speed, gradually beat in the pistachio mixture and flour. Do not over beat. • Spoon the mixture into the prepared pan and bake until lightly browned and firm to the touch, 25–30 minutes. • Cool the cake completely in the pan on a wire rack. • Chocolate Mousse: Place the chocolate in large bowl. • Place the milk in small saucepan over medium-low heat and bring to a boil. Pour over the chocolate in the bowl. Let stand until the chocolate is melted, then whisk until smooth. Let cool to room temperature. • Beat the cream in a large bowl at high speed until stiff peaks form. Fold one-third of the cream into chocolate mixture. Fold in the remaining cream. • Remove the frangipan from the pan and cut into 1/2-inch (1-cm) cubes. Arrange enough cubes in each of 8 martini glasses so that they come one-third to halfway up sides of each glass. Splash about 2 teaspoons of amaretto onto the frangipan cubes in each glass to moisten. Spoon the mouse over the cubes, filling each glass about three-quarters full. • Chill in the refrigerator for at least 1 hour.

Pistachio Frangipan

- 3/3 cup (150 g) shelled pistachios
- 1/2 cup (100 g) granulated sugar
- 1/2 cup (125 g) unsalted butter, softened
- 2 large eggs
- 3 tablespoons all-purpose (plain) flour

Chocolate Mousse

- 1 1/3 lb (650 g) bittersweet (dark) chocolate, finely chopped
- 1 cup (250 ml) milk
- 2 cups (500 ml) heavy (double) cream
- 1/3 cup (90 ml) amaretto (almond) liqueur

Meringue

- 6 large egg whites
- 1 cup (200 g) granulated sugar

Serves: 8
Preparation: 30 minutes
  + 1 hour to chill
Cooking: 30 minutes
Level: 2

Meringue: just before serving, pour enough water
into a medium saucepan so that it comes one-third
of the way up the side and bring to a simmer.
• Place the egg whites and sugar in a large bowl.
Place the bowl in the saucepan and whisk
continuously until the whites register 160°F (80°C)
on an instant-read thermometer. Remove the bowl
from the saucepan and beat on high speed until the
mixture is cool and the meringue is shiny and forms
stiff peaks. • Place the meringue in a pastry bag
fitted with medium star tip. Pipe a generous
amount of meringue onto each mousse. Using
a small butane or propane torch, gently brown
the meringue.

TRIPLE CHOCOLATE CREAM

Place the cream and vanilla bean in a medium saucepan and bring to a gentle simmer over medium heat. Remove from the heat and let infuse for 10 minutes. • Melt the three types of chocolate separately in heatproof bowls sitting over saucepans half filled with barely simmering water. Remove each bowl from the heat and let cool. • Pour enough water into a medium saucepan so that it comes one-third of the way up the sides and bring to a simmer. • Place the egg yolks in a medium bowl. Place the bowl in the saucepan and whisk continuously until the yolks register 160°F (80°C) on an instant-read thermometer. Let cool. • Add two egg yolks to each bowl and beat until smooth. • Combine the sugar and salt in a small bowl and stir one-third of the mixture into each bowl of chocolate until the sugar is completely dissolved. • Remove the vanilla bean from the cream and gently stir one-third of the cream into each chocolate mixture until well blended. • Replace the bowls over saucepans of simmering water and simmer each mixture, stirring constantly, until it coats the back of a spoon. • Layer the three chocolate mixtures in six serving glasses and chill until set, at least three hours.

1½ cups (375 ml) light (single) cream

1 vanilla bean, split lengthwise and scraped

3 oz (90 g) bittersweet (dark) chocolate, minimum 60% cocoa content, finely chopped

3 oz (90 g) milk chocolate, finely chopped

3 oz (90 g) white chocolate, finely chopped

6 large egg yolks

½ cup (100 g) granulated sugar

¼ teaspoon salt

Serves: 6
Preparation: 30 minutes + 3 hours to chill
Level: 2

CHOCOLATE POTS DE CRÈME

410

Preheat the oven to 325°F (170°C/gas 3). • Place 6–8 pots de crème molds or ramekins in a medium roasting pan. • Place the milk, cream, and both types of chocolate in a medium saucepan over medium heat. Bring almost to a simmer. Remove from the heat and stir until the chocolate is melted. • Whisk the egg yolks, sugar, and salt in a medium bowl. While whisking, add a little of the hot milk mixture. Add the remaining milk mixture and whisk to combine. Stir in the vanilla. Strain the mixture through a fine mesh sieve. • Pour about 1/2 cup (125 ml) of the mixture into each of the prepared pots de crème molds or ramekins. • Place the roasting pan to the oven. Fill the pan with enough boiling water to come halfway up the sides of the molds. • Bake until the pots de crème are just set in the center, about 35 minutes. • Remove the roasting pan from the oven. Remove the pots de crème from the water and place on a wire rack to cool. • When completely cooled, cover, and chill for at least 4 hours or overnight in the refrigerator. • Serve topped with the cream and chocolate curls.

1 cup (250 ml) milk

1 cup (250 ml) heavy (double) cream

2 oz (60 g) milk chocolate, coarsely chopped

2 oz (60 g) bittersweet (dark) chocolate, coarsely chopped

5 large egg yolks

1/3 cup (70 g) granulated sugar

1/4 teaspoon salt

2 teaspoons vanilla extract (essence)

Whipped cream, to serve

Milk chocolate curls, to serve (see page 694)

Serves: 6–8
Preparation: 30 minutes
+ 4 hours to chill
Level: 2

CHOCOLATE MOLD WITH CHOCOLATE SAUCE

<u>Chocolate Mold</u>: Preheat the oven to 375°F (190°C/gas 5). • Butter a 9-inch (23-cm) ring mold. Dust with cocoa. • Place the flour and salt in a small bowl and stir in a little milk until smooth. • Bring the remaining milk, sugar, and butter to a boil in a medium saucepan over medium-low heat, stirring often. Beat in the flour mixture with an electric mixer at low speed until well blended. Set aside to cool. • Beat in the cocoa until smooth. • With mixer at high speed, beat the egg yolks in a large bowl until pale in color. • With mixer at high speed, beat the egg whites in a large bowl until stiff peaks form. • Stir the milk mixture into the egg yolks. Use a large rubber spatula to fold in the beaten whites. • Spoon the batter into the prepared mold. • Bake until a toothpick inserted into the center comes out clean, 25–30 minutes. • Cool the cake in the mold for 10 minutes. Turn out onto a serving dish. • <u>Chocolate Sauce</u>: Stir the chocolate, cream, and milk in a double boiler over barely simmering water until melted. • Pour the hot sauce over the mold. Serve immediately.

Chocolate Mold

- ½ cup (75 g) all-purpose (plain) flour
- ¼ teaspoon salt
- 1 cup (250 ml) milk
- ½ cup (100 g) granulated sugar
- ⅓ cup (90 g) butter
- 4 large eggs, separated
- 4 tablespoons unsweetened cocoa powder
- ½ cup (75 g) coarsely chopped walnuts

Chocolate Sauce

- 6 oz (180 g) bittersweet (dark) chocolate, coarsely chopped
- ½ cup (125 ml) heavy (double) cream
- ¼ cup (60 ml) milk

Serves: 6–8
Preparation: 30 minutes
Cooking: 25–30 minutes
Level: 1

CHOCOLATE MOUSSE WITH FRUIT

Preheat the oven to 300°F (150°C/gas 2). • Butter a 9-inch (23-cm) springform pan. Dust with cocoa. • Melt the chocolate, butter, and coffee granules in a double boiler over barely simmering water. Transfer to a large bowl. Cool to lukewarm. • Whisk the egg yolks and milk in a saucepan until well blended. Simmer over low heat, stirring constantly with a wooden spoon, until the mixture lightly coats a metal spoon or registers 160°F (80°C) on an instant-read thermometer. Immediately plunge the pan into a bowl of ice water and stir until the egg mixture has cooled. Transfer to a large bowl. • Use a large rubber spatula to fold the beaten yolks into the chocolate mixture. • Stir the whites, sugar, and cream of tartar in a double boiler until blended. Cook over low heat, beating constantly with a mixer at low speed until the whites register 160°F (80°C) on an instant-read thermometer. Transfer to a bowl and beat at high speed until stiff peaks form. Use a large rubber spatula to fold them into the chocolate mixture • Spoon two-thirds of the mixture into the prepared pan. Cover and refrigerate the remaining mousse. • Bake until just firm in the center, 30–40 minutes. • Cool completely in the pan on a rack. Loosen and remove the pan sides. Place on a serving plate. Refrigerate for 1 hour. • Spread the remaining mousse over the top and sides of the cake. • Refrigerate overnight before serving decorated with fresh fruit and whipped cream.

12 oz (350 g) semisweet (dark) chocolate, coarsely chopped

1 cup (250 g) unsalted butter

1 teaspoon instant coffee granules

10 large eggs, separated

¼ cup (60 ml) milk

1½ cups (300 g) granulated sugar

¼ cup (60 ml) water

1 teaspoon cream of tartar

Whipped cream, to serve

Fresh fruit, to serve

Serves: 6–8
Preparation: 30 minutes
  + 12 hours to chill
Cooking 30–40 minutes
Level: 1

CHOCOLATE MOUSSE

416

Stir the chocolate in a double boiler over barely simmering water until melted. Set aside until tepid. • Beat the egg yolks and confectioners' sugar in a medium bowl with an electric mixer at high speed until pale and creamy. • Add the melted chocolate and return to the heat for a few minutes, stirring all the time. Set aside to cool. • Beat the egg whites until stiff peaks form and fold into the chocolate mixture. Beat the cream until stiff and fold into the chocolate mixture. • Spoon into six small molds and chill in the refrigerator for 12 hours before serving.

12 oz (350 g) semi-sweet (dark) chocolate

6 large eggs, separated

4 tablespoons confectioners' (icing) sugar

½ cup (125 ml) heavy (double) cream

White chocolate curls, to decorate

Serves: 6
Preparation: 30 minutes + 12 hours to chill
Level: 1

CHOCOLATE BAVARIAN CREAM

418

Sprinkle the gelatin over the cold water in a saucepan. Let stand for 1 minute. Place over low heat and stir until the gelatin has completely dissolved. Set aside. • Heat the milk to a gentle simmer in a medium saucepan over medium heat. • Beat the egg yolks and sugar in a bowl with an electric mixer at high speed until pale and creamy. • Gradually stir in the milk. • Return the mixture to the saucepan and simmer, stirring continuously, until it coats the back of a spoon. • Remove from the heat and add the gelatin mixture and chocolate. Let stand for 1 minute, then stir until the chocolate has melted. Let cool. • Place the disk of sponge cake in a 9-inch (23-cm) springform pan. Moisten with the rum. • Beat the cream until stiff then fold it into the cooled chocolate mixture. • Spoon the mixture into the pan over the cake, spreading it evenly. Chill in the refrigerator until set, at least 4 hours. • Decorate with the white chocolate curls just before serving.

1   tablespoon unflavored gelatin

¼   cup (60 ml) water

¾   cup (180 ml) milk

4   large egg yolks

½   cup (100 g) granulated sugar

4   oz (125 g) bittersweet (dark) chocolate, coarsely chopped

2   cups (500 ml) heavy (double) cream

1   (9-inch/23-cm) disk ready-made sponge cake (about 1-inch/ 2.5-cm thick)

2   tablespoons rum

White chocolate curls (see page 694), to decorate

Serves: 6–8
Preparation: 35 minutes
   + 4 hours to chill
Cooking:15 minutes
Level: 1

CHOCOLATE SULTANA MOUSSE

420

Place the golden raisins in a small bowl with the rum. Let stand for 15 minutes. • Place the cocoa, flour, and sugar in a medium saucepan and mix well. Gradually stir in the milk and vanilla. • Place over medium heat and bring to a boil. Simmer, stirring constantly, for 4 minutes. • Add the golden raisins, and butter and simmer for 4 more minutes. Remove from the heat and let cool. • Spoon the mixture into four dessert bowls or glasses. Chill in the refrigerator for at least 2 hours. • Just before serving, Beat the cream until stiff. Decorate the mousses with the cream and dust with a little of the extra cocoa.

2 oz (60 g) golden raisins (sultanas)

¼ cup (60 ml) rum

½ cup (75 g) unsweetened cocoa powder + extra, to dust

½ cup (75 g) all-purpose (plain) flour

⅓ cup (70 g) granulated sugar

2 cups (500 ml) milk

1 teaspoon vanilla extract (essence)

¼ cup (60 g) butter

½ cup (125 ml) heavy (double) cream

Serves: 4
Preparation: 20 minutes
    + 2 hours to chill
Cooking: 10 minutes
Level: 1

TIRAMISÙ

Beat the egg yolks and sugar in a large bowl with an electric mixer at high speed until pale and creamy. • Carefully fold in the mascarpone. • Beat the egg whites and salt with an electric mixer at high speed until very stiff. Fold into the mixture. • Spread a thin layer of cream over the bottom of a large oval serving dish or in 8 individual serving dishes. • Dip some of the ladyfingers briefly in the red liqueur then soak them briefly in the coffee. Place a layer over the cream on the bottom of the dish. • Cover with another layer of cream and sprinkle with a little chocolate. • Continue in this way until all the ingredients are in the dish. • Finish with a layer of cream and chocolate. Dust with the cocoa. • Chill in the refrigerator for at least 3 hours before serving.

5 large eggs, separated

1 cup (200 g) granulated sugar

2 cups (500 g) mascarpone cheese, softened

¼ teaspoon salt

30 ladyfingers

1 cup (250 ml) strong black coffee, cold

¼ cup (60 ml) Alkermes liqueur

8 oz (250 g) bittersweet (dark) chocolate, coarsely grated

2 tablespoons unsweetened cocoa powder

Serves: 6–8
Preparation: 20 minutes
+ 3 hours to chill
Level: 1

■ ■ ■ *This classic Italian dessert uses raw eggs. Since raw eggs can be a health risk you may prefer to use pasteurized eggs. Alkermes liqueur is bright red and adds cheerful color to the dessert. If you can't get it, replace with cherry brandy brightened with a few drops of red food coloring.*

CHOCOLATE MASCARPONE CREAM

424

Beat the egg yolks and sugar in a medium bowl with an electric mixer at high speed until pale and creamy. • Carefully stir in the mascarpone and Marsala. Divide the mixture evenly between two bowls. • Stir the chocolate and milk in a double boiler over barely simmering water until the chocolate has melted. Set aside to cool. • Mix the chocolate and milk into one bowl of the mascarpone mixture. • Crumble the meringues in the bottom of 4 serving glasses or bowls and spoon in the plain mascarpone and chocolate mixtures. • Blend the surfaces of the two mixtures with a knife to give a marbled effect. • Chill in the refrigerator for at least 2 hours. Top with the chocolate curls just before serving.

2 large egg yolks

½ cup (100 g) granulated sugar

1⅓ cups (300 g) mascarpone cheese, softened

1 tablespoon Marsala wine

4 oz (125 g) bittersweet (dark) chocolate, chopped

3 tablespoons milk

6 ready-made plain meringues

Chocolate curls (see page 694), to decorate

Serves: 4
Preparation: 30 minutes
+ 2 hours to chill
Level: 1

CHOCOLATE CHESTNUT MOUSSE

426

Melt the chocolate in a double boiler over barely simmering water. • Remove from the heat and transfer to a bowl. Add the chestnut purée and 3/4 cup (180 ml) of cream. Mix well. • Beat the egg whites and salt in a medium bowl with an electric mixer at high speed until soft peaks form. • Gradually add the sugar, beating until stiff peaks from. • Stir into the chestnut and chocolate mixture. • Chill in the refrigerator for at least 1 hour. • Spoon into dessert glasses or bowls. Beat the remaining cream and spoon a little over each of the mousses. Top with fresh berries.

8 oz (250 g) canned chestnut purée

4 oz (125 g) semisweet (dark) chocolate

1¼ cups (300 ml) heavy (double) cream

2 large egg whites

¼ teaspoon salt

½ cup (100 g) granulated sugar

Fresh berries, to top

Serves: 4–6
Preparation: 20 minutes + 1 hour to chill
Level: 1

CHOCOLATE HAZELNUT STEAMED PUDDING

Pudding: Butter a 6-cup (1.5-liter) pudding basin or heatproof bowl. • Mix the flour and baking powder in a large bowl. • Beat the eggs and sugar in a large bowl with an electric mixer at high speed until pale and fluffy. • With mixer on medium speed, gradually beat in the butter. • Use a large rubber spatula to fold in the hazelnuts, chocolate, bread crumbs, and dry ingredients. • Spoon the batter into the prepared basin. Cover with parchment paper and a layer of aluminum foil. Secure with kitchen string or cover with a lid. • Place the basin in a large saucepan and pour in enough boiling water to reach halfway up the sides. Cover and simmer until firm, about 2 hours. • Coffee Cream: Mix the cream, egg, coffee liqueur, and sugar in a small saucepan over low heat. Stir constantly until the cream thickens slightly. • Serve the pudding with the coffee cream and sliced apricots and walnuts.

Pudding

- ½ cup (75 g) all-purpose (plain) flour
- ½ teaspoon baking powder
- 4 large eggs
- 1 cup (200 g) superfine (caster) sugar
- ½ cup (125 g) butter
- 1 cup (150 g) finely ground hazelnuts
- 8 oz (250 g) semisweet (dark) chocolate, coarsely grated
- 2 cups (250 g) fine dry bread crumbs

Coffee Cream

- 1¼ cups (310 ml) heavy (double) cream
- 1 large egg, lightly beaten
- 2 tablespoons coffee liqueur
- 1 tablespoon superfine (caster) sugar

Fresh or canned apricots, to serve

Coarsely chopped walnuts, to serve

Serves: 6–8
Preparation: 35 minutes
Cooking: 2 hours
Level: 2

429

CHOCOLATE SLICE WITH STRAWBERRIES AND CREAM

Preheat the oven to 325°F (170°C/gas 3). • Butter a 9 x 5-inch (23 x 13-cm) loaf pan. Line with aluminum foil, letting the edges overhang. Butter the foil. • Melt the chocolate and butter in a double boiler over barely simmering water. Let cool. • Beat the eggs and egg yolk in a double boiler over barely simmering water with an electric mixer at medium speed until pale and thick. Fold into the chocolate mixture. • With mixer at high speed, beat the egg whites in a medium bowl until stiff peaks form. Fold into the chocolate mixture. • Spoon the batter into the prepared pan. • Place the pan in a baking dish and pour in enough boiling water to come halfway up the sides of the loaf pan. • Bake until a toothpick inserted into the center comes out clean, about 55 minutes. • Cool the loaf in the pan on a rack. Refrigerate for 12 hours. • Using the foil as a lifter, remove the loaf from the pan. Carefully remove the foil. • Beat the cream and confectioners' sugar until thick. • Serve in slices decorated with the cream and strawberries.

8 oz (250 g) bittersweet (dark) chocolate, chopped

½ cup (125 g) butter

4 large eggs + 1 large egg yolk

2 large egg whites

1 cup (250 ml) heavy (double) cream

1 tablespoon confectioners' (icing) sugar

8 oz (250 g) fresh strawberries, hulled and sliced

Serves: 6–8
Preparation: 30 minutes
  + 12 hours to chill
Cooking: 55 minutes
Level: 1

MOCHA MOUSSE

432

Preheat the oven to 300°F (150°C/gas 2). • Butter a 10-inch (25-cm) springform pan. Dust with cocoa. • Melt the chocolate, butter, and coffee in a double boiler over barely simmering water. Transfer to a large bowl. Cool to warm. • Beat the egg yolks and milk in a large bowl with an electric mixer at high speed until pale and thick. Fold into the chocolate mixture. • With mixer at high speed, beat the egg whites and sugar in a large bowl until stiff peaks form. Fold into the chocolate mixture. • Spoon the mixture into the prepared pan. • Bake until just firm in the center, about 1 hour. • Cool completely in the pan on a rack. Loosen and remove the pan sides. • Chill in the refrigerator for at least 2 hours. • Decorate with a little cream and the coffee beans just before serving

12 oz (350 g) semisweet (dark) chocolate, coarsely chopped

1 cup (250 g) butter

1 teaspoon instant coffee granules

10 large eggs, separated

¼ cup (60 ml) milk

1½ cups (300 g) granulated sugar

½ cup (125 ml) whipped cream, to decorate

Coffee beans, to decorate

Serves: 8–10
Preparation: 30 minutes
    + 2 hours to chill
Cooking: 35 minutes
Level: 1

KAHLUA MOUSSE

Melt the chocolate with the butter and egg yolks in a double boiler over barely simmering water.
• In a large bowl, combine the confectioners' sugar, Kahlua, and coffee powder. • Stir the chocolate mixture into the bowl. • Whip the cream until stiff and fold it into the Kahlua and chocolate mixture. • Beat the egg whites until just stiff (do not over beat). Fold them into the mixture.
• Spoon the mixture into 8 individual serving bowls.
• Refrigerate for at least 4 hours before serving. If liked, decorate the mousse with extra whipped cream flavored with vanilla extract or Kahlua.

1 lb (500 g) bittersweet (dark) chocolate, chopped

3 oz (90 g) butter

3 large eggs, separated

1/3 cup (50 g) confectioners' (icing) sugar

1/4 cup (60 ml) Kahlua (coffee liqueur)

1 teaspoon instant coffee granules

2 cups (500 ml) heavy (double) cream

Serves: 8
Preparation: 15 minutes
+ 4 hours to chill
Cooking: 15 minutes
Level: 1

435

CHOCOLATE ORANGE MOUSSE

436

Melt the chocolate and butter with the Grand Marnier in a double boiler over barely simmering water. Set aside to cool. • Beat the egg yolks and sugar until the mixture fall in ribbons. This will take about 10 minutes. • In a large bowl, combine the chocolate with the egg mixture. • In another bowl, beat the egg whites until stiff peaks form. • Fold the egg whites into the chocolate mixture until just combined. • Beat the cream until stiff and fold it into the chocolate mixture. • Spoon into 6 individual serving bowls and refrigerate for at least 3 hours. • Decorate each dish with segments of mandarin just before serving.

12 oz (350 g) bittersweet (dark) chocolate

1 cup (250 g) butter

¼ cup (60 ml) Grand Marnier

8 large eggs, separated

¾ cup (150 g) granulated sugar

2½ cups (625 ml) heavy (double) cream

Mandarin segments, to decorate

Serves: 6
Preparation: 15 minutes
  + 3 hours to chill
Cooking: 15 minutes
Level: 1

CHOCOLATE FONDUE WITH FRESH FRUIT

438

Rinse and dry the fruit. Cut the larger pieces into bite-sized chunks. • If using apple, pear, or banana, immerse the chunks in water and lemon juice for a few seconds to prevent the flesh from browning, then dry carefully. • Arrange the fruit in an attractive bowl or serving dish. • Melt the chocolate in a double-boiler over barely simmering water. Dilute with the cream, add the butter and sugar and stir until the sugar has dissolved. • Pour the chocolate mixture into the fondue bowl and keep warm over the flame. • Place bowls filled with the almonds, hazelnuts, and coconut on the table, so that your guests can dip their pieces of fruit into them, after having dipped them in the chocolate sauce.

2 lb (1 kg) mixed fresh fruit (grapes, figs, strawberries, bananas, apples, apricots, plums, peaches)

2 cups (500 ml) water

Juice of 1 lemon

1 lb (500 g) bittersweet (dark) chocolate, chopped

1 cup (250 ml) heavy (double) cream

¼ cup (60 g) butter

4 tablespoons superfine (caster) sugar

⅓ cup (50 g) each chopped toasted almonds and hazelnuts

½ cup (60 g) shredded (desiccated) coconut

Serves: 6–8
Preparation: 15 minutes
+ 3 hours to chill
Cooking: 15 minutes
Level: 1

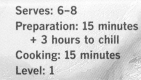

CHOCOLATE RICE PUDDING

440

Heat the milk and sugar in a large saucepan over medium-low heat. • When the milk is boiling, add the rice and simmer until the rice is tender and the milk has all been absorbed, about 25 minutes. Depending on the quality of the rice, you may need to add a little more milk during cooking or strain a little milk off the mixture when the rice is cooked.
• Add three-quarters of the chocolate and the cinnamon and stir until the chocolate is melted.
• Remove from the heat and pour into a deep serving bowl. Sprinkle with the remaining chocolate and serve while still warm.

4 cups (1 liter) milk

½ cup (100 g) granulated sugar

1 cup (200 g) short-grain rice

8 oz (250 g) bittersweet (dark) chocolate, grated

Dash of ground cinnamon

Serves: 6–8
Preparation: 10 minutes
Cooking: 30 minutes
Level: 1

BAKED CHOCOLATE AND AMARETTI CUSTARDS

Preheat the oven to 300°F (150°C/gas 2). • Place half the sugar in a small saucepan with the lemon juice and water over medium heat. • As soon as the sugar caramelizes to golden brown, pour it into 6–8 small pudding molds. Tip the mold to coat the inside evenly before the caramel hardens. Set aside. • Heat the milk gently until just tepid. • Use a balloon whisk or electric beater to beat the eggs very thoroughly in a bowl with the remaining sugar. Add the cocoa and mix well. • Stir in the warm milk, followed by the amaretti cookies and rum. • Pour this mixture into the caramel-lined molds. Cover the molds with pieces of foil and place in a baking dish half filled with cold water. Bake until set, about 1 hour. • Let the molds cool for 15–20 minutes before unmolding carefully onto serving dishes. • Chill for at least 4 hours in the refrigerator. Decorate with a little whipped cream and slivered almonds just before serving.

1 cup (200 g) granulated sugar

½ teaspoon freshly squeezed lemon juice

2 tablespoons cold water

3½ cups (800 ml) milk

6 large eggs

4 tablespoons unsweetened cocoa powder

2 oz (60 g) amaretti cookies (biscuits), finely pounded

3 tablespoons rum

Whipped cream and slivered almonds, to decorate

Serves: 6–8
Preparation: 25 minutes + 4 hours to chill
Cooking: 1 hour
Level: 2

PEARS WITH CUSTARD AND CHOCOLATE SAUCE

444

Pears: Peel the pears, and without removing the cores, place them whole in a high-sided narrow saucepan. Cover with cold water. Stir in the sugar and cinnamon. • Simmer over low heat until cooked but still firm. Remove from the saucepan and let cool. • Custard: Beat the egg yolks and sugar with an electric mixer at high speed until pale and creamy, then stir in the flour. • Bring the milk to a boil with the salt and vanilla. • Stir the hot milk into the egg mixture, then simmer over very low heat, stirring constantly, until thickened. Pour into a medium bowl, cover with plastic wrap (cling film) and set aside. • Sauce: Melt the chocolate in a double-boiler over barely simmering water. • Bring the cream to a boil then use it to dilute the liquid chocolate. • Remove the plastic wrap, warm the custard, and pour into a serving dish. • Serve the pears covered with the melted chocolate on the bed of custard, sprinkled with the crumbled amaretti cookies.

Pears

- 6 large ripe yellow pears (Kaiser or Williams)
- 1½ cups (300 g) granulated sugar
- Dash of ground cinnamon

Custard

- 5 large egg yolks
- ¾ cup (150 g) granulated sugar
- ⅓ cup (50 g) all-purpose (plain) flour
- 2 cups (500 ml) milk
- ⅛ teaspoon salt
- 1 teaspoon vanilla extract (essence)

Sauce

- 5 oz (150 g) bittersweet (dark) chocolate
- 5 tablespoons light (single) cream
- 6 amaretti cookies (biscuits), crumbled

Serves: 6
Preparation: 30 minutes
Cooking: 1 hour
Level: 1

445

WHITE CHOCOLATE MOUSSE WITH COINTREAU

446

Melt the chocolate in a double-boiler over barely simmering water. • Beat the egg yolks and sugar in a large bowl with an electric mixer on high speed until pale and creamy. • Fold in the melted chocolate followed by the dissolved gelatin. Stir in the Cointreau. • Whip the cream until thick then fold into the cooled chocolate mixture. • Pour into 4–6 serving dishes. • Chill in the refrigerator for 4 hours before serving.

5   oz (150 g) white chocolate

5   large egg yolks

4   tablespoons granulated sugar

2   teaspoons gelatin dissolved in 2 tablespoons warm water

2   tablespoons Cointreau

1   cup (250 ml) heavy (double) cream

Serves: 4–6
Preparation: 30 minutes
    + 4 hours to chill
Level: 1

CHOCOLATE ICE CREAM

448

Place the milk and cream in a medium saucepan over medium heat. Add $^3/_4$ cup (150 g) of sugar and the vanilla. Bring to a boil then remove from the heat. • Add the chocolate, stirring until dissolved. • Beat the egg yolks and remaining sugar in a medium bowl with an electric mixer at high speed until pale and creamy. • Beat the cocoa into the egg yolk mixture. • Gradually pour the milk and cream mixture into the egg yolk mixture, stirring well with a wooden spoon. • Return the mixture to the saucepan over low heat and, stirring constantly with a wooden spoon, cook until it coats the back of the spoon. Make sure the mixture does not boil. • Remove from the heat and strain into a chilled bowl. Let cool. • Place in an ice cream maker and prepare according to the instructions. • Serve with the candied mandarins.

2 **cups (500 ml) milk**

2 **cups (500 ml) heavy (double) cream**

1¼ **cups (250 g) granulated sugar**

1 **teaspoon vanilla extract (essence)**

4 **oz (125 g) bittersweet (dark) chocolate, coarsely grated**

8 **large egg yolks**

⅓ **cup (50 g) unsweetened cocoa powder**

Candied mandarins, to decorate

Serves: 4–6
Preparation: 30 minutes
+ time to freeze
Level: 1

ITALIAN CHOCOLATE CHIP ICE CREAM

450

Place the milk and cream in a medium saucepan over medium heat. Add $3/4$ cup (150 g) of sugar and the vanilla. Bring to a boil then remove from the heat. • Beat the egg yolks and remaining sugar in a medium bowl with an electric mixer at high speed until pale and creamy. • Gradually pour the milk and cream mixture into the egg yolk mixture, stirring well with a wooden spoon. • Return the mixture to the saucepan over low heat and, stirring constantly with a wooden spoon, simmer until it coats the back of the spoon. Make sure the mixture does not boil. • Remove from the heat and strain into a chilled bowl. Let cool, stirring from time to time. • Place in an ice cream maker and prepare according to the manufacturers' instructions.
• Melt the chocolate in a double boiler over barely simmering water. Let cool a little and add to the ice cream in the ice cream maker just before it is ready. The chocolate should solidify into small lumps.
• Serve with the Florentine cookies, if liked.

2 cups (500 ml) milk

2 cups (500 ml) cream

1½ cups (300 g) granulated sugar

1 teaspoon vanilla extract (essence)

8 large egg yolks

4 oz (125 g) bittersweet chocolate, coarsely grated

2 tablespoons rum

White Florentine cookies, to serve (see page 86), optional

Serves: 6–8
Preparation: 30 minutes
  + time to freeze
Level: 1

CHOCOLATE SPONGE PUDDING

Preheat the oven to 350°F (180°C/gas 4). • Place the butter in a small bowl. Sift in the flour and cocoa, add the sugar and then stir in the orange zest and juice. Mix thoroughly. • Beat the egg whites until stiff but not dry. • Beat the egg yolks and milk together then stir into the chocolate mixture. • Fold the whites carefully into the mixture. • Pour into 4 ramekins and scatter with the chocolate. • Place in a baking dish half filled with cold water and bake for 50–60 minutes. • Serve warm.

1 tablespoon butter, melted

2 tablespoons self-raising flour

2 tablespoons unsweetened cocoa powder

½ cup (100 g) granulated sugar

1 tablespoon finely grated orange zest

¼ cup (60 ml) freshly squeezed orange juice

2 large eggs, separated

1 cup (250 ml) milk

4 oz (125 g) bittersweet (dark) chocolate, coarsely chopped

Serves: 4
Preparation: 10 minutes
Cooking: 50–60 minutes
Level: 1

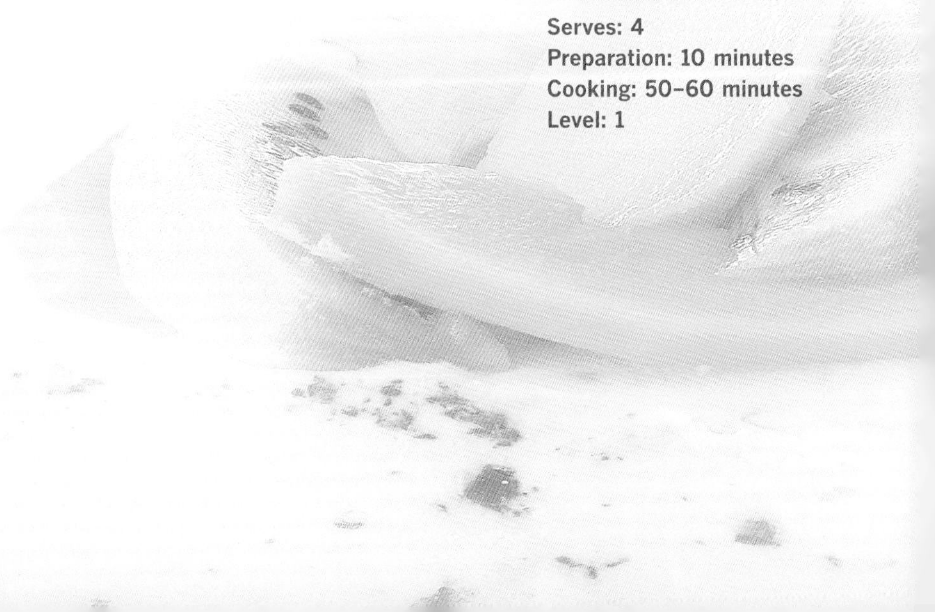

454

COCONUT AND CHOCOLATE SEMIFREDDO

Dampen a sheet of parchment paper with the orange flower water. Use the paper to line a 9 x 5-inch (23 x 13-cm) loaf pan. • Process the ricotta, sugar, coconut, and vanilla in a food processor or blender until smooth. • Stir in the chocolate. • Beat the cream in a large bowl until stiff, then carefully fold it into the mixture. • Spoon the mixture into the prepared pan. • Freeze for 4 hours. • Cut the kiwi fruit and star anise into slices and the mango and papaya into thin segments. • Turn the semifreddo out onto a serving platter. • Decorate with the fruit and serve in thick slices.

1 teaspoon orange flower water

1¼ cups (300 g) fresh ricotta cheese, drained

¾ cup (150 g) granulated sugar

¾ cup (90 g) shredded (desiccated) coconut

½ teaspoon vanilla extract (essence)

4 oz (125 g) semisweet (dark) chocolate, chopped

2 cups (500 ml) heavy (double) cream

2 kiwi fruit

2 star anise

1 ripe mango

1 ripe papaya (pawpaw)

Serves: 4–6
Preparation: 25 minutes
    + 4 hours to freeze
Level: 2

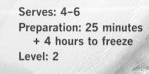

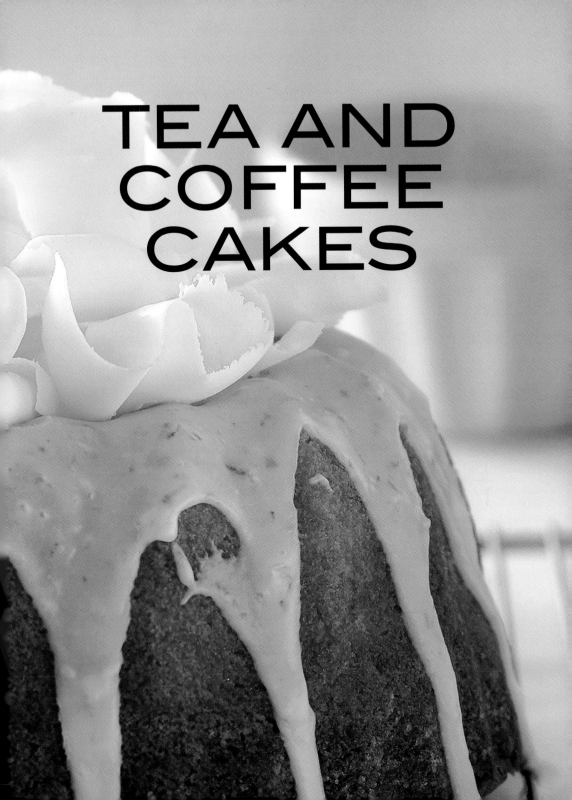

TEA AND COFFEE CAKES

CRUNCHY CHOCOLATE CHIP COFFEE CAKE

458

Preheat the oven to 350°F (180°C/gas 4). • Butter and flour a 13 x 9-inch (32 x 23-cm) baking pan. Topping: Stir the sugar and flour in a medium bowl. Use a pastry blender to cut in the butter until the mixture resembles fine crumbs. Stir in the chocolate chips and walnuts. • Cake: Mix the flour, baking powder, baking soda, and salt in a large bowl. • Beat the butter, cream cheese, sugar, and vanilla in a large bowl with an electric mixer at medium speed until creamy. • Add the eggs, one at a time, beating until just blended after each addition. • With mixer at low speed, gradually beat in the dry ingredients, alternating with the milk. • Spoon the batter into the prepared pan. Sprinkle with the topping. • Bake until a toothpick inserted into the center comes out clean, 50–60 minutes. • Cool the cake completely in the pan on a wire rack.

Topping

½ cup (100 g) firmly packed dark brown sugar

½ cup (75 g) all-purpose (plain) flour

¼ cup (60 g) butter

1 cup (180 g) semisweet (dark) chocolate chips

½ cup (60 g) walnuts, coarsely chopped

Cake

2½ cups (375 g) all-purpose (plain) flour

2 teaspoons baking powder

½ teaspoon baking soda (bicarbonate of soda)

¼ teaspoon salt

¾ cup (180 g) butter

8 oz (250 g) cream cheese, softened

1½ cups (300 g) granulated sugar

1 teaspoon vanilla extract (essence)

3 large eggs

¾ cup (180 ml) milk

Serves: 10–12
Preparation: 20 minutes
Cooking: 50–60 minutes
Level: 1

FROSTED MARBLE CAKE

Preheat the oven to 350°F (180°C/gas 4). • Butter and flour a 9-inch (23-cm) tube pan. • Mix the flour, baking powder, and salt into a large bowl. • Beat the butter, sugar, and vanilla in a large bowl with an electric mixer at high speed until creamy. • With mixer at medium speed, add the eggs one at a time, beating until just combined after each addition. • With mixer at low speed, gradually beat in the dry ingredients, alternating with the milk. • Divide the batter evenly among three small bowls. Stir the cocoa into one bowl and the red food coloring into another. Leave one bowl plain. • Drop alternate spoonfuls of the batters into the prepared pan, swirling them together with a knife to create a marbled effect. • Bake until a toothpick inserted into the center comes out clean, 40–50 minutes. • Cool the cake completely in the pan on a wire rack. • Spread with the frosting.

2⅓ cups (350 g) all-purpose (plain) flour

2½ teaspoons baking powder

¼ teaspoon salt

1 cup (250 g) butter

1 cup (100 g) granulated sugar

1 teaspoon vanilla extract (essence)

3 large eggs

¾ cup (180 ml) milk

4 tablespoons unsweetened cocoa powder

1 teaspoon red food coloring

1 recipe chocolate frosting (see page 688)

Serves: 8–10
Preparation: 30 minutes
Cooking: 40–50 minutes
Level: 1

CHOCOLATE CARROT CAKE

462

Cake: Preheat the oven to 350°F (180°C/gas 4). • Butter and flour a 13 x 9-inch (33 x 23-cm) baking pan. • Mix the flour, walnuts, raisins, cocoa, cinnamon, baking powder, baking soda, ginger, and salt in a large bowl. • Melt the chocolate in a double boiler over barely simmering water. Set aside to cool. • Beat the eggs, sugar, and oil in a large bowl with an electric mixer at medium speed until creamy. • With mixer at low speed, gradually beat in the dry ingredients, alternating with the chocolate and carrots. • Spoon the batter into the prepared pan. • Bake until a toothpick inserted into the center comes out clean, 40–50 minutes. • Cool the cake completely in the pan on a wire rack. • Milk Chocolate Frosting: Melt the chocolate in a double boiler over barely simmering water. Set aside to cool. • With mixer at medium speed, beat the cream cheese and confectioners' sugar in a large bowl. Beat in the melted chocolate. • Spread the cake with the frosting.

Cake

2 cups (300 g) all-purpose (plain) flour

½ cup (50 g) chopped walnuts

½ cup (90 g) raisins

⅓ cup (50 g) unsweetened cocoa powder

1 teaspoon ground cinnamon

1 teaspoon baking powder

½ teaspoon baking soda

½ teaspoon ground ginger

¼ teaspoon salt

5 oz (150 g) milk chocolate, grated

3 large eggs

¾ cup (150 g) firmly packed dark brown sugar

½ cup (125 ml) vegetable oil

3 cups (300 g) finely shredded carrots

Milk Chocolate Frosting

6 oz (180 g) milk chocolate, chopped

8 oz (250 g) cream cheese, softened

2 cups (300 g) confectioners' (icing) sugar

Serves: 8–10
Preparation: 30 minutes
Cooking: 50 minutes
Level: 1

CINNAMON MARBLE CAKE

Preheat the oven to 350°F (180°C/gas 4). • Butter and flour a 13 x 9-inch (32 x 23-cm) baking pan. • Mix the flour, baking powder, and salt in a medium bowl. • Mix 1/2 cup (100 g) of sugar, the cocoa, and cinnamon in a small bowl. • Beat the butter and cream cheese in a large bowl with an electric mixer at medium speed until creamy. Gradually beat in the remaining sugar and vanilla until smooth. • Add the eggs, one at a time, beating until just blended after each addition. • With mixer at low speed, gradually beat in the flour mixture. • Stir in the chocolate chips. • Spread two-thirds of the batter in the prepared pan. Sprinkle with the cocoa mixture. Spoon the remaining batter on top and run a knife through the layers to create a marbled effect. • Bake until a toothpick inserted into the center comes out clean, 40–50 minutes. • Cool the cake completely in the pan on a wire rack.

2⅓ cups (350 g) all-purpose (plain) flour

1½ teaspoons baking powder

¼ teaspoon salt

2 cups (400 g) granulated sugar

2 tablespoons unsweetened cocoa powder

2 tablespoons ground cinnamon

1 cup (250 g) butter

8 oz (250 g) cream cheese

2 teaspoons vanilla extract (essence)

4 large eggs

¾ cup (100 g) semisweet (dark) chocolate chips

Serves: 8–10
Preparation: 25 minutes
Cooking: 40–50 minutes
Level: 1

465

STRAWBERRY MARBLE CAKE

Cake: Preheat the oven to 350°F (180°C/gas 4).
• Butter a deep 9-inch (23-cm) square baking pan. Line with parchment paper. Butter the paper. • Mix the flour, baking powder, and salt in a medium bowl. • Beat the butter and sugar in a large bowl with an electric mixer at high speed until creamy. • Add the eggs, one at a time, beating until just blended after each addition. • With mixer at low speed, gradually beat in the dry ingredients, alternating with the milk and vanilla. • Place half the batter in a separate bowl. Stir the cocoa into one bowl and the red food coloring into the other. • Drop alternate spoonfuls of the two batters into the prepared pan, swirling them together with a knife to create a marbled effect. • Bake until a toothpick inserted into the center comes out clean, 30–40 minutes. • Cool the cake in the pan for 15 minutes. Turn out onto a wire rack. Carefully remove the parchment paper and let cool completely. • Cream Cheese Frosting: With mixer at medium speed, beat the cream cheese and confectioners' sugar in a large bowl until creamy. Add the cocoa and milk and beat until smooth and spreadable. Spread the top and sides of the cake with the frosting. • Decorate with the strawberries.

Cake

2 cups (300 g) all-purpose (plain) flour

1½ teaspoons baking powder

¼ teaspoon salt

¾ cup (180 g) butter, softened

¾ cup (150 g) granulated sugar

2 large eggs

½ cup (125 ml) milk

1 teaspoon vanilla extract (essence)

⅓ cup (50 g) unsweetened cocoa powder

½ teaspoon red food coloring

Cream Cheese Frosting

8 oz (250 g) cream cheese, softened

2 cups (300 g) confectioners' (icing) sugar

¼ cup (35 g) unsweetened cocoa powder

1 tablespoon hot milk

Fresh strawberries, to decorate

Serves: 8–10
Preparation: 30 minutes
Cooking: 30–40 minutes
Level: 1

IRISH CREAM CAKE

Cake: Preheat the oven to 350°F (180°C/gas 4).
• Butter and flour a 10-inch (25-cm) tube pan.
• Mix the flour, sugar, baking powder, and salt in a large bowl. • Melt the chocolate with the oil, liqueur, water, and coffee granules in a double boiler over barely simmering water. • Transfer to a large bowl and beat in the egg yolks with a wooden spoon until well blended. • Add the dry ingredients and stir until smooth. • Beat the egg whites in a large bowl with an electric mixer at high speed until stiff peaks form. Use a large rubber spatula to fold them into the batter. • Spoon the batter into the prepared pan.
• Bake until firm to the touch and a slightly sugary crust had formed, 30–40 minutes. • Cool the cake in the pan for 15 minutes. Turn out onto a wire rack to cool completely. • Coffee Frosting: Beat the coffee mixture and butter into the confectioners' sugar until the frosting is thick and spreadable. Spread over the top and sides of the cake.

Cake

2 cups (300 g) all-purpose (plain) flour

1½ cups (300 g) granulated sugar

2 teaspoons baking powder

¼ teaspoon salt

5 oz (150 g) bittersweet (dark) chocolate, coarsely chopped

½ cup (125 ml) vegetable oil

⅓ cup (90 ml) Irish cream liqueur

⅓ cup (90 ml) water

2 tablespoons instant coffee granules

7 large eggs, separated

Coffee Frosting

1 tablespoon instant coffee granules dissolved in 2 tablespoons Irish cream liqueur

3 tablespoons butter, melted

2 cups (300 g) confectioners' (icing) sugar

Serves: 10–12
Preparation: 20 minutes
Cooking: 30–40 minutes
Level: 2

BANANA-CHOCOLATE BRUNCH CAKE

Preheat the oven to 350°F (180°C/gas 4). • Butter and flour a 9-inch (23-cm) springform pan. • Mix the flour, sugar, baking powder, baking soda, salt, and cinnamon in a large bowl. • Combine the banana, milk, and egg in a medium bowl, stirring until well blended. • Add the banana mixture to the flour mixture, stirring just until moist. Gently fold in half the chocolate. • Spoon the batter into the prepared pan. • Bake until a toothpick inserted in center comes out clean, 30–40 minutes. • Cool in pan for 5 minutes on a wire rack, then remove from pan and let cool completely. • Place the remaining chocolate and water in a small saucepan over low heat until melted. Stir until smooth. Drizzle the glaze over the cooled cake.

2   cups (300 g) all-purpose (plain) flour

1   cup (200 g) firmly packed light brown sugar

1½ teaspoons baking powder

½ teaspoon baking soda (bicarbonate of soda)

¼ teaspoon salt

½ teaspoon ground cinnamon

2   cups mashed banana (about 3 large bananas)

½ cup (125 ml) milk

1   large egg

5   oz (150 g) bittersweet (dark) chocolate, grated

2½ tablespoons boiling water

Serves: 8–10
Preparation: 15 minutes
Cooking: 30–40 minutes
Level: 1

CHOCOLATE MARBLE CAKE WITH GANACHE

Cake: Preheat the oven to 350°F (180°C/gas 4).
• Butter and flour a 9 x 5-inch (23 x 13-cm) loaf pan.
• Mix the flour, salt, and baking powder in a medium bowl. • Melt the chocolate in a double boiler over barely simmering water. • Beat the butter with an electric mixer on low speed until smooth, 2–3 minutes. Add the sugar and increase speed to medium. Beat the butter and sugar until pale and creamy. • Add the eggs, one at a time, beating until just combined after each addition. • Reduce speed to low and gradually beat in the sifted dry ingredients, alternating with the milk. • Spoon half the batter into the melted chocolate and stir well. • Drop alternate tablespoons of plain and chocolate batter into the prepared pan. Use a table knife to cut through the batter with a swirling motion to create a marbled effect. • Bake until a toothpick inserted into the center comes out clean, 50–60 minutes. • Let cool slightly in the pan on a wire rack for 10 minutes. Run a thin knife around edges of the pan to loosen and unmold. Let cool completely on a rack.
Ganache: Place the chocolate in a medium bowl. Heat the cream in a small saucepan over medium heat until just about to simmer. Pour the cream over chocolate and stir until smooth. Let stand for 10 minutes to thicken slightly. • Using a small spatula, spread the ganache over the cooled cake. Let stand for about 1 hour before serving.

Cake

1   cup (250 g) butter, softened

1⅓ cups (200 g) all-purpose (plain) flour

½ teaspoon salt

¾ teaspoon baking powder

5   oz (150 g) semisweet (dark) chocolate, coarsely chopped

¾ cup (150 g) granulated sugar

4   large eggs

½ cup (125 ml) milk

Ganache

4   oz (125 g) semisweet (dark) chocolate, coarsely chopped

¼ cup (60 ml) heavy (double) cream

Serves: 6–8
Preparation: 20 minutes
Cooking: 50–60 minutes
Level: 1

CHOCOLATE GINGERBREAD

Preheat the oven to 325°F (170°C/gas 3). • Butter an 8-inch (20-cm) square pan. • Mix the flour, ginger, baking powder, salt, pepper, and cloves in a medium bowl. Stir in the brown sugar. • Melt the butter in the water in a small saucepan over medium heat. • Pour the butter mixture into the dry ingredients, stirring until smooth. • Add the molasses and egg, stirring until just blended. • Spoon half the batter into prepared pan. Drizzle half the chocolate over the batter. Spoon the remaining batter over the top and drizzle the remaining chocolate over the batter. • Bake until a toothpick inserted in the center comes out clean, about 30 minutes. • Let cool in the pan on a wire rack for 15 minutes, then turn onto the rack to cool completely.

1¾ cups (230 g) all-purpose (plain) flour

1½ teaspoons ground ginger

1 teaspoon baking powder

¼ teaspoon salt

⅛ teaspoon freshly ground black pepper

⅛ teaspoon ground cloves

½ cup (100 g) firmly packed light brown sugar

½ cup (125 g) unsalted butter

½ cup (125 ml) water

½ cup (125 ml) molasses

1 large egg, lightly beaten

3 oz (90 g) bittersweet (dark) chocolate, melted and slightly cooled

Serves: 6–8
Preparation: 15 minutes
Cooking: 30 minutes
Level: 1

■ ■ ■ *Serve this moist gingerbread as is at breakfast or brunch. Later in the day, serve it with whipped cream sprinkled with coarsely chopped candied ginger.*

CHOCOLATE CHIP POUND CAKE

476

Preheat the oven to 350°F (180°C/gas 4). • Butter and flour a deep 10-inch (25-cm) tube pan. • Mix the flour, baking powder, and salt in a large bowl. • Beat the butter, sugar, and vanilla in a large bowl with an electric mixer at high speed until creamy. • Add the eggs, one at a time, beating until just blended after each addition. • With mixer at low speed, gradually beat in the dry ingredients, alternating with the buttermilk. • By hand, stir in the chocolate chips. • Spoon the batter into the prepared pan. Bake until a toothpick inserted into the center comes out clean, 1 hour 15–25 minutes. • Run a knife around the edges of the pan to loosen the cake. Cool the cake in the pan for 15 minutes. Turn out onto a wire rack to cool completely.

2½ cups (375 g) all-purpose (plain) flour

1 teaspoon baking powder

¼ teaspoon salt

1½ cups (375 g) butter, softened

2¼ cups (250 g) granulated sugar

2 teaspoons vanilla extract (essence)

5 large eggs

¾ cup (180 ml) buttermilk

1 cup (180 g) semisweet (dark) chocolate chips

Serves: 10–12
Preparation: 25 minutes
Cooking: 1 hour 15–25 minutes
Level: 1

PEPPERMINT-FROSTED CHOCOLATE POUND CAKE

Cake: Preheat the oven to 350°F (180°C/gas 4).
• Butter and flour a deep 10-inch (25-cm) tube pan.
• Mix the flour, cocoa, baking powder, and salt in a large bowl. • Beat the butter, shortening, sugar, and vanilla in a large bowl with an electric mixer at medium speed until creamy. • Add the eggs, one at a time, beating until just blended after each addition. • With mixer at low speed, gradually beat in the dry ingredients, alternating with the milk.
• Spoon the batter into the prepared pan. • Bake until a toothpick inserted into the center comes out clean, 1 hour 35–45 minutes. • Run a knife around the edges of the pan to loosen the cake. Cool the cake in the pan for 15 minutes. Turn out onto a wire rack to cool completely. • Peppermint Frosting: With mixer at medium speed, beat the confectioners' sugar and butter in a large bowl until creamy. Add the cocoa, milk, and peppermint and beat until smooth. • Spread the top and sides of the cake with the frosting.

Cake

3½ cups (525 g) all-purpose (plain) flour

1 cup (150 g) unsweetened cocoa powder

1 teaspoon baking powder

½ teaspoon salt

1 cup (250 g) butter

½ cup (125 g) vegetable shortening

3 cups (600 g) granulated sugar

1 tablespoon vanilla extract (essence)

5 large eggs

1¼ cups (325 ml) milk

Peppermint Frosting

2 cups (300 g) confectioners' (icing) sugar

¼ cup (60 g) butter, softened

⅓ cup (50 g) unsweetened cocoa powder

1 tablespoon milk

½ teaspoon peppermint extract

■ ■ ■ *If preferred, leave the peppermint extract out of the frosting or replace it with 1 teaspoon of vanilla extract (essence).*

Serves: 12–14
Preparation: 25 minutes
Cooking: 1 hour 35–45 minutes
Level: 1

WHITE CHOCOLATE POUND CAKE

Cake: Preheat the oven to 350°F (180°C/gas 4).
• Butter and flour a deep 10-inch (25-cm) Bundt pan. Sprinkle the pan with 2 tablespoons of the sugar. • Melt the chocolate in a double boiler over barely simmering water. Set aside to cool. • Stir the flour, baking powder, baking soda, and salt into a large bowl. • Beat the butter, remaining sugar, and vanilla and almond extracts in a large bowl with an electric mixer at medium speed until creamy. • Add the eggs, one at a time, beating until just blended after each addition. • With mixer at low speed, gradually beat in the dry ingredients, alternating with the yogurt and melted chocolate. • Spoon the batter into the prepared pan. • Bake until a toothpick inserted into the center comes out clean, 1 hour 15–25 minutes. • Run a knife around the edges of the pan to loosen the cake. Cool the cake in the pan for 15 minutes. Turn out onto a wire rack to cool completely. Glaze: Melt both types of chocolate separately in a double boiler over barely simmering water. • Drizzle alternate spoonfuls of the melted chocolate over the cake.

Cake

2	cups (400 g) granulated sugar
8	oz (250 g) white chocolate, coarsely chopped
3	cups (450 g) all-purpose (plain) flour
1	teaspoon baking powder
½	teaspoon baking soda (bicarbonate of soda)
½	teaspoon salt
1	cup (250 g) butter
2	teaspoons vanilla extract (essence)
1	teaspoon almond extract (essence)
5	large eggs
1	cup (250 ml) plain yogurt

Glaze

3	oz (90 g) white chocolate
3	oz (90 g) milk chocolate

Serves: 12–14
Preparation: 25 minutes
Cooking: 75–85 minutes
Level: 1

■ ■ ■ *Serve this cake with fresh raspberries or strawberries; the chocolate and fruit go together beautifully.*

SUSAN'S EASY CHOCOLATE CAKE

Cake: Preheat the oven to 325°F (170°/gas 3).
• Butter a 9-inch (23-cm) square baking pan. Dust the pan with cocoa. • Place all the ingredients in a food processor and process until smooth and well blended, 1–2 minutes. (Or place in a large bowl and beat with an electric mixer at low speed until just blended.) • Spoon the batter into the prepared pan.
• Bake until a toothpick inserted into the center comes out clean, 50–60 minutes. • Cool the cake completely in the pan on a wire rack. • Chocolate Sour Cream Frosting: Melt the chocolate in a double boiler over barely simmering water. Remove from the heat. Stir in the sour cream and confectioners' sugar. Do not let the frosting cool completely or it will be too thick to spread. Top with the walnut halves.

■ ■ ■ *This cake is so very to make. Serve it plain for breakfast, or spread with the sour cream frosting and top with walnuts for morning or afternoon tea.*

Cake

1⅓ cups (200 g) all-purpose (plain) flour

1 cup (200 g) granulated sugar

½ cup (75 g) unsweetened cocoa powder

½ cup (125 g) butter

½ cup (125 ml) plain yogurt or sour cream

¼ cup + 2 tablespoons strong cold coffee

1 large egg

1 teaspoon baking powder

1 teaspoon baking soda (bicarbonate of soda)

1 teaspoon vanilla extract (essence)

¼ teaspoon salt

Sour Cream Frosting

8 oz (250 g) semisweet (dark) chocolate, coarsely chopped

½ cup (125 ml) sour cream

1 cup (150 g) confectioners' (icing) sugar

Walnuts halves

Serves: 8–10
Preparation: 10 minutes
Cooking: 50–60 minutes
Level: 1

CHOCOLATE COFFEE CAKE

484

Cake: Preheat the oven to 350°F (180°C/gas 4). • Butter and flour a 13 x 9-inch (33 x 23-cm) baking pan. • Stir the flour, cocoa, baking soda, baking powder, and salt in a large bowl. • Beat the butter, sugar, and vanilla in a large bowl with an electric mixer at medium speed until creamy. • Add the eggs, one at a time, beating until just blended after each addition. • With mixer at low speed, gradually beat in the dry ingredients, alternating with the buttermilk and coffee. • Spoon the batter into the prepared pan. • Bake until a toothpick inserted into the center comes out clean, 30–40 minutes. • Cool the cake completely in the pan on a wire rack. • Walnut Frosting: Melt the chocolate and butter in a double boiler over barely simmering water. Set aside to cool. • Beat in the confectioners' sugar, vanilla, and lemon juice. Stir in the walnuts and chocolate. Spread over the cooled cake.

Cake

2 cups (300 g) all-purpose (plain) flour

1 cup (150 g) unsweetened cocoa powder

2 teaspoons baking soda

1 teaspoon baking powder

½ teaspoon salt

½ cup (125 g) butter

1½ cups (300 g) granulated sugar

2 teaspoons vanilla extract (essence)

2 large eggs

1 cup (250 ml) buttermilk

½ cup (125 ml) strong cold coffee

Walnut Frosting

4 oz (125 g) semisweet (dark) chocolate, chopped

⅓ cup (90 g) butter

2½ cups (375 g) confectioners' (icing) sugar

1 teaspoon vanilla extract (essence)

1 tablespoon freshly squeezed lemon juice

1 cup walnuts, chopped

Serves: 12–14
Preparation: 30 minutes
Cooking: 30–40 minutes
Level: 1

CHOCOLATE CHIP OATMEAL CAKE

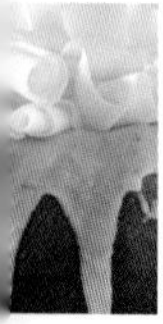

Preheat the oven to 350°F (180°C/gas 4). • Butter and flour a 10-inch (25-cm) round cake pan. • Stir together the water and oats in a large bowl and let rest for 10 minutes. • Stir in both types of sugar, the butter, and eggs. Mix in the flour, cocoa, baking soda, and salt. • Spoon the batter into the prepared pan. Sprinkle with the chocolate chips and walnuts. • Bake until lightly browned, 15–20 minutes. • Cool the cake in the pan for 15 minutes. Turn out onto a wire rack to cool completely. Dust with the confectioners' sugar just before serving.

1²/₃ cups (400 ml) boiling water

1³/₄ cups (250 g) old-fashioned rolled oats

1 cup (200 g) granulated sugar

½ cup (100 g) firmly packed dark brown sugar

½ cup (125 g) butter, softened

2 large eggs

1¹/₃ cups (200 g) all-purpose (plain) flour

1 tablespoon unsweetened cocoa powder

1 teaspoon baking soda

¼ teaspoon salt

1 cup (180 g) semisweet (dark) chocolate chips

1 cup (100 g) walnuts, coarsely chopped

4 tablespoons confectioners' (icing) sugar, to dust

Serves: 8–10
Preparation: 20 minutes
Cooking: 20 minutes
Level: 1

CHOCOLATE POTATO CAKE

Preheat the oven to 350°F (180°C/gas 4). • Butter and flour a 10-inch (25-cm) tube pan. • Mix the flour, cocoa, baking powder, and salt in a medium bowl. • Beat the butter and sugar in a large bowl with an electric mixer at medium speed until creamy. • Add the eggs, one at a time, beating until just blended after each addition. • With mixer at low speed, gradually beat in the potato, followed by the dry ingredients, alternating with the milk. • Spoon the batter into the prepared pan. • Bake until a toothpick inserted into the center comes out clean, 30–40 minutes. • Cool the cake in the pan for 30 minutes. Turn out onto a rack to cool completely. • Spread the top and sides of the cake with the frosting.

½ cup (75 g) unsweetened cocoa powder

2 cups (300 g) all-purpose (plain) flour

2½ teaspoons baking powder

¼ teaspoon salt

½ cup (125 g) butter

¾ cup (150 g) granulated sugar

3 large eggs

1 cup (200 g) cold unseasoned mashed potato

½ cup (125 ml) milk

1 recipe chocolate frosting (see page 688)

Serves: 8–10
Preparation: 20 minutes
Cooking: 30–40 minutes
Level: 1

CHOCOLATE RAISIN CAKE WITH RUM FROSTING

<u>Cake</u>: Preheat the oven to 350°F (180°C/gas 4).
• Butter an 8-inch (20-cm) square baking pan.
• Stir together the raisins and rum in a small bowl.
Cover and soak for 1 hour. • Beat the egg and
brown sugar in a large bowl with an electric mixer
at medium speed until creamy. • Melt the chocolate
and butter in a double boiler over barely simmering
water. • With mixer at medium speed, beat the
chocolate into into the egg mixture. • Use a large
rubber spatula to fold in the flour, baking powder,
salt, and raisin mixture. • Spoon the batter into the
prepared pan. • Bake until firmly set, 30–35
minutes. Cool completely in the pan on a wire rack.
<u>Rum Fudge Frosting</u>: Beat the egg yolks, sugar,
cream, and rum in a medium saucepan until well
blended. Simmer over low heat, stirring constantly
with a wooden spoon, until the mixture lightly coats
a metal spoon, or registers 160°F (80°C) on an
instant-read thermometer. Immediately plunge the
pan into a bowl of ice water and stir until cooled.
• Beat the butter in a small bowl until creamy. Stir
in the cocoa powder. Gradually fold the cocoa butter
into the egg yolk mixture. • Cover and refrigerate for
10 minutes. • Use a thin metal spatula to spread the
frosting over the cake. • Cut into squares to serve.

1 cup (90 g) raisins

3 tablespoons dark rum

1 large egg

³/₄ cup (150 g) firmly packed dark brown sugar

8 oz (250 g) milk chocolate, coarsely chopped

¹/₂ cup (125 g) butter

1¹/₃ cups (180 g) all-purpose (plain) flour

1 teaspoon baking powder

¹/₄ teaspoon salt

Rum Fudge Frosting

4 large egg yolks

¹/₃ cup (80 g) superfine (caster) sugar

¹/₄ cup (60 ml) light (single) cream

2 teaspoons dark rum

2 tablespoons butter

1 teaspoon unsweetened cocoa powder

Serves: 8–10
Preparation: 15 minutes
+ 10 minutes to chill
+ 1 hour to soak
Cooking: 30–35 minutes
Level: 1

CHOCOLATE PEANUT BUTTER CAKE

Cake: Preheat the oven to 325°F (170°C/gas 3).
• Butter a 9-inch (23-cm) square baking pan.
• Mix the flour, baking powder, and salt in a large bowl. • Melt the chocolate in a double boiler over barely simmering water. Set aside to cool. • Beat the butter, sugar, and vanilla in a large bowl with an electric mixer at medium speed until creamy.
• Add the egg yolks one at a time, beating until just blended after each addition. • With mixer at low speed, gradually beat in the chocolate and peanut butter, followed by the dry ingredients, alternating with the milk. • With mixer at high speed, beat the egg whites in a large bowl until stiff peaks form. Use a large rubber spatula to fold them into the chocolate batter. • Spoon the batter into the prepared pan. • Bake until a toothpick inserted into the center comes out clean, 1 hour and 15–25 minutes. • Cool the cake in the pan for 10 minutes. Turn out onto a wire rack and let cool completely.
Peanut Butter Frosting: With mixer at high speed, beat the confectioners' sugar, butter, and peanut butter in a large bowl until smooth. • Spread the top and sides of the cake with the frosting.

Cake

- 2 cups (300 g) all-purpose (plain) flour
- 2 teaspoons baking powder
- 1/4 teaspoon salt
- 6 oz (180 g) semisweet (dark) chocolate, coarsely chopped
- 1/2 cup (125 g) butter
- 1 3/4 cups (350 g) granulated sugar
- 1 teaspoon vanilla extract (essence)
- 4 large eggs, separated
- 1/2 cup (125 g) smooth peanut butter
- 1 cup (250 ml) milk

Peanut Butter Frosting

- 1 1/2 cups (225 g) confectioners' (icing) sugar
- 1/2 cup (125 g) butter, melted
- 1/2 cup (125 g) smooth peanut butter

Serves: 8–10
Preparation: 20 minutes
Cooking: 1 hour 15–25 minutes
Level: 1

CHOCOLATE CHIP LOAF

Cake: Preheat the oven to 350°F (180°C/gas 4).
• Butter a 9 x 5-inch (23 x 13-cm) loaf pan. Line
with aluminum foil, letting the edges overhang.
Butter the foil. • Mix the flour, baking powder,
baking soda, and salt in a medium bowl. • Beat
the butter, sugar, and vanilla in a large bowl with
an electric mixer at medium speed until creamy.
• Add the egg, beating until just blended. • With
mixer at low speed, gradually beat in the dry
ingredients, alternating with the sour cream. • Stir
in the chocolate chips. • Spoon the batter into the
prepared pan. • Bake until springy to the touch and
a toothpick inserted into the center comes out
clean, 45–55 minutes. • Cool the loaf in the pan for
5 minutes. Using the foil as a lifter, remove the loaf
from the pan. Carefully remove the foil and let cool
completely on a rack. • Orange Frosting: Mix the
confectioners' sugar, butter, and orange zest in a
medium bowl. Add enough orange juice to make
a thick, spreadable frosting. • Spread the frosting
over the top of the cake.

Cake

1½ cups (225 g) all-
   purpose (plain) flour

1   teaspoon baking powder

½ teaspoon baking soda
   (bicarbonate of soda)

¼ teaspoon salt

⅓ cup (85 g) butter

¾ cup (150 g) granulated
   sugar

1   teaspoon vanilla extract
   (essence)

1   large egg

1   cup (250 ml) sour
   cream

¾ cup (100 g) bittersweet
   or semisweet (dark)
   chocolate chips

Orange Frosting

1½ cups (225 g)
   confectioners' (icing)
   sugar

3   tablespoons butter,
   melted

1   tablespoon grated
   orange zest

2   tablespoons freshly
   squeezed orange juice

Serves: 6–8
Preparation: 20 minutes
Cooking: 45–55 minutes
Level: 1

PINEAPPLE CHOCOLATE SNACKING CAKE

Preheat the oven to 350°F (180°C/gas 4). • Butter and flour a 13 x 9-inch (33 x 23-cm) baking pan. • Mix the flour, cocoa, baking powder, cinnamon, and salt in a medium bowl. • Beat the butter, sugar, and vanilla in a large bowl with an electric mixer at medium speed until creamy. • Add the eggs, one at a time, beating until just blended after each addition. • With mixer at low speed, gradually beat in the dry ingredients. • By hand, stir in the pineapple and walnuts. • Spoon the batter into the prepared pan. • Bake until a toothpick inserted into the center comes out clean, 35–45 minutes. • Cool the cake completely in the pan on a rack. • Spread with the frosting.

1 cup (150 g) all-purpose (plain) flour

1/2 cup (75 g) unsweetened cocoa powder

1 teaspoon baking powder

1 teaspoon ground cinnamon

1/4 teaspoon salt

3/4 cup (180 g) butter, softened

1 1/2 cups (300 g) granulated sugar

1 teaspoon vanilla extract (essence)

3 large eggs

1 cup (200 g) crushed drained canned pineapple

1/4 cup (60 g) walnuts, chopped

1 recipe chocolate frosting (see page 688)

Serves: 10–12
Prep 20 minutes
Cooking: 35–45 minutes
Level: 1

QUICK-MIX CHOCOLATE APPLE CAKE

Cake: Preheat the oven to 350°F (180°C/gas 4).
• Butter and flour a 13 x 9-inch (33 x 23-cm) baking pan. Line with parchment paper. Butter the paper.
• Beat the apples, flour, butter, sugar, eggs, cocoa, water, baking powder, baking soda, and salt in a large bowl with an electric mixer at low speed until just blended. • Spoon the batter into the prepared pan.
• Bake until a toothpick inserted into the center comes out clean, 50–60 minutes. • Cool the cake in the pan for 10 minutes. Turn out onto a wire rack. Carefully remove the parchment paper and let cool completely. • Rich Chocolate Frosting: Bring the sugar and 1 cup (250 ml) of cream to a boil in a saucepan over medium heat. Simmer for 1 minute, then remove from the heat. • Stir in the chocolate.
• Return the saucepan to medium heat and simmer, without stirring, until the mixture reaches 238°F (115°C), or the soft-ball stage. Remove from the heat.
• Add the butter and vanilla, without stirring, and place the saucepan in a larger pan of cold water for 5 minutes. • Beat with a wooden spoon until the frosting begins to lose its sheen, 5–10 minutes. Immediately stir in 1 tablespoon of cream. Do not let the frosting harden too much before adding the cream. • Let stand for 3–4 minutes, then stir until spreadable. Add more cream, 1 teaspoon at a time, if it is too stiff. • Spread the top and sides of the cake with the frosting.

Cake

1   lb (500 g) tart apples (about 2 large apples), coarsely grated
2   cups (300 g) all-purpose (plain) flour
1½ cups (325 g) butter
1¼ cups (250 g) granulated sugar
3   large eggs
⅓ cup (50 g) unsweetened cocoa powder
⅓ cup (90 ml) water
2   teaspoons baking powder
½ teaspoon baking soda (bicarbonate of soda)
¼ teaspoon salt

Rich Chocolate Frosting

2   cups (400 g) granulated sugar
1   cup (250 ml) heavy (double) cream + extra, as needed
8   oz (250 g) bittersweet (dark) chocolate, coarsely chopped
2   tablespoons butter
1   teaspoon vanilla extract (essence)

Serves 10–12
Preparation: 10 minutes
Cooking: 50–60 minutes
Level: 1

CHOCOLATE APPLESAUCE CAKE

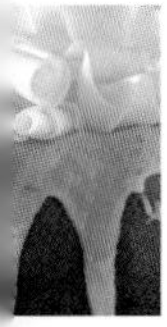

Preheat the oven to 350°F (180°C/gas 4). • Butter and flour an 8-inch (20-cm) square baking pan. • Mix the flour, cocoa, baking soda, and salt in a medium bowl. • Beat the butter, sugar, and vanilla in a large bowl with an electric mixer at medium speed until creamy. • Add the eggs, one at a time, beating until just blended after each addition. • With mixer at low speed, gradually beat in the dry ingredients, alternating with the applesauce. • Spoon the batter into the prepared pan. Sprinkle with the chocolate chips and walnuts. • Bake until a toothpick inserted into the center comes out clean, 30–35 minutes. • Cool the cake completely in the pan on a rack.

1 cup (150 g) all-purpose (plain) flour

2 tablespoons unsweetened cocoa powder

3/4 teaspoon baking soda (bicarbonate of soda)

1/4 teaspoon salt

1/4 cup (60 g) butter

3/4 cup (150 g) granulated sugar

1 teaspoon vanilla extract (essence)

2 large eggs

1 cup (250 g) unsweetened applesauce

1/2 cup (90 g) semisweet (dark) chocolate chips

1/2 cup (50 g) walnuts, chopped

Serves: 6–8
Preparation: 20 minutes
Cooking: 35 minutes
Level: 1

EASY CHOCOLATE ORANGE CAKE

Cake: Preheat the oven to 350°F (180°C/gas 4).
• Butter an 11 x 7-inch (28 x 15-cm) baking pan.
• Beat the flour, sugar. cocoa, butter, orange zest and juice, eggs, water, baking powder, baking soda, and salt in a large bowl with an electric mixer at low speed until just blended. Increase mixer speed to medium and beat until the batter is smooth, about 5 minutes. • Spoon the batter into the prepared pan. • Bake until a toothpick inserted into the center comes out clean, 35–45 minutes.
• Cool the cake completely in the pan on a wire rack. • Marbled Frosting: With mixer at high speed, beat the butter and orange zest in a large bowl until creamy. Gradually beat in the confectioners' sugar and milk. • Place half the mixture in another bowl. Stir in the cocoa. • Place spoonfuls of orange and chocolate frosting next to each other on top of the cake. Swirl them together with a knife to create a marbled effect.

Cake

- 2 cups (300 g) all-purpose (plain) flour
- 1½ cups (300 g) granulated sugar
- ½ cup (75 g) unsweetened cocoa powder
- ½ cup (125 g) butter, softened
- 2 tablespoons finely grated orange zest
- ½ cup (125 ml) freshly squeezed orange juice
- 3 large eggs
- ¼ cup (60 ml) water
- 1½ teaspoons baking powder
- ½ teaspoon baking soda (bicarbonate of soda)
- ¼ teaspoon salt

Marbled Frosting

- ¼ cup (60 g) butter
- 1 tablespoon finely grated orange zest
- 2 cups (300 g) confectioners' (icing) sugar
- 2 tablespoons milk
- 2 tablespoons unsweetened cocoa powder

Serves: 8–10
Preparation: 25 minutes
Cooking: 35–45 minutes
Level: 1

DEATH-BY-CHOCOLATE CAKE

504

Cake: Preheat the oven to 350°F (180°C/gas 4).
• Butter and flour a 9-inch (23-cm) springform pan.
• Melt the chocolate in a double boiler over barely
simmering water. Let cool. • Mix the flour, baking
powder, and salt in a medium bowl. Stir in the
almonds. • Beat the butter and sugar in a large
bowl with an electric mixer at medium speed until
creamy. • Add the egg yolks, one at a time, beating
until just blended after each addition. • With mixer
at low speed, gradually beat in the cooled
chocolate, dry ingredients, and liqueur. • With mixer
at high speed, beat the egg whites in a large bowl
until stiff peaks form. Use a large rubber spatula to
fold them into the batter. • Spoon the batter into the
prepared pan. • Bake until springy to the touch and
a toothpick inserted into the center comes out
clean, 40–50 minutes. • Cool the cake in the pan
for 5 minutes. Turn out onto a wire rack and let cool
completely. • Chocolate Frosting: Melt the chocolate
and butter in a double boiler over barely simmering
water. Set aside until cool enough to spread (make
sure it doesn't set). • Warm the marmalade and
liqueur in a small saucepan over low heat. • Split
the cake horizontally. Place one layer on a serving
plate. Spread with the marmalade and one-third
of the frosting. Top with the remaining layer and
spread the top and sides with the remaining
frosting. • Spoon the ganache into a pastry bag
and decorate the top of the cake.

Cake

8 oz (250 g) bittersweet (dark) chocolate, coarsely chopped

²⁄₃ cup (100 g) all-purpose (plain) flour

1 teaspoon baking powder

¼ teaspoon salt

¹⁄₃ cup (50 g) almonds, finely ground

½ cup (125 g) butter

³₄ cup (150 g) granulated sugar

3 large eggs, separated

3 tablespoons orange liqueur

Chocolate Frosting

8 oz (250 g) bittersweet chocolate, coarsely chopped

½ cup (125 g) butter

¼ cup (60 g) orange marmalade

2 tablespoons orange liqueur

½ recipe chocolate ganache (see page 686)

Serves: 8–10
Preparation: 45 minutes
Cooking: 40–50 minutes
Level: 1

GOLDEN MUD CAKE

Cake: Preheat the oven to 325°F (160°/gas 3).
• Butter and flour a 9-inch (23-cm) springform pan.
• Stir the butter, chocolate, sugar, milk, and corn syrup in a large saucepan over low heat until smooth. Do not boil. Set aside to cool. • Stir in the flour and baking powder. Add the eggs one at a time, beating until just blended after each addition.
• Spoon the batter into the prepared pan. • Bake until golden brown and a toothpick inserted into the center comes out clean, 1 hour 10–15 minutes.
• Cool the cake in the pan for 10 minutes. Loosen and remove the pan sides. Invert the cake onto a wire rack. Loosen and remove the pan bottom and let cool completely. • White Chocolate Ganache: Heat the cream almost to a boil in a small saucepan over low heat. Place the chocolate in a large bowl. Pour the cream over the chocolate and stir until the chocolate is melted and smooth. • Refrigerate until thickened and spreadable, about 30 minutes, stirring occasionally. • Spread the top and sides of the cake with the ganache.

Cake

- ¾ cup (180 g) butter
- 5 oz (150 g) white chocolate, coarsely chopped
- 1 cup (200 g) firmly packed brown sugar
- 1 cup (250 ml) milk
- ⅓ cup (90 g) corn syrup (golden syrup)
- 2 cups (300 g) all-purpose (plain) flour
- 2 teaspoons baking powder
- 2 large eggs, lightly beaten

White Chocolate Ganache

- ½ cup (125 ml) heavy (double) cream
- 12 oz (350 g) white chocolate, coarsely chopped

Serves: 8–10
Preparation: 25 minutes
Cooking: 1 hour 10–15 minutes
Level: 1

OLD-FASHIONED DEVIL'S FOOD CAKE

Cake: Preheat the oven to 350°F (180°C/gas 4).
• Butter two 9-inch (23-cm) round cake pans. Line with parchment paper. Butter the paper. • Melt the chocolate in a double boiler over barely simmering water. Set aside to cool. • Stir together the milk and lemon juice to make sour milk. Set aside. • Mix the flour, baking powder, baking soda, and salt in a large bowl. • Beat both sugars, the butter, and vanilla in a large bowl with an electric mixer at medium speed until creamy. • Add the eggs, one at a time, beating until just blended after each addition. • With mixer at low speed, gradually beat in the dry ingredients, food coloring, and chocolate, alternating with the sour milk. • Spoon the batter into the prepared pans. • Bake until a toothpick inserted into the centers comes out clean, 30–35 minutes. • Cool the cakes in the pans for 5 minutes. Turn out onto racks. Carefully remove the paper and let cool completely. • Mock Cream: Beat the butter, sugar, water, and vanilla in a medium bowl with an electric mixer at medium speed until creamy. • The mixture may curdle as you beat; continue beating until smooth. • Place one cake on a serving plate.

Cake

5 oz (150 g) semisweet (dark) chocolate

1 cup (250 ml) milk

1 tablespoon freshly squeezed lemon juice

2 cups (300 g) all-purpose (plain) flour

1 teaspoon baking powder

1 teaspoon baking soda (bicarbonate of soda)

¼ teaspoon salt

¾ cup (150 g) granulated sugar

¾ cup (150 g) firmly packed brown sugar

½ cup (125 g) butter

1 teaspoon vanilla extract (essence)

2 large eggs

1 teaspoon red food coloring

½ cup (125 g) raspberry jam or preserves

1 recipe chocolate frosting (see page 688)

Spread with the raspberry jam, followed by the mock cream. Top with the remaining cake.

• Spread the top and sides with the frosting.

Mock Cream

½ cup (125 g) butter

½ cup (100 g) granulated sugar

½ cup (125 ml) boiling water

1 teaspoon vanilla extract (essence)

Serves: 8–10
Preparation: 45 minutes
Cooking: 30–35 minutes
Level: 2

GLAZED PEAR AND WHITE CHOCOLATE BUNDT CAKE

Cake: Preheat the oven to 325°F (160°C/gas 3).
• Butter and flour a 9-inch (23-cm) Bundt pan.
• Melt the chocolate in a double boiler over barely simmering water. Set aside to cool. • Mix the flour, baking powder, and salt in a medium bowl. • Beat the butter and sugar in a large bowl with an electric mixer at medium speed until creamy. • Add the egg yolks one at a time, beating until just blended after each addition. • With mixer at low speed, gradually beat in the chocolate, followed by the dry ingredients, alternating with the milk. • With mixer at high speed, beat the egg whites in a large bowl until stiff peaks form. Use a large rubber spatula to fold them into the batter. • Spoon half the batter into the prepared pan. Top with the sliced pears. Spoon the remaining batter over the pears. • Bake until a toothpick inserted into the center comes out clean, 45–55 minutes. • Cool the cake in the pan for 10 minutes. Turn out onto a wire rack to cool completely. • Glaze: Mix the confectioners' sugar and butter in a medium bowl. Beat in enough of the reserved pear syrup to make a fairly thick glaze. Drizzle the glaze over the cake, letting it run down the sides.

Cake

4 oz (125 g) white chocolate, coarsely chopped

1½ cups (225 g) all-purpose (plain) flour

1½ teaspoons baking powder

¼ teaspoon salt

½ cup (125 g) butter, softened

½ cup (100 g) granulated sugar

3 large eggs, separated

½ cup (125 ml) milk

1 (15 oz/450-g) can pear halves, drained and sliced (syrup reserved)

Glaze

1 cup (150 g) confectioners' (icing) sugar

2 tablespoons butter, melted

Reserved pear syrup (see above)

Serves: 8–10
Preparation: 30 minutes
Cooking: 45–55 minutes
Level: 1

CHOCOLATE ZUCCHINI BUNDT Cake

514

Cake: Preheat the oven to 350°F (180°C/gas 4).
• Butter and flour a 10-inch (25-cm) Bundt pan.
• Mix the flour, cocoa, baking powder, baking soda, cinnamon, and salt in a large bowl. • Beat the butter, sugar, and vanilla in a large bowl with an electric mixer at medium speed until creamy.
• Add the eggs one at a time, beating until just blended after each addition. • With mixer at low speed, gradually beat in the dry ingredients and zucchini, alternating with the milk. • Spoon the batter into the prepared pan. • Bake until a toothpick inserted into the center comes out clean, 55–65 minutes. • Cool the cake in the pan for 10 minutes. Turn out onto a wire rack to cool completely. • Orange Glaze: Stir the confectioners' sugar, orange zest, and vanilla in a medium bowl. Stir in enough of the orange juice to make a thick glaze. Drizzle the glaze over the warm cake.

Cake

2²/₃ cups (250 g) all-purpose (plain) flour

²/₃ cup (100 g) unsweetened cocoa powder

2   teaspoons baking powder

1   teaspoon baking soda

1   teaspoon ground cinnamon

¼ teaspoon salt

³/₄ cup (180 g) butter

2   cups (400 g) granulated sugar

2   teaspoons vanilla extract

3   large eggs

2   cups (250 g) grated zucchini

½ cup (125 ml) milk

1   cup (100 g) walnuts, chopped

Orange Glaze

2   cups (300 g) confectioners' (icing) sugar

1   tablespoon finely grated orange zest

2   teaspoons vanilla extract

2   tablespoons freshly squeezed orange juice

Serves: 10–12
Preparation: 30 minutes
Cooking: 55–65 minutes
Level: 1

WHITE CHOCOLATE AND LIME BUNDT CAKE

Cake: Preheat the oven to 350°F (180°C/gas 4).
• Butter and flour a 9-inch (23-cm) Bundt pan. •
Melt the chocolate in a double boiler over barely
simmering water. Set aside to cool. • Stir the flour,
baking powder, and salt in a medium bowl. • Beat
the butter, sugar, and lime zest in a large bowl with
an electric mixer at medium speed until creamy. •
Add the egg yolks, one at a time, beating until just
blended after each addition. • With mixer at low
speed, gradually beat in the chocolate, followed by
the dry ingredients, alternating with the milk. • With
mixer at high speed, beat the egg whites in a
medium bowl until stiff peaks form. Use a large
rubber spatula to fold them into the batter. • Spoon
the batter into the prepared pan. • Bake until a
toothpick inserted into the center comes out clean,
40–50 minutes. • Cool the cake in the pan for
10 minutes. Turn out onto a wire rack to cool
completely. • Lime Frosting: Mix the confectioners'
sugar, butter, and lime zest in a large bowl. Beat in
enough lime juice to make a thick, spreadable
frosting. Spread the frosting over the top of the
cake. Sprinkle with the grated chocolate.

■ ■ ■ *On special occasions, serve this cake topped with*
one recipe of white chocolate curls (see page 694).

Cake

5 oz (150 g) white chocolate, coarsely chopped

2 cups (300 g) all-purpose (plain) flour

2 teaspoons baking powder

¼ teaspoon salt

1 cup (250 g) butter, softened

½ cup (100 g) granulated sugar

2 tablespoons finely grated lime zest

3 large eggs, separated

¼ cup (60 ml) milk

Lime Frosting

1 cup (150 g) confectioners' (icing) sugar

1 tablespoon butter, melted

1 tablespoon finely grated lime zest

2 tablespoons freshly squeezed lime juice

Serves: 10–12
Preparation: 20 minutes
Cooking: 40–50 minutes
Level: 1

LAYER CAKES

CHOCOLATE LAYER CAKE WITH FRESH FIGS

Prepare the chocolate sponge. • Chocolate Filling: Beat the butter in a large bowl with an electric mixer at medium speed until creamy. • Gradually beat in the cocoa, confectioners' sugar, and vanilla until creamy. • Split the cake in three horizontally. • Place one layer on a serving plate. Drizzle with one-third of the liqueur and spread with one-third of the preserves followed by one-third of the filling. Top with another layer of sponge. Drizzle with one-third of the liqueur and spread with one-third of the preserves followed by one-third of the filling. Top with the final layer of sponge. Drizzle with the remaining liqueur and spread with the remaining preserves followed by the remaining filling. Decoration: Melt the chocolate in a double boiler over barely simmering water. • Cover a work surface with parchment paper and use a pencil to mark out about twenty-five 2 x 5-inch (5 x 12-cm) strips. Turn the paper over. • Use a metal spatula to spread the melted chocolate to fit into the marked strips. Set aside to cool. • Trim one end of the chocolate strips so that they are the same height as the cake, and arrange them around the sides of the cake, slightly overlapping each strip. • Arrange the figs on the top of the cake.

1 recipe basic chocolate sponge (see page 696)

Chocolate Filling

1 cup (250 g) butter, softened

⅓ cup (50 g) unsweetened cocoa powder

⅓ cup (50 g) confectioners' (icing) sugar

1 teaspoon vanilla extract (essence)

½ cup (125 ml) orange liqueur

½ cup (125 g) raspberry preserves (jam)

Decoration

12 oz (350 g) bittersweet (dark) chocolate, coarsely chopped

8 fresh green or black figs, stemmed and halved

Serves: 10–12
Preparation: 1 hour
Cooking: 50–60 minutes (to cook the sponge)
Level: 3

CREAMY CHOCOLATE LAYER CAKE

522

Cake: Preheat the oven to 350°F (180°C/gas 4). • Butter two 9-inch (23-cm) round cake pans. Line with parchment paper. Butter the paper. • Mix the flour, baking powder, and salt in a large bowl. • Melt the chocolate with the water in a double boiler over barely simmering water. Set aside to cool. • Beat the butter, brown sugar, and vanilla in a large bowl with an electric mixer at medium speed until creamy. • Add the eggs, one at a time, beating until just blended after each addition. • With mixer at low speed, gradually beat in the chocolate mixture, followed by the yogurt and dry ingredients. • Spoon half the batter into each of the prepared pans. • Bake until a toothpick inserted into the centers comes out clean, 30–40 minutes. • Turn out onto racks and let cool completely. • Filling: With mixer at high speed, beat the cream, confectioners' sugar, and vanilla in a medium bowl until stiff. • Frosting: Melt the chocolate in a double boiler over barely simmering water. Remove from the heat. Stir in the sour cream and confectioners' sugar. Do not let the frosting cool completely or it will be too thick to spread. • Split each cake horizontally. Place one layer on a serving plate. Spread with one-third of the raspberry jam and a layer of frosting. Spread with one-third of the cream. Repeat with the remaining cake layers. Top with a plain cake layer. • Spread the top and sides with the remaining frosting.

Cake

2½ cups (375 g) all-purpose (plain) flour

2 teaspoons baking powder

¼ teaspoon salt

6 oz (180 g) semisweet (dark) chocolate

½ cup (125 ml) water

¾ cup (180 g) butter

1¾ cups (150 g) firmly packed dark brown sugar

1 teaspoon vanilla extract

3 large eggs

½ cup (125 ml) plain yogurt

Filling

1½ cups (375 ml) heavy (double) cream

3 tablespoons confectioners' (icing) sugar

½ teaspoon vanilla extract

1 cup (250 g) raspberry jelly

Frosting

12 oz (350 g) semisweet (dark) chocolate

¾ cup (180 ml) sour cream

1½ cups (225 g) confectioners' (icing) sugar

Serves: 8–10
Preparation: 45 minutes
Cooking: 30–40 minutes
Level: 3

PEPPERMINT CREAM CAKE

Cake: Preheat the oven to 350°F (180°C/gas 4).
• Butter a 9-inch (23-cm) round cake pan. Line with parchment paper. Butter the paper. • Melt the chocolate and water in a double boiler over barely simmering water. Set aside to cool. • Mix the flour, cocoa, baking powder, baking soda, and salt in a medium bowl. • Beat the butter and sugar in a large bowl with an electric mixer at medium speed until creamy. • Add the eggs, one at a time, beating until just blended after each addition. • With mixer at low speed, gradually beat in the dry ingredients, alternating with the milk and chocolate. • Spoon the batter into the prepared pan. • Bake until a toothpick inserted into the center comes out clean, 30–40 minutes. • Cool the cake in the pan for 10 minutes. Turn out onto a rack. Carefully remove the parchment paper and let cool completely. • Peppermint Filling: With mixer at high speed, beat the confectioners' sugar and butter in a medium bowl until creamy. Stir in the milk and peppermint extract. • Split the cake horizontally. • Place one layer on a serving plate. Spread with the filling. Top with the remaining layer. Spread the top and sides with the chocolate frosting.

Cake

4 oz (125 g) bittersweet (dark) chocolate, coarsely chopped

¼ cup (60 ml) water

1⅓ (200 g) cups all-purpose (plain) flour

2 tablespoons unsweetened cocoa powder

1 teaspoon baking powder

1 teaspoon baking soda

¼ teaspoon salt

½ cup (125 g) butter, melted

1½ cups (300 g) granulated sugar

2 large eggs, at room temperature

⅓ cup (90 ml) milk

Peppermint Filling

3 cups (450 g) confectioners' (icing) sugar

½ cup (125 g) butter

1 tablespoon milk

½ teaspoon peppermint extract

1 recipe chocolate frosting (see page 688)

Serves: 8–10
Preparation: 40 minutes
Cooking: 30–40 minutes
Level: 2

SACHERTORTE

Cake: Preheat the oven to 325°F (160°C/gas 3). • Set out a 9-inch (23-cm) springform pan. • Melt the chocolate in a double boiler over barely simmering water. Set aside to cool. • Beat the butter and sugar in a large bowl with an electric mixer at medium speed until creamy. • Add the egg yolks, one at a time, beating until just blended after each addition. • Use a large rubber spatula to fold in the chocolate and flour. • With mixer at high speed, beat the egg whites until stiff peaks form. Fold them into the batter. • Spoon the batter into the prepared pan. • Bake until a toothpick inserted into the center comes out clean, 55–60 minutes. • Cool the cake in the pan for 20 minutes. Loosen and remove the pan sides and let cool completely. • Split the cake horizontally. Place one layer on a serving plate. Spread with the preserves. Top with the remaining cake. • Frosting: Melt the butter and chocolate in a double boiler over barely simmering water. Add the coffee, confectioners' sugar and vanilla. Beat until smooth and creamy. • Spread the top and sides of the cake with the frosting.

Cake

5 oz (150 g) semisweet (dark) chocolate, coarsely chopped

⅓ cup (90 g) butter, softened

½ cup (100 g) granulated sugar

5 large eggs, separated

⅔ cup (100 g) all-purpose (plain) flour

⅓ cup (90 g) apricot preserves (jam)

Frosting

1 tablespoon butter

4 oz (125 g) semisweet (dark) chocolate, coarsely chopped

⅓ cup (90 ml) strong black coffee, cold

2 cups (300 g) confectioners' (icing) sugar

2 teaspoons vanilla extract (essence)

Serves: 8–10
Preparation: 25 minutes
Cooking: 55–60 minutes
Level: 2

BLACK FOREST CAKE

Cake: Preheat the oven to 350°F (180°C/gas 4).
• Butter two 9-inch (23-cm) round cake pans. Line
with parchment paper. Butter the paper. • Mix the
flour, baking powder, and salt in a large bowl. • Melt
the chocolate and water in a double boiler over
barely simmering water. Set aside to cool. • Beat
the butter and brown sugar in a large bowl with an
electric mixer at medium speed until creamy. • Add
the eggs, one at a time, beating until just blended
after each addition. • With mixer at low speed,
gradually beat in the chocolate mixture, sour cream,
and dry ingredients. • Spoon half the batter into
each of the prepared pans. • Bake until a toothpick
inserted into the centers comes out clean, 45–55
minutes. • Cool the cakes in the pans for 10
minutes. Turn out onto racks. Carefully remove the
parchment paper and let cool completely. • Split the
cakes horizontally. • **Cherry Cream Filling:** Mix the
jam and kirsch. • With mixer at high speed, beat the
cream in a medium bowl until stiff. • **Chocolate
Frosting:** Melt the chocolate and butter in a double
boiler over barely simmering water. • Place one
cake layer on a serving plate. Spread with one-third
of the preserves mixture and one-third of the
whipped cream. Repeat with the remaining cake
layers, finishing with a plain layer. Spread the
frosting over the top and sides of the cake.
Decorate with the candied cherries.

Cake

1²⁄₃ cups (250 g) all-
   purpose (plain) flour

1½ teaspoons baking powder

¼ teaspoon salt

5 oz (150 g) bittersweet
   (dark) chocolate,
   coarsely chopped

½ cup (125 ml) water

½ cup (125 g) butter,
   softened

1¼ cups (250 g) firmly
   packed dark brown sugar

2 large eggs

½ cup (125 ml) sour cream

Cherry Cream Filling

1½ cups (375 g) cherry jam
   or preserves

3 tablespoons kirsch

2 cups (500 ml) heavy
   (double) cream

Chocolate Frosting

8 oz (250 g) bittersweet
   (dark) chocolate,
   coarsely chopped

2 tablespoons butter

Candied cherries,
   to decorate

Serves: 8–10
Preparation: 30 minutes
Cooking: 45–55 minutes
Level: 2

CHOCOLATE LAYER CAKE WITH TRUFFLES

Truffles: Melt the chocolate, cream, and butter in a double boiler over barely simmering water. Remove from the heat and stir in the confectioners' sugar and orange liqueur. • Let cool a little, then, roll spoonfuls of the mixture into marble-sized balls, dusting your hands with cocoa, if needed. Transfer to a plate and chill in the refrigerator for 30 minutes. • Cake: Preheat the oven to 350°F (180°C/gas 4). • Butter two 9-inch (23-cm) springform pans. • Mix the flour, cocoa, baking powder, baking soda, and salt in a large bowl. • Melt the chocolate in a double boiler over barely simmering water. Set aside to cool. • Beat the butter, sugar, and cream cheese in a large bowl with an electric mixer at medium speed until creamy. • Add the eggs, one at a time, beating until just blended after each addition. • With mixer at low speed, gradually beat in the chocolate, orange liqueur, and vanilla. Beat in the dry ingredients, alternating with the water. • Spoon half the batter into each of the prepared pans. • Bake until a toothpick inserted into the centers comes out clean 25–35 minutes. • Cool the cakes in the pans for 10 minutes. Loosen and remove the pan sides. Invert the cakes onto racks. Loosen and remove the pan bottoms. • Filling: Melt the chocolate and cream in a double boiler over barely simmering water. Set aside to cool. • Frosting: Melt the chocolate in a double boiler over barely simmering water. Set aside to cool. • With mixer at medium

Truffles

4 oz (125 g) bittersweet (dark) chocolate, coarsely chopped

3 tablespoons heavy (double) cream

1 tablespoon butter

1/3 cup (50 g) confectioners' (icing) sugar

2 tablespoons orange liqueur

1/3 cup (50 g) unsweetened cocoa powder

Cake

2 cups (300 g) all-purpose (plain) flour

1/3 cup (50 g) unsweetened cocoa powder

1 teaspoon baking powder

1/2 teaspoon baking soda

1/4 teaspoon salt

2 oz (60 g) bittersweet (dark) chocolate, coarsely chopped

1/3 cup (90 g) butter

3/4 cup (150 g) granulated sugar

3 oz (90 g) cream cheese, softened

2 large eggs

1 tablespoon orange liqueur

speed, beat the butter in a medium bowl until creamy. Beat the butter into the chocolate until glossy and smooth. Cover and set aside. • Split each cake horizontally. Place one layer on a serving plate. Spread with one-third of the filling. Repeat with 2 more layers. Top with the remaining layer. • Spread the top and sides of the cake with the frosting. Decorate with the truffles.

531

1 teaspoon vanilla extract (essence)

³/₄ cup (180 ml) water

Filling

8 oz (250 g) bittersweet (dark) chocolate, coarsely chopped

¹/₃ cup (90 ml) heavy (double) cream

Frosting

5 oz (150 g) bittersweet (dark) chocolate, coarsely chopped

²/₃ cup (150 g) butter, softened

Serves: 12–14
Preparation: 45 minutes
  + 30 minutes to chill
Cooking: 25–35 minutes
Level: 3

RICH CHOCOLATE CAKE

534

Cake: Preheat the oven to 350°F (180°C/gas 4).
• Butter and flour an 8-inch (20-cm) springform pan. • Mix the flour, cocoa, and baking powder in a large bowl. • Beat the butter and sugar with an electric mixer at medium speed until creamy.
• Add the egg yolks, one at a time, beating until just blended after each addition. • With mixer at low speed, gradually beat in the dry ingredients and milk. • With mixer at high speed, beat the egg whites and salt until stiff peaks form. Use a large rubber spatula to fold them into the batter. • Spoon the batter into the prepared pan. • Bake until a toothpick inserted into the center comes out clean, 40–45 minutes. • Cool the cake in the pan for 5 minutes. Loosen and remove the pan sides. Invert onto a rack and remove the pan bottom. Let cool completely. • Dust the top of the cake with the cocoa powder. Creamy Chocolate Frosting: Melt the chocolate, butter, and condensed milk in a double boiler over barely simmering water. Let cool a little, then spoon the frosting into a pastry bag and pipe around the sides of the cake in a decorative manner.
• Decorate the sides of the cake with the flaked chocolate.

Cake

1²⁄₃ cups (250 g) all-purpose (plain) flour

¹⁄₃ cup (50 g) unsweetened cocoa powder

1 teaspoon baking powder

³⁄₄ cup (180 g) butter

³⁄₄ cup (150 g) superfine (caster) sugar

2 large eggs, separated

¹⁄₂ cup (125 ml) milk

¹⁄₈ teaspoon salt

Unsweetened cocoa powder, to dust

Creamy Chocolate Frosting

6 oz (180 g) semisweet (dark) chocolate, coarsely chopped

¹⁄₃ cup (90 g) butter

¹⁄₂ cup (125 g) sweetened condensed milk

6 oz (180 g) semisweet (dark) chocolate, flaked

Serves: 10–12
Prep: 15 minutes
Cooking: 40–45 minutes
Level: 2

GLAZED CHOCOLATE CREAM CAKE

Cake: Preheat the oven to 350°F (180°C/gas 4). • Butter a 9-inch (23-cm) round cake pan. Dust with cocoa. • Mix the flour, cocoa, baking powder, baking soda, and salt in a large bowl. Stir in the sugar. • Beat in the milk, butter, egg, and vanilla with an electric mixer at medium speed until well blended. • Spoon the batter into the prepared pan. • Bake until a toothpick inserted into the center comes out clean, 40–50 minutes. • Cool the cake in the pan for 10 minutes. Turn out onto a rack and let cool completely. • Chocolate Cream: Stir together the sugar, cocoa and cornstarch in a medium saucepan. Gradually stir in the cream. • Simmer over medium heat, stirring constantly, until the mixture thickens and begins to boil. Boil for 1 minute, stirring constantly. Remove from the heat. • Stir in the butter and vanilla. Transfer to a bowl. Cover with plastic wrap (cling film) pressed directly onto the surface. Let cool to room temperature then chill in the refrigerator until cold. • Glaze: Melt the butter with the water in a small saucepan. Remove from the heat and stir in the cocoa. Gradually beat in the confectioners' sugar and vanilla until smooth. Set aside to cool slightly. • Split the cake horizontally. • Place one layer on a serving plate. Spread with the chocolate cream. Top with the remaining cake. Pour the glaze over the cake, allowing some to drizzle down the sides. • Chill in the refrigerator for one hour before serving.

Cake

- 1 cup (150 g) all-purpose (plain) flour
- ⅓ cup (50 g) cocoa powder
- 1 teaspoon baking powder
- ½ teaspoon baking soda
- ¼ teaspoon salt
- 1 cup (200 g) sugar
- 1 cup (250 ml) milk
- ⅓ cup (90 g) butter
- 1 large egg
- 1 teaspoon vanilla extract

Chocolate Cream

- ½ cup (100 g) sugar
- ⅓ cup (50 g) cocoa powder
- 2 tablespoons cornstarch
- 1½ cups (375 ml) heavy (double) cream
- 1 tablespoon butter
- 1 teaspoon vanilla extract

Glaze

- 1 tablespoon butter
- 2 tablespoons water
- 3 tablespoons cocoa
- 1 cup (150 g) confectioners' (icing) sugar
- ½ teaspoon vanilla extract

Serves: 8–10
Preparation: 30 minutes + 2 hours to chill
Cooking: 40–50 minutes
Level: 2

CHOCOLATE ORANGE ROULADE

<u>Cake</u>: Preheat the oven to 350°F (180°C/gas 4).
• Butter a 15^1/$_2$ x 10^1/$_2$-inch (35 x 26-cm) jelly-roll (Swiss roll) pan. Line with parchment paper.
• Melt the chocolate in a double boiler over barely simmering water. Set aside to cool. • Beat the sugar and egg yolks in a large bowl with an electric mixer at high speed until pale and thick. • With mixer at medium speed, gradually beat in the chocolate.
• With mixer at high speed, beat the egg whites and salt in a large bowl until stiff peaks form. • Use a large rubber spatula to fold them into the chocolate mixture. • Spoon the batter into the prepared pan.
• Bake until springy to the touch and a toothpick inserted into the center comes out clean, 15–20 minutes. • Cool the cake in the pan for 5 minutes. Dust a clean kitchen cloth with cocoa and turn the cake out onto it. • Using the cloth as a guide carefully roll up the cake. Let cool. • <u>Orange Mascarpone Cream</u>: Beat the egg yolks and ^{1}/$_2$ cup (100 g) of sugar in a large bowl with an electric mixer at high speed until pale and thick. • With mixer at low speed, gradually beat in the mascarpone and liqueur. • Stir the egg whites and remaining sugar in a saucepan. Stir over low heat, beating constantly, until the whites register 160°F (80°C) on an instant-read thermometer. Transfer to a bowl and beat at high speed until stiff peaks form. Use a large rubber spatula to fold them into the cream. • Unroll the cake and spread with the filling, leaving a 1-inch (2.5-cm) border. • Reroll the cake and dust with the cocoa.

Cake

8   oz (250 g) bittersweet (dark) chocolate, coarsely chopped

1^1/$_4$ cups (250 g) granulated sugar

8   large eggs, separated

^{1}/$_4$ teaspoon salt

Orange Mascarpone Cream

6   large eggs, separated

^{3}/$_4$ cup (150 g) granulated sugar

1^2/$_3$ cups (400 g) mascarpone cheese

1   cup (250 ml) orange liqueur

Unsweetened cocoa powder, to dust

Serves: 8
Preparation: 45 minutes
Cooking: 15–20 minutes
Level: 3

ALMOND WHITE CHOCOLATE CAKE

Cake: Preheat the oven to 350°F (180°C/gas 4).
• Butter two 9-inch (23-cm) round cake pans. Line with parchment paper. Butter the paper. • Beat the egg yolks and sugar in a large bowl with an electric mixer at high speed until pale and thick. • With mixer at low speed, gradually beat in the butter. • Gradually beat in the pecans, almonds, flour, vanilla, and almond extract. • With mixer at high speed, beat the egg whites in a large bowl until stiff peaks form. Use a large rubber spatula to fold them into the batter. • Spoon half the batter into each of the prepared pans. • Bake until a toothpick inserted into the centers comes out clean, 45–50 minutes. • Cool the cakes in the pans for 10 minutes. Turn out onto racks to cool completely. • Transfer the cakes to high-sided plates. use a thin skewer to poke holes all over the cakes.
Syrup: Bring the water and sugar to a boil in a small saucepan over medium heat. Simmer for 20 minutes. Remove from the heat and stir in the kirsch. Spoon the hot syrup over the cakes. Set aside until the cakes have absorbed the syrup. • White Chocolate Ganache: Bring the cream almost to a boil in a small saucepan over low heat. Place the chocolate in a large bowl. Pour the cream over the chocolate and stir until the chocolate is melted and smooth. Refrigerate until thickened and spreadable, about 30 minutes, stirring occasionally. • Place one cake layer on a serving plate. Spread with one-third of the ganache. Top with the remaining layer. Spread the top and sides with the remaining ganache. • Top with the chocolate curls.

Cake

10 large eggs, separated

1½ cups (300 g) sugar

1¼ cups (310 g) butter, melted

2 cups (250 g) pecans, finely ground

2 cups (250 g) almonds, finely ground

⅓ cup (50 g) all-purpose (plain) flour

1 teaspoon vanilla extract

¼ teaspoon almond extract

Syrup

1½ cups (375 ml) water

¾ cup (150 g) granulated sugar

¼ cup (60 ml) kirsch

1 recipe white chocolate curls (see page 694)

White Chocolate Ganache

½ cup (125 ml) heavy (double) cream

13 oz (380 g) white chocolate, coarsely chopped

Serves: 10–12
Prep: 1 hour 30 minutes
Cooking: 45–50 minutes
Level: 2

CHOCOLATE HAZELNUT CREAM CAKE

Cake: Butter and flour two 8-inch (20-cm) springform pans. • Melt the chocolate in a double boiler over barely simmering water. Set aside to cool. • Mix the flour, baking powder, and salt in a medium bowl. • Beat the egg yolks, sugar, and almond extract in a medium bowl with an electric mixer at high speed until pale and thick. • With mixer at low speed, gradually beat in the dry ingredients, alternating with the chocolate and cream. • Beat the egg whites until thickened. Fold into the batter. • Spoon half the batter into each of the prepared pans. • Turn the oven on to 400°F (200°C/gas 6) and put the cakes in while the oven is still cold. Bake for 25 minutes, then turn the oven down to 300°F (150°C/gas 2) and bake for 15 more minutes. • Cool the cakes in the pans for 10 minutes. Loosen and remove the pan sides. Invert onto wire racks to cool completely. • Chocolate Hazelnut Cream: Bring the cream to a boil in a medium saucepan over low heat. Remove from the heat and add the chocolate hazelnut cream and butter. Stir until melted. Chill in the refrigerator for 30 minutes. • Split the cakes horizontally. • Place one layer on a serving plate. Spread with some of the filling. Repeat with the second layer and more filling. Top with the third layer and more filling. Finish with the remaining layer. Spread the remaining filling over the cake. • Dust with the cocoa and decorate with the raspberries.

Cake

- 4 oz (125 g) bittersweet chocolate, coarsely chopped
- 1⅓ cups (200 g) all-purpose (plain) flour
- 1½ teaspoons baking powder
- ¼ teaspoon salt
- 3 large eggs, separated
- ⅓ cup (70 g) granulated sugar
- ½ teaspoon almond extract
- ½ cup (125 ml) heavy (double) cream

Chocolate Hazelnut Cream

- 1 cup (250 ml) heavy (double) cream
- 1½ cups (375 g) chocolate hazelnut cream (Nutella or other)
- ⅓ cup (90 g) butter

- ⅓ cup (50 g) unsweetened cocoa powder, to dust
- Fresh raspberries, to decorate

Serves: 8–10
Preparation: 45 minutes
Cooking: 40 minutes
Level: 2

CHOCOLATE MOUSSE CAKE

544

Cake: Preheat the oven to 375°F (190°C/gas 5).
• Butter and flour two 9-inch (23-cm) round cake pans.
• Beat the eggs and sugar with an electric mixer at high speed until pale and creamy. • Mix the flour, cornstarch, and cocoa in a large bowl. Use a large rubber spatula to gently fold in the egg mixture. Stir in the melted butter and vanilla. • Spoon half the batter into each of the prepared pans. • Bake until a toothpick inserted into the centers comes out clean, 35–40 minutes. • Cool the cakes in the pans for 15 minutes. Turn out onto wire racks to cool completely. • Rum Syrup: Bring the sugar and water to a boil. Simmer until the sugar has dissolved, 3 minutes. Set aside to cool. • Stir in the rum. Chocolate Mousse: Melt the chocolate and milk in a double boiler over barely simmering water. • Beat the egg yolks and sugar in a double boiler until well blended. Stir in the chocolate mixture. Stir over low heat until the mixture lightly coats a metal spoon. Plunge the pan into a bowl of ice water and stir until the egg mixture has cooled. • Beat the cream in a large bowl until stiff. Fold it into the chocolate mixture. • Beat the egg whites and sugar until stiff peaks form. • Fold into the chocolate mixture. • Refrigerate for 4 hours.
• Split a cake horizontally. Sprinkle one layer with the rum syrup. Spread with one-third of the chocolate mousse. Top with the remaining layer. Spread the top and sides of the cake with the remaining mousse. • Cut the remaining cake into small cubes. Arrange over the assembled cake. •Decorate with the berries and dust with the confectioners' sugar.

Cake

10 large eggs

1½ cups (300 g) sugar

1 cup (125 g) finely ground almonds

1 cup (150 g) cornstarch (cornflour)

⅔ cup (100 g) unsweetened cocoa powder

⅔ cup (180 g) butter, melted

1 teaspoon vanilla extract

Rum Syrup

¼ cup (50 g) sugar

1 tablespoon water

¼ cup (60 ml) dark rum

Chocolate Mousse

12 oz (350 g) bittersweet (dark) chocolate

½ cup (125 ml) milk

6 large eggs, separated

½ cup (75 g) confectioners' sugar + extra, to dust

¾ cup (180 ml) heavy (double) cream

Berries, to decorate

Serves: 10–12
Preparation: 1 hour
+ 4 hours to chill
Cooking: 35–40 minutes
Level: 3

CHOCOLATE MOUSSE CAKE

546

Cake: Preheat the oven to 350°F (180°C/gas 4). • Butter a 9-inch (23-cm) springform pan. Dust with cocoa. • Mix the flour, cocoa, baking powder, and salt in a large bowl. Stir in the sugar. • Make a well in the center and beat in the coffee, oil, egg, and vanilla with an electric mixer at medium speed. • Pour the batter into the prepared pan. • Bake until a toothpick inserted into the center comes out clean, 40–45 minutes. • Cool the cake completely in the pan on a wire rack. • Loosen and remove the pan sides. Invert the cake onto a rack. Loosen and remove the pan bottom. • Split the cake horizontally. Place one layer in a 10-inch springform pan. Spread with one-third of the chocolate mousse. Top with the remaining cake layer. Spread the remaining mousse over the top and sides of the cake. • Cover and chill in the refrigerator until completely set, about 24 hours. • Loosen and remove the pan sides. Gently press the chopped nuts into the side of the mousse. Drizzle with the ganache.

Cake

1²/₃ cups (250 g) all-purpose (plain) flour

¹/₃ cup (50 g) unsweetened cocoa powder

2 teaspoons baking powder

¹/₄ teaspoon salt

1 cup (100 g) granulated sugar

1 cup (250 ml) lukewarm strong coffee

¹/₃ cup (90 ml) vegetable oil

1 large egg, at room temperature

1 tablespoon vanilla extract (essence)

1 recipe Chocolate Mousse (see page 544)

1 cup (120 g) walnuts, coarsely chopped

¹/₂ recipe Chocolate Ganache (see page 686)

Serves: 8–10
Preparation: 1 hour + 24 hours to chill
Cooking: 40–45 minutes
Level: 3

CHOCOLATE COFFEE CREAM ROLL

Cake: Preheat the oven to 400°F (200°C/gas 6).
• Butter and flour a 17 x 12½-inch (42 x 30-cm) jelly-roll (Swiss roll) pan. Line with parchment paper.
• Mix the flour, ⅓ cup (50 g) cocoa, and baking powder in a large bowl. • Beat the egg yolks, ¼ cup (50 g) of sugar, and butter in a large bowl with an electric mixer at high speed until pale and thick. Add the vanilla. • Use a large rubber spatula to fold in the dry ingredients. • With mixer at medium speed, beat the egg whites and salt in a large bowl until frothy. With mixer at high speed, gradually add the remaining ½ cup (100 g) of sugar, beating until stiff, glossy peaks form. Fold them into the batter.
• Spoon into the prepared pan. • Bake until springy to the touch, 10–12 minutes. • Dust a clean kitchen cloth with cocoa and turn the cake out onto it.
• Using the cloth as a guide carefully roll up the cake. Let cool. • Irish Coffee Cream: Beat the egg yolks, sugar, and liqueur until pale and thick.
• Bring the milk to a boil. Place the flour and salt in a bowl. Pour in a little of the boiling milk and stir until smooth. Pour in the remining milk and then stir into the egg and sugar. Simmer over low heat, stirring constantly, until thickened. Let cool. • Unroll the cake and spread evenly with most of the cream, leaving a 1-inch (2.5-cm) border at the ends. Reroll the cake. Spread with the remaining cream and dust with cocoa.

Cake

½ cup (75 g) all-purpose (plain) flour

⅓ cup (50 g) + 2 tablespoons unsweetened cocoa powder

½ teaspoon baking powder

5 large eggs, separated

¾ cup (150 g) granulated sugar

2 tablespoons butter, melted

1 teaspoon vanilla extract (essence)

½ teaspoon salt

Irish Coffee Cream

5 large egg yolks

⅔ cup (120 g) granulated sugar

2 tablespoons Irish coffee liqueur

⅓ cup (50 g) all-purpose (plain) flour

2 cups (500 ml) milk

¼ teaspoon salt

½ teaspoon vanilla extract (essence)

Serves: 8–10
Preparation: 15 minutes
  + 1 hour to cool
Cooking: 10–12 minutes
Level: 1

549

WHITE CHOCOLATE RASPBERRY ROLL

Cake: Preheat the oven to 375°F(190°C/gas 5).
• Butter a 15$1/2$ x 10$1/2$-inch (35 x 26-cm) jelly-roll (Swiss roll) pan. Line with parchment paper.
• Melt the chocolate in a double boiler over barely simmering water. Set aside to cool. • Mix the flour, baking powder, baking soda, and salt in a medium bowl. • Beat the eggs and granulated sugar in a large bowl with an electric mixer at high speed until pale and thick. Add the vanilla. • Use a large rubber spatula to fold the dry ingredients into the egg mixture, alternating with the water. Add the chocolate. • Spoon the batter into the prepared pan.
• Bake until springy to the touch, 15–20 minutes.
• Dust a clean kitchen cloth with confectioners' sugar and turn the cake out onto it. • Using the cloth as a guide, carefully roll up the cake. Let cool.
Chantilly Cream: Beat the cream, sugar, and vanilla in a large bowl with an electric mixer at high speed until stiff. • Unroll the cake and spread evenly with the chantilly cream, leaving a 1-inch (2.5-cm) border. Sprinkle with the raspberries. • Reroll the cake and dust with confectioners' sugar.

Cake

- 4 oz (125 g) white chocolate, coarsely chopped
- $1/2$ cup (75 g) all-purpose (plain) flour
- $1/2$ teaspoon baking powder
- $1/2$ teaspoon baking soda (bicarbonate of soda)
- $1/4$ teaspoon salt
- 4 large eggs
- $3/4$ cup (150 g) granulated sugar
- 1 teaspoon vanilla extract (essence)
- 2 tablespoons cold water
- 4 tablespoons confectioners' (icing) sugar

Chantilly Cream

- 1 cup (250 ml) heavy cream
- 2 tablespoons granulated sugar
- $1/2$ teaspoon vanilla extract (essence)
- 2 cups fresh raspberries

Serves: 8
Preparation: 20 minutes
Cooking: 15–20 minutes
Level: 1

OPERA

Cake: Preheat the oven to 350°F (180°C/gas 4).
• Butter a 9-inch (23-cm) cake pan. Line with
parchment paper. • Beat the whole eggs and sugar
in a large bowl with an electric mixer at high speed
until pale and thick. • With mixer at high speed, beat
the egg whites in a large bowl until stiff peaks form. •
Mix the almonds, flour, and salt in a large bowl. • Fold
the flour mixture and butter into the batter. Fold in the
beaten whites. • Spoon the batter into the pan. • Bake
until a toothpick inserted into the center comes out
clean, 25–30 minutes. • Cool the cake in the pan for 5
minutes. Invert onto a rack. Carefully remove the paper
and let cool completely. • Stir the rum into the
chocolate ganache. • Syrup: Bring the sugar and water
to a boil in a small pan. Let cool then stir in the rum.
• Buttercream: Stir the coffee and sugar in a saucepan
over medium heat until the sugar has dissolved. Cook,
without stirring, until the mixture reaches 238°F
(115°C), or soft-ball stage. • Beat the egg yolks in a
double boiler with an electric mixer at high speed until
pale. • Beat the syrup into the yolks. • Beat the butter
in a large bowl until creamy. Stir into the egg mixture.
• Split the cake in three horizontally. • Place one layer
on a serving plate. Brush with one-third of the syrup.
Spread with the buttercream. Top with a cake layer
and brush with half the remaining syrup. Spread with
one-third of the ganache. Top with the remaining layer
and brush with the remaining syrup. • Spread the cake
with the remaining ganache. Dust with the cocoa.
Refrigerate for 1 hour before serving.

Cake

5 large eggs + 5 egg whites

1 cup (200 g) granulated
 sugar

1⅓ cups (160 g) finely
 ground almonds

⅓ cup (50 g) all-purpose
 (plain) flour

¼ teaspoon salt

¼ cup (60 g) butter,
 melted

1 recipe chocolate
 ganache (see page 686)

1 tablespoon rum

Syrup

½ cup (100 g) granulated
 sugar

½ cup (125 ml) water

5 tablespoons rum

Buttercream

½ cup (125 ml) strong
 black coffee, lukewarm

¾ cup (150 g) granulated
 sugar

3 large egg yolks

1 cup (250 g) butter

2 tablespoons unsweeten-
 ed cocoa powder

Serves: 10–12
Preparation: 1 hour 15
 minutes + 1 hour to chill
Cooking: 25–30 minutes
Level: 2

VIENNESE WALNUT TORTE

554

Cake: Preheat the oven to 350°F (180°C/gas 4).
• Butter and flour a 9-inch (23-cm) springform pan.
• Mix the walnuts, flour, baking powder, and salt in a medium bowl. • Beat the butter, half the sugar, and vanilla in a large bowl with an electric mixer at medium speed until creamy. • Add the egg yolks, one at a time, beating until just blended after each addition. • With mixer at medium speed, beat the egg whites in a large bowl until frothy. With mixer at high speed, gradually beat in the remaining sugar until stiff, glossy peaks form. • Use a large rubber spatula to fold them into the batter. Fold in the dry ingredients. • Spoon the batter into the prepared pan. • Bake until a toothpick inserted into the center comes out clean, 50–60 minutes. • Cool the cake in the pan for 10 minutes. Loosen and remove the pan sides. Invert onto a rack. Loosen and remove the pan bottom and let cool completely.
Chocolate Glaze: Melt the chocolate in a double boiler over barely simmering water. Remove from the heat and gradually stir in the butter until glossy. Stir in the cream. • Split the cake horizontally. Place one layer on a serving plate. Spread with the marmalade. Top with the remaining cake layer. Drizzle with the glaze.

Cake

2¼ cups (300 g) walnuts, finely ground

⅓ cup (50 g) all-purpose (plain) flour

½ teaspoon baking powder

¼ teaspoon salt

1 cup (250 g) butter, softened

1¼ cups (250 g) granulated sugar

5 large eggs, separated

1 teaspoon vanilla extract (essence)

Chocolate Glaze

5 oz (150 g) semisweet (dark) chocolate, coarsely chopped

½ cup (125 g) butter, softened

2 tablespoons heavy (double) cream

½ cup (125 g) orange marmalade

Serves: 8–10
Preparation: 35 minutes
Cooking: 50–60 minutes
Level: 1

WHITE CHOCOLATE MOUSSE CAKE WITH LEMON AND KIWI

Butter Cake: Preheat the oven to 350°F (180°C/gas 4). • Butter and flour a 9-inch (23-cm) round cake pan. Line with parchment paper. • Mix the flour, baking powder, and salt in a large bowl. • Beat the butter, sugar, and vanilla in a large bowl with an electric mixer at medium speed until creamy. • Add the eggs, one at a time, beating until just blended after each addition. • With mixer at low speed, beat in the dry ingredients, alternating with the milk. • Spoon the batter into the prepared pan. • Bake until a toothpick inserted into the center comes out clean, 45–55 minutes. • Cool the cake in the pan for 10 minutes. Turn out onto a rack. Carefully remove the parchment paper and let cool. • Mousse: Melt the chocolate in a double boiler over barely simmering water. Let cool. • Beat the cream cheese and sugar in a large bowl with an electric mixer at medium speed. • Add the chocolate. • Sprinkle the gelatin over the orange juice in a saucepan. Let stand 1 minute. Stir over low heat until the gelatin is dissolved. Let cool for 30 minutes. • Beat into the cream cheese mixture. • Beat the cream until stiff. • Use a rubber spatula to fold into the cream cheese mixture. • Cut the rounded top off the cake. • Place the cake in a 9-inch (23-cm) springform pan. Pour in the mousse and refrigerate for 6 hours. • Topping: Stir the lemon juice and sugar in a saucepan over low heat until the sugar has dissolved. Remove from heat and stir in the gelatin until dissolved. Let cool. • Pour the topping over the cake and refrigerate until set, 6 hours. • Loosen and remove the pan sides. Decorate with slices of kiwi.

Butter Cake

- 1½ cups (225 g) all-purpose (plain) flour
- 1½ teaspoons baking powder
- ¼ teaspoon salt
- 1 cup (250 g) butter
- 1 cup (200 g) sugar
- 2 teaspoons vanilla extract (essence)
- 4 large eggs
- ¾ cup (180 ml) milk

Mousse

- 6 oz (180 g) white chocolate, chopped
- 6 oz 180 g) cream cheese
- ¼ cup (50 g) sugar
- 4 teaspoons gelatin
- ⅓ cup (90 ml) freshly squeezed orange juice
- 1½ cups (375 ml) heavy (double) cream

Topping

- ½ cup (125 ml) freshly squeezed lemon juice
- ¼ cup (50 g) sugar
- 1 teaspoon gelatin
- 3 kiwi fruit

Serves: 8–10
Preparation: 1 hour
  + 12 hours to chill
Cooking: 45–55 minutes
Level: 2

ITALIAN RICOTTA CAKE

Cake: Preheat the oven to 375°F (190°C/gas 5).
• Butter two 9-inch (23-cm) round cake pans. Line
with parchment paper. • Mix the almonds, flour,
cocoa, baking powder, and salt in a large bowl. • Beat
the egg yolks, 1 cup (200 g) sugar, vanilla, and
almond extract in a large bowl with an electric mixer
at high speed until pale and very thick. • With mixer
at low speed, gradually beat in the dry ingredients,
alternating with the milk. • With mixer at medium
speed, beat the egg whites in a large bowl until frothy.
• With mixer at high speed, gradually add the
remaining sugar, beating until stiff, glossy peaks form.
• Use a large rubber spatula to fold them into the
batter. • Spoon half the batter into each of the
prepared pans. • Bake until a toothpick inserted into
the center comes out clean, 20–25 minutes. • Cool
the cakes in the pans for 10 minutes. Turn out onto
racks. Carefully remove the paper and let cool
completely. • Ricotta Filling: With mixer at high speed,
beat the cream in a medium bowl until stiff. • Process
the ricotta, confectioners' sugar, and orange peel in a
food processor until smooth. Transfer to a large bowl.
• Use a large rubber spatula to fold the cream into the
ricotta mixture. • Chocolate Topping: With mixer at
high speed, beat the cream, confectioners' sugar,
cocoa, and vanilla in a large bowl until stiff. • Split the
cakes horizontally. Place one layer on a serving plate.
Spread with one-third of the filling. Repeat with two
more layers. Place the remaining layer on top. •
Spread with the topping. Decorate with the chocolate.

Cake

1½ cups (180 g) almonds,
    finely ground

⅔ cup (100 g) all-purpose
    (plain) flour

⅔ cup (100 g) cocoa

2 teaspoons baking powder

8 large eggs, separated

1½ cups (300 g) sugar

2 teaspoons vanilla
    extract (essence)

½ teaspoon almond extract

½ cup (125 ml) milk

Chocolate curls
    (see page 694)

Ricotta Filling

1 cup (250 ml) heavy
    (double) cream

1 lb (500 g) ricotta cheese

½ cup (75 g) confec-
    tioners' (icing) sugar

½ cup chopped orange peel

Chocolate Topping

2 cups (500 ml) heavy
    (double) cream

⅔ cup (100 g) con-
    fectioners' (icing) sugar

⅓ cup (50 g) cocoa

1 teaspoon vanilla

Serves: 8–10
Preparation: 50 minutes
Cooking: 20–25 minutes
Level: 2

CAPPUCCINO LAYER CAKE

Prepare the butter cake. • <u>Coffee Liqueur Truffles</u>:
Melt the chocolate with the cream in a double
boiler over barely simmering water. Set aside to
cool. • Dissolve the coffee in the liqueur and stir
into the chocolate mixture. Chill in the refrigerator
until thick, about 1 hour. • Roll teaspoonfuls of the
chocolate mixture into round truffles and place on a
dish lined with parchment paper. This should yield
about 12 truffles. Cover and refrigerate until firm.
<u>Coffee Buttercream</u>: Melt the white chocolate with
the cream in a double boiler over barely simmering
water. Set aside to cool. • Beat the butter in a large
bowl with an electric mixer at high speed until
creamy. Gradually beat in the confectioners' sugar.
• Beat in the chocolate mixture and dissolved
coffee. • Split the cake horizontally. Place one layer
on a serving plate and spread with a quarter of the
buttercream. Place the remaining layer on top.
Spread the top and sides with the remaining
buttercream. • Press the hazelnuts into the sides
of the cake and arrange the truffles on top.
Dust with cocoa.

1 **Butter Cake**
   (see page 556)

Coffee Liqueur Truffles

4 oz (125 g) bittersweet
   (dark) chocolate,
   coarsely chopped

3 tablespoons heavy
   (double) cream

2 teaspoons freeze-dried
   coffee granules

½ tablespoon coffee
   liqueur

Coffee Buttercream

10 oz (300 g) white
   chocolate, chopped

⅔ cup (180 ml) heavy
   (double) cream

1¾ cups (430 g) unsalted
   butter, softened

1 cup (150 g) confec-
   tioners' (icing) sugar

1 tablespoon coffee
   granules dissolved
   in 1 tablespoon boiling
   water, cooled

1 cup (120 g) hazelnuts,
   toasted and chopped

   Unsweetened cocoa
   powder, to dust

Serves 8–10
Preparation: 1 hour
Cooking: 1 hour
Level: 2

CHOCOLATE DACQUOISE

562

Dacquoise: Preheat the oven to 300°F (150°/gas 2).
• Cut out three 9-inch (23-cm) rounds of parchment paper and place on baking sheets. • Beat the egg whites and salt in a large bowl with an electric mixer at medium speed until frothy. With mixer at high speed, gradually add the sugar, beating until stiff peaks form. • Fold in the almonds and cornstarch. • Spoon into a pastry bag fitted with a 1/2-inch (1-cm) plain tip. Pipe the meringue in a spiral to fill the rounds, leaving a 1/2-inch (1-cm) border around the edge. • Bake until crisp, 1 hour 20–30 minutes. • Let cool for 10 minutes. Transfer to racks. Remove the paper and let cool completely. • Filling: Melt the chocolate in a double boiler over barely simmering water. Let cool. • Beat the butter in a medium bowl with an electric mixer at medium speed until creamy. • With mixer at high speed, beat the egg yolks in a large bowl until pale and thick. • Bring the sugar and water to a boil over medium heat. Wash down the sides of the pan with a pastry brush dipped in cold water to prevent sugar crystals from forming. Cook, without stirring, until the mixture reaches 238°F (115°C), or the soft-ball stage. • Remove from the heat and slowly beat into the egg yolks. Beat until the mixture is cool. Gradually beat in the butter, followed by the chocolate and vanilla. • Place one dacquoise on a serving plate and spread with one-third of the filling. Top with another dacquoise and spread with one-third of the filling. Cover with the remaining dacquoise. Spread with the remaining filling. Top with hazelnuts.

Dacquoise

6 large egg whites, at room temperature

1/8 teaspoon salt

1 1/2 cups (300 g) granulated sugar

1 1/2 cups (180 g) almonds, finely ground

1 tablespoon cornstarch (cornflour)

Filling

8 oz (250 g) bittersweet (dark) chocolate, coarsely chopped

1 1/2 cups (375 g) unsalted butter, softened

6 large egg yolks

1 cup (200 g) granulated sugar

1/2 cup (125 ml) water

2 teaspoons vanilla extract (essence)

Toasted hazelnuts, to decorate

Serves: 8–10
Preparation: 30 minutes
Cooking: 1 hour 20–30 minutes
Level: 2

CHOCOLATE LEMON MERINGUE SPONGE

Prepare the chocolate sponge (or use storebought chocolate sponge to save time). • Preheat the oven to 250°F (125°C/gas 1). • Meringue: Cut out three 9-inch (23-cm) rounds of parchment paper and place on two baking sheets. • Beat the egg whites in a large bowl with an electric mixer at medium speed until frothy. • With mixer at high speed, gradually add the superfine sugar, beating until stiff, glossy peaks form. • Spread one-third of the meringue onto each parchment round. • Bake until crisp, 50–60 minutes. Turn the oven off and leave the meringues inside with door ajar until cool. Remove from the oven and carefully remove the parchment paper. • Lemon Curd: Beat the eggs, sugar, and lemon zest and juice in a saucepan until well blended. Cook over low heat, stirring constantly with a wooden spoon, until the mixture lightly coats a wooden spoon or registers 160°F (80°C) on an instant-read thermometer. • Add the butter, stirring until it has melted before adding more. Immediately plunge the pan into a bowl of ice water and stir until the mixture has cooled. • Transfer to a bowl, cover with plastic wrap (cling film), and let cool to room temperature. Chill in the refrigerator for at least 1 hour. • Lemon Syrup: Stir the sugar, lemon juice, and water in a saucepan over medium heat until the sugar has dissolved. Set aside to cool. • With mixer at high speed, beat the cream, confectioners' sugar, and vanilla in a medium bowl until stiff. • Split the

1   basic chocolate sponge
    (see page 696)

Meringue

4   large egg whites
1   cup (200 g) superfine
    (caster) sugar

Lemon Curd

3   large eggs
½   cup (100 g) granulated
    sugar
3   tablespoons finely
    grated lemon zest
⅓   cup (90 ml) freshly
    squeezed lemon juice
½   cup (125 g) butter,
    cut up

Lemon Syrup

½   cup (100 g) granulated
    sugar
¼   cup (60 ml) freshly
    squeezed lemon juice
2   tablespoons water

½   cup (125 ml) heavy
    (double) cream
2   tablespoons
    confectioners' (icing)
    sugar

sponge cake in three thin layers horizontally. Place one cake layer on a serving plate. Drizzle with the syrup and spread with lemon curd. Top with a meringue round, trimming the edges if needed. Spread the meringue with lemon curd and top with another cake layer. Repeat, using all the lemon curd and lemon syrup. Place the remaining layer on top.
• Spread the top of the cake with the cream. Sprinkle with the almonds.

½ **teaspoon vanilla extract (essence)**

½ **cup (60 g) sliced almonds, to decorate**

Serves: 10–12
Preparation: 1 hour + time to make the sponge cake
Cooking: 1 hour
Level: 3

CHOCOLATE ORANGE GÂTEAU

Cake: Preheat the oven to 350°F (180°c/gas 4). • Line a 9-inch (23-cm) springform pan with parchment paper. • Beat the egg yolks and water in a large bowl with an electric mixer at high speed until pale and thick. Beat in two-thirds of a cup (120 g) of sugar and the lemon zest and juice. • With mixer at medium speed, beat the egg whites in a large bowl until frothy. With mixer at high speed, gradually beat in the remaining sugar, beating until stiff, glossy peaks form. Use a large rubber spatula to fold them into the egg yolk mixture. • Fold the flour and baking powder into the batter. • Spoon the batter into the prepared pan. • Bake until a toothpick inserted into the center comes out clean, 35–40 minutes. • Cool the cake in the pan for 15 minutes. Loosen and remove the pan sides. Invert onto the rack. Loosen and remove the pan bottom. Carefully remove the paper and let cool completely. • Filling: Beat the egg yolks, orange zest, and sugar in a saucepan until well blended. Cook over low heat, stirring constantly until the mixture lightly coats a metal spoon or registers 160°F (80°C) on an instant-read thermometer. Plunge the pan into a bowl of ice water and stir until the egg mixture has cooled. • Sprinkle the gelatin over the orange and lemon juices in a saucepan. Let stand 1 minute. Stir over low heat until the gelatin has dissolved. • Heat the juice mixture over low heat until thickened. • Remove from the heat. Gradually fold the egg mixture into the gelatin mixture. • With mixer at high speed, beat the

Cake

- 4 large eggs, separated
- ¼ cup (60 ml) hot water
- 1 cup (200 g) granulated sugar

  grated zest and juice of ½ lemon
- 1 cup (150 g) all-purpose (plain) flour
- ⅓ cup (50 g) unsweetened cocoa powder
- ½ teaspoon baking powder

Filling

- 4 large egg yolks

  Grated zest of 1 orange
- ½ cup (100 g) granulated sugar
- 2 tablespoons gelatin

  Juice of 3 oranges
- 1 tablespoon freshly squeezed lemon juice
- ¾ cup (180 ml) heavy (double) cream
- 2 tablespoons orange liqueur
- ¾ cup (100 g) flaked almonds

cream in a large bowl until stiff. Fold the cream into the egg mixture. • Split the cake horizontally. Sprinkle with the orange liqueur. • Place one layer on a serving plate and surround with the pan sides. Spread with the filling. Top with the remaining layer. • Refrigerate for 3 hours. • Remove the pan sides. • <u>Topping</u>: Melt the butter and sugar in a saucepan over low heat. Add the oranges and cook until they begin to caramelize, about 10 minutes. Decorate the cake with the oranges, star fruit, and candied cherries.

Topping

¼ **cup (60 g) butter**

½ **cup (100 g) granulated sugar**

3 **oranges, thinly sliced**

Sliced star fruit and candied cherries, to decorate

569

Serves: 10–12
Preparation: 1 hour
+ 3 hours to chill
Cooking: 35–40 minutes
Level: 2

CHOCOLATE SPONGE DACQUOISE

Prepare the chocolate sponge (or use storebought chocolate sponge to save time). • Chocolate Cream Frosting: Melt the chocolate with the cream in a double boiler over barely simmering water. Add the vanilla. Transfer to a medium bowl. Cover and refrigerate until thick and spreadable, about 12 hours. • Dacquoise: Preheat the oven to 300°F (150°C/gas 2). • Butter three 9-inch (23-cm) round cake pans. Line with parchment paper. • Beat the egg whites in a large bowl with an electric mixer at medium speed until frothy. • With mixer at high speed, gradually beat in the sugar, beating until stiff, glossy peaks form. • Use a large rubber spatula to fold the almonds and almond extract into the mixture. • Spoon the batter evenly into the prepared pans. • Bake until pale gold and crisp, 60–70 minutes. • Cool the dacquoise in the pans for 10 minutes. Invert onto parchment paper and let cool completely. • Split the chocolate sponge cakes horizontally. Place one layer on a serving plate. Brush with the rum and spread with some of the frosting. Top with a meringue layer and spread with frosting. Top with a cake layer. Repeat until all the cake, frosting, rum, and dacquoise have been used, finishing with a layer of frosted cake. • Refrigerate for 1–2 hours to soften the meringue a little so that the cake can be cut. • Garnish with the berry fruit.

2 basic chocolate sponge cakes (see page 696)

Chocolate Cream Frosting

6 oz (180 g) bittersweet (dark) chocolate, coarsely chopped

1½ cups (375 ml) heavy (double) cream

1 teaspoon vanilla extract (essence)

Dacquoise

4 large egg whites

1 cup (200 g) granulated sugar

¾ cup (100 g) almonds, finely ground

1 teaspoon almond extract

½ cup (125 ml) rum

Mixed berryfruit, to garnish

Serves: 10–12
Preparation: 45 minutes
+ 12 hours to chill
Cooking: 60–70 minutes
Level: 2

CANDY

HOT EASTER EGGS

Filling: Place the chocolate and cream in a double boiler over barely simmering water. Stir occasionally until the mixture is smooth and shiny. • Remove from the heat and stir in the butter and chile powder. Pour the mixture into a pouring pitcher (jug) and let cool. • Eggs: Wipe two 12-hole mini Easter egg trays with cotton wool dipped in a little vegetable oil. Remove any excess oil. • Color the white chocolate with the red food coloring. Be sure to use an oil-based coloring as a water based coloring will turn the chocolate solid. Drizzle lines across the egg trays and let cool and set firmly before proceeding with the semisweet chocolate. • Using a small paintbrush, brush the insides of the egg trays with the melted semisweet chocolate coating evenly with a thin layer of chocolate. Let set completely. Reserve a little of the melted chocolate to sandwich the eggs together. • Fill to just below the edge of each egg. Chill in the refrigerator until the filling is firm, about 30 minutes. • Reheat the remaining melted chocolate and spoon a little over the filling in each egg. Smooth the top with a spatula. Let the chocolate almost set before sandwiching the two halves together.

Filling

12 oz (350 g) semisweet (dark) chocolate

½ cup (125 ml) heavy (double) cream

2 tablespoons butter

¼ teaspoon chile powder

Eggs

2 tablespoons vegetable oil

2 drops red oil-based food coloring

2 oz (60 g) white chocolate, melted

12 oz (350 g) semisweet (dark) chocolate, melted

Makes: 24 whole eggs
Preparation: 35–40 minutes + 30 minutes to chill
Level: 1

CHAMPAGNE TRUFFLES

578

Truffles: Place both types of chocolate, the glucose, and cream in a double boiler over barely simmering water. Stir until smooth and shiny. • Remove from the heat and stir in the liqueur, cognac, and butter. • Pour the mixture onto a tray and cover with plastic wrap (cling film). Chill in the refrigerator until cold and firm, 1–2 hours. • Using your hands, roll teaspoon-sized balls of the chocolate mixture, placing them on a tray ready for finishing. • Chill in the refrigerator for 30 minutes. • To Finish: Melt the chocolate in a double boiler over barely simmering water. Let cool for a few minutes. • Sift the confectioners' sugar onto a plate. • Place a little of the chocolate in the palm of your hand. Roll the truffle in this chocolate then roll in the confectioners' sugar.

Truffles

1¼ lb (600 g) milk chocolate

8 oz (250 g) bittersweet (dark) chocolate

2 tablespoons glucose

2 cups (500 ml) heavy (double) cream

3 tablespoons petit liqueur

3 tablespoons cognac

2 tablespoons butter

To Finish

5 oz (150 g) bittersweet (dark) chocolate

1 cup (150 g) confectioners' (icing) sugar

Makes: About 60
Preparation: 20 minutes
    + 2 hours to chill
Level: 1

CASSIS TRUFFLES

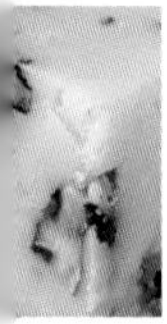

Truffles: Place both types of chocolate, the glucose, and cream in a double boiler over barely simmering water. Stir until smooth and shiny. • Remove from the heat and stir in the liqueur and butter. • Pour the mixture into a tray and cover with plastic wrap (cling film). Chill in the refrigerator until cold and firm, 1–2 hours. • Using your hands, roll teaspoon-sized balls of the chocolate mixture, placing them on a tray ready for finishing. • Chill in the refrigerator for 30 minutes. • To Finish: Place confectioners' sugar and cocoa in a bowl and mix well. • Melt the chocolate in a double boiler over barely simmering water. Let cool for a few minutes. • Place a little of the chocolate in the palm of your hand. Roll the truffle in this chocolate then roll in the confectioners' sugar mixture.

Truffles

1¼ lb (600 g) milk chocolate

5 oz (150 g) bittersweet (dark) chocolate

2 tablespoons glucose

2 cups (500 ml) heavy (double) cream

¼ cup (60 ml) cassis liqueur

2 tablespoons butter

To Finish

1 cup (150 g) confectioners' (icing) sugar

⅔ cup (100 g) unsweetened cocoa powder

5 oz (150 g) bittersweet (dark) chocolate

Makes: About 60
Preparation: 20 minutes + 2 hours to chill
Level: 1

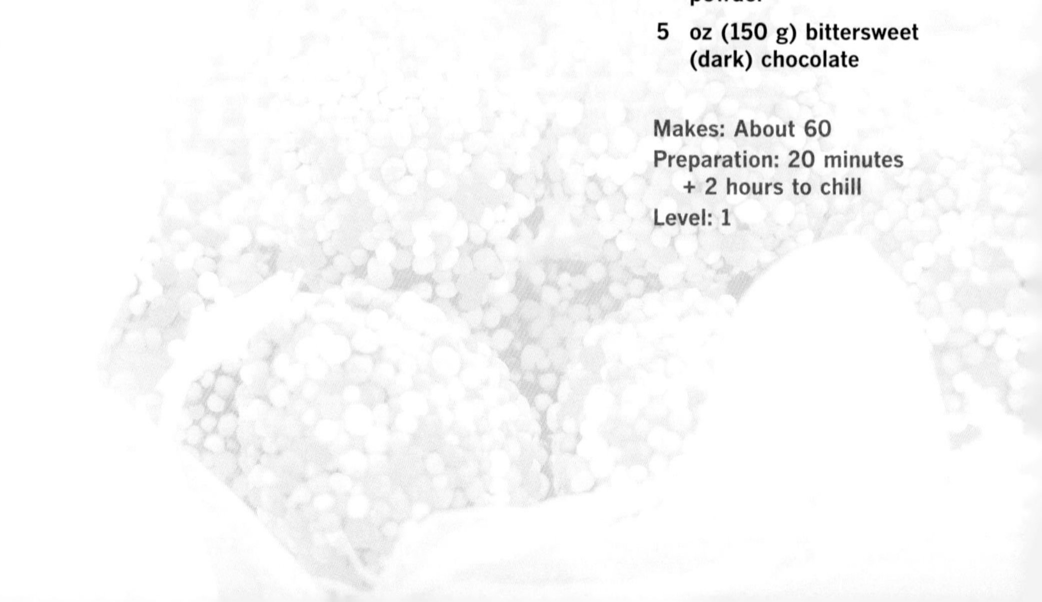

CHOCOLATE BRANDY SNAPS

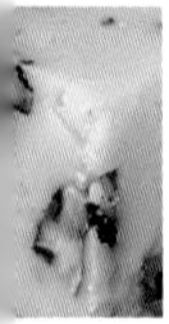

Preheat the oven to 350°F (180°C/gas 4). • Line a baking sheet with parchment paper. • Stir the butter, sugar, and corn syrup in a saucepan over low heat until the sugar has dissolved. Remove from the heat. • Sift the flour and cocoa together and stir into the sugar mixture a little at a time, making sure no lumps form. Let cool for 10 minutes. • Place teaspoonfuls of the mixture onto the baking sheet, spacing them well so that there is room to spread; they will at least double in size during baking. • Bake until the mixture begins to bubble, about 10 minutes. • Take out of the oven and let cool just enough so that they can be lifted with a spatula without breaking. • Drape each brandy snap over a rolling pin until cool and firm.

3 tablespoons butter

2 tablespoons dark brown sugar

2 tablespoons corn (golden) syrup

$1/3$ cup (50 g) all-purpose (plain) flour

2 tablespoons unsweetened cocoa powder

Makes: About 25
Preparation: 10 minutes
Cooking: 10 minutes
Level: 2

WHITE CHOCOLATE LOGS

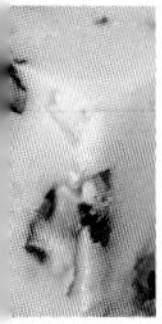

Logs: Place the white chocolate, cream, and glucose in a double boiler over barely simmering water. Stir until the mixture is smooth and shiny. • Remove from the heat and stir in the liqueur and butter.
• Pour the mixture into a tray and cover with plastic wrap (cling film). Chill in the refrigerator until cold and firm, 1–2 hours. • Using your hands, roll teaspoon-sized balls of the chocolate mixture into logs, placing them on a tray ready for finishing.
• Chill in the refrigerator for 30 minutes. • To Finish: Place the grated or flaked chocolate on a plate. Take the logs out of the refrigerator. • Melt the chopped white chocolate in a double boiler over barely simmering water. Let cool for a few minutes.
• Place a little of the chocolate in the palm of your hand. Roll the log in the chocolate and then roll in the flaked chocolate. Place in mini paper cups and chill in the refrigerator until ready to serve.

Logs

1¼ lb (600 g) white
   chocolate

1¼ cups (300 ml) heavy
   (double) cream

4 tablespoons glucose

3 tablespoons kirsch

2 tablespoons butter

To Finish

3 oz (90 g) white
   chocolate, grated
   or flaked

5 oz (150 g) white
   chocolate, chopped

Makes: 40 logs
Preparation: 15 minutes
  + 2 hours to chill
Level: 1

WHITE CHOCOLATE AND RASPBERRY FRIANDS

Preheat the oven to 350°F (180°C/gas 4). • Oil a 24-hole mini oval friand pan. • Place the almonds, confectioners' sugar, flour, and baking powder in a large bowl. • Pour in the butter and mix until smooth. • Add the egg whites and mix until well combined. • Spoon the batter into the prepared pans so that they are about half full. Push a few raspberries into the top of each and sprinkle with the chocolate. Bake until golden and firm, but still moist in the center, 8–10 minutes. • Turn out onto a wire rack to cool. Oil the friand pan and repeat the process for another batch.

1 cup (120 g) ground almonds

1 cup (150 g) confectioners' (icing) sugar

²/₃ cup (100 g) all-purpose (plain) flour

½ teaspoon baking powder

¹/₃ cup (90 g) butter, melted

6 large egg whites, lightly beaten

½ cup (60 g) frozen raspberries

2 oz (60 g) white chocolate, finely chopped

Makes: 48
Preparation: 10 minutes
Cooking: 10 minutes
Level: 1

WHITE CHOCOLATE AND PECAN FUDGE

Oil an 8 x 10-inch (20 x 25-cm) baking pan.
• Place the butter, milk, and sugar in a saucepan over medium heat. Bring to a boil and stir until the sugar begins to dissolve. Simmer the mixture until it reaches the soft ball stage. At this temperature, if you drop a spoonful of the mixture into ice water, it will make a limp, sticky ball that flattens when you remove from the water. • Remove from the heat and beat until it starts to thicken, about 5 minutes. • Add the chocolate and stir until it has melted. Fold in the pecan nuts and vanilla extract. • Pour the mixture into the prepared pan. Let cool to room temperature then chill in the refrigerator until set, 2–3 hours. • Cut into 1 inch (2.5 cm) pieces.

1   cup (250 g) butter

1½ cups (375 ml) milk

2½ cups (500 g) granulated sugar

4   oz (125 g) white chocolate, finely chopped

1   cup (120 g) pecans, chopped

1   teaspoon vanilla extract (essence)

Makes: About 30 pieces
Preparation: 30 minutes
    + 2–3 hours to chill
Level: 1

COCONUT AND WHITE CHOCOLATE TRUFFLES

Heat the chocolate and cream in a double boiler over barely simmering water. Stir until the mixture is smooth and shiny.• Remove from the heat and stir in the liqueur and butter. • Pour the mixture into a tray and cover with plastic wrap (cling film). Chill in the refrigerator until cold and firm, 1–2 hours. • Using your hands, roll teaspoon-sized balls of the chocolate mixture into logs, placing them on a tray ready for finishing. • Chill in the refrigerator for 30 minutes. • Preheat the oven to 350°F (180°C/gas 4). • Place the shredded coconut on a baking sheet. • Bake until golden in color, 50–10 minutes. • Let cool completely on the baking sheet. • Take the truffles out of the refrigerator and roll each ball in your hands just warming the surface. Roll immediately in the coconut. Repeat with all the truffles.

12 oz (300 g) white chocolate

1/3 cup (90 ml) heavy (double) cream

3 tablespoons Grand Marnier

2 tablespoons butter

3/4 cup (80 g) toasted shredded coconut

Makes: About 20
Preparation: 15 minutes + 2 hour 30 minutes to chill
Level: 1

CHOCOLATE MARSHMALLOWS

Place the gelatin and water in the bowl of an electric mixer and let rest until the gelatin begins to swell, about 3 minutes. • Place the sugar, corn syrup and water in a heavy-based pan over medium heat. Bring to a boil and simmer until it reaches the soft ball stage. • Remove from the heat and let cool for a few minutes. • In the meantime, add the cocoa to the gelatin mixture and beat until frothy. • With mixer on low speed, slowly and carefully pour in the sugar. Add the vanilla extract and continue to beat until the batter is glossy and smooth, about 10 minutes. • Transfer the mixture to a piping bag fitted with a plain $1/2$-inch (1-cm) nozzle. • Pipe drops onto a baking sheet or large platter lined with parchment paper and dusted with confectioners' sugar. Once you have piped them all out, dust again with the confectioners' sugar. Let stand for 10 minutes while they firm up. • If liked, serve in mini paper cups.

$1/2$ cup (75 g) unsweetened cocoa powder

1 tablespoon vanilla extract (essence)

3 tablespoons gelatin

$1/2$ cup (125 ml) water

$2^{1}/_{4}$ cups (450 g) granulated sugar

$1/3$ cup (90 g) corn (golden) syrup

$1/4$ cup (60 ml) water

$1/4$ teaspoon salt

Confectioners' (icing) sugar, to dust

Makes: About 60
Preparation: 20 minutes + 10 minutes to set
Level: 2

PISTACHIO LOGS

Preheat the oven to 350°F (180°C/gas 4). • Line a baking sheet with parchment paper. • Place the marzipan, egg, egg yolk, pistachios, and lemon zest in the bowl of an electric mixer. Using the paddle attachment, mix to a paste on medium speed. • Spoon the mixture into a piping bag fitted with a $1/2$-inch (1-cm) plain nozzle and pipe out lines of the mix. • Bake until firm to the touch, about 10 minutes. • Remove from the oven and let cool completely on the baking sheet. • Cut into logs about 1 inch (2.5 cm) long. • Heat the chocolate in a double boiler over barely simmering water, stirring until melted. • Dip the logs into the chocolate, submerging each one. Remove from the chocolate with two forks. • Gently place the chocolates on a wire rack so that the excess chocolate can drip off. • Sprinkle the slivered pistachios on top for decoration. • Let set before serving.

5 oz (150 g) raw marzipan

1 large egg yolk

1 large egg

$1/2$ cup (60 g) pistachios, finely ground

Finely grated zest of 1 lemon

12 oz (350 g) semisweet (dark) chocolate

$1/2$ cup (60 g) slivered pistachios

Makes: About 25
Preparation: 20 minutes
Cooking: 10 minutes
Level: 2

PANFORTE

Preheat the oven to 350°F (180°C/gas 4). • Place the hazelnuts and brazil nuts on a baking sheet and toast until golden, 5–10 minutes. • Use a cloth to rub the skins from the nuts. • Toast the almonds until golden, about 10 minutes. Leave the oven on but turn down to 300°F (150°C/gas 2). • Combine the nuts in a food processor and chop very coarsely. • Place the nuts, zests, candied fruit, figs, flour, cocoa and all the spices in a large bowl and mix well. • Butter the base and sides of a 9-inch (23-cm) springform pan. Line with parchment paper and butter the paper. • Heat the honey, sugar, and butter in a heavy saucepan over low heat. Stir constantly until it registers 242–248°F (soft ball stage) on a candy thermometer. • Add to the nut mixture and stir until well combined. • Spoon into the prepared pan, smoothing the top with the back of the spoon. You will need to work quickly as the mixture becomes very sticky. • Bake for 35–40 minutes. The panforte will seem uncooked but hardens as it cools. • Cool on a rack until firm and cool. Dust with confectioners' sugar before serving.

1 cup (120 g) hazelnuts

½ cup (60 g) brazil nuts

1 cup (120 g) whole blanched almonds

1 cup (130 g) roughly chopped candied peel

1 cup (150 g) dried figs quartered

Finely grated zest of 1 lemon

Finely grated zest of 1 orange

½ cup (75 g) all-purpose (plain) flour

2 tablespoons unsweetened cocoa powder

1 teaspoon cinnamon

½ teaspoon ground nutmeg

¼ teaspoon ground coriander

¼ teaspoon ground cloves

1¼ cups (300 g) honey

½ cup (100 g) sugar

¼ cup (60 g) butter

½ teaspoon ground nutmeg

Confectioners' (icing) sugar to dust

Serves: 10–12
Preparation: 30 minutes
Cooking: 35–40 minutes
Level: 1

EASTER EGGS

Melt the white chocolate in a double boiler over barely simmering water. • Wipe two 12-hole mini Easter egg trays with cotton wool dipped in a little vegetable oil. Remove any excess oil. • Drizzle the white chocolate in lines across the egg trays and let cool and set firmly. • Place the semisweet chocolate and cream in a double boiler over barely simmering water. Stir occasionally until the mixture is smooth and shiny. • Remove from the heat and stir in the butter. • Set $1/2$ cup (125 g) of the mixture aside. Pour the rest into the egg trays, filling to just below the edge of each egg. Chill in the refrigerator until firm. • Reheat the remaining melted chocolate and spoon a little over each egg. Smooth the top with a spatula. Let the chocolate almost set before sandwiching the two halves together.

2 oz (60 g) white chocolate, chopped

$1^{1}/4$ lb (600 g) semisweet (dark) chocolate, chopped

$2/3$ cup (180 ml) heavy (double) cream

$1/4$ cup (60 g) butter

Makes: 24 whole eggs
Preparation: 35–40 minutes + 30 minutes to chill
Level: 1

EASTER EGGS WITH SPRINKLES

Heat 1¹/₄ lb (600 g) of the chocolate with the cream in a double boiler over barely simmering water. Stir occasionally until the mixture is smooth and shiny. • Pour the mixture into a tray and cover with plastic wrap (cling film). Chill in the refrigerator until cold and firm, 1–2 hours. • Using your hands, roll teaspoon-sized balls of the chocolate mixture into balls, placing them on a tray ready for finishing. • Chill in the refrigerator for 30 minutes. • Melt the remaining chocolate in a double boiler over barely simmering water. • Put the sprinkles into a bowl. Take a little of the melted chocolate in your hands and roll each egg in the chocolate and then immediately roll the egg in the sprinkles. Make sure the eggs are thoroughly coated in the sprinkles.

1¹/₂ lb (750 g) semisweet (dark) chocolate, chopped

²/₃ cup (180 ml) heavy (double) cream

¹/₄ cup (60 g) butter

2 cups colored sprinkles to finish

Makes: About 20 eggs
Preparation: 25 minutes + 2 hours 30 minutes to chill
Level: 1

CHOCOLATE CANDIED PEEL

Score the fruit in sections 2 inches (5 cm) wide, cutting through the peel but not the fruit. Pull off the peel. Set the fruit aside for another use. • Place the peel in a saucepan and pour in enough water to cover. • Bring to a boil, drain, and rinse briefly under cold water. repeat this blanching process twice. • Drain the peel, rinse under cold water, and remove as much of the white pith as possible using a small sharp knife. • Cut the peel into strips about $1/4$ inch (5 mm) wide. • Place the sugar and water in heavy-based saucepan. Bring to a boil, stirring well to dissolve the sugar. • Simmer, without stirring, over low heat until the mixture becomes a thin syrup, about 1 hour. You will have about 1 cup (250 ml) of syrup. • Cover the blanched peel with cold water and bring to a boil. Simmer until the peel begins to lose its raw look, 5–10 minutes. • Drain well and place in a large bowl. • Cover with the hot sugar syrup and set aside to candy, about 1 hour. • Shake the candied fruit to remove excess sugar. Place on a rack over a plate to catch any dripping sugar. Place in a warm oven (250°F/120°C) to dry, about 1 hour. • Leave at room temperature to finish drying, 1–2 days. • Dip the peel in the melted chocolate. Place on a tray lined with parchment paper to set.

1 lb (500 g) orange or lemons,

1 cup (250 ml) water

1 cup (200 g) granulated sugar

12 oz (350 g) semisweet (dark) chocolate

Makes: About 24 pieces
Preparation: 3 hours + 1–2 days to dry
Level: 1

■ ■ ■ *If you are short of time, use pre-candied fruits to make these delicious treats.*

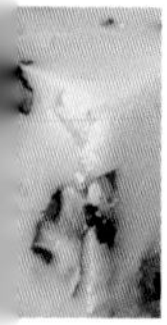

DIPPED BRAZILS

Line a baking sheet with parchment paper and lightly grease the paper. • Place the sugar and water in a heavy-based pan and bring to a boil over medium heat. Occasionally brush down the sides with a wet, pastry brush, collecting any crystals that may have formed. • When the sugar begins to bubble rapidly reduce the heat. When it turns golden brown and starts to caramelize, remove from the heat immediately and plunge the pan into a bowl half filled with cold water. • Remove the pan from the water and very carefully drop in a brazil nut, roll it over with 2 forks, then transfer to the prepared tray. Repeat with all the brazil nuts. You may need to put the caramel back over a low heat to keep it warm enough to coat the nuts evenly. • Let the dipped nuts cool completely. • Melt the chocolate in a double boiler over barely simmering water. • Dip the nuts in the melted chocolate, coating half of each one. Return to the tray. Let the chocolate set before serving.

1 cup (200 g) granulated sugar

½ cup (125 ml) water

About 30 whole brazil nuts

5 oz (150 g) bittersweet (dark) chocolate, chopped

Makes: About 30 nut
Preparation: 20 minutes
Cooking: 20 minutes
Level: 1

GRAND MARNIER TRUFFLES

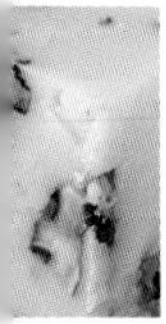

Heat the chocolate and cream in a double boiler over barely simmering water. Stir until the mixture is smooth and shiny.• Remove from the heat and stir in the liqueur and butter. • Pour the mixture into a tray and cover with plastic wrap (cling film). Chill in the refrigerator until cold and firm, 1–2 hours. • Using your hands, roll teaspoon-sized balls of the chocolate mixture into logs, placing them on a tray ready for finishing. • Chill in the refrigerator for 30 minutes. • Take the truffles out of the refrigerator and roll each ball in your hands, just warming the surface. Roll immediately in the chocolate. Repeat with all the truffles.

12 oz (300 g) bittersweet (dark) chocolate

$\frac{1}{3}$ cup (90 ml) heavy (double) cream

3 tablespoons Grand Marnier

2 tablespoons butter

2 oz (60 g) grated or flaked chocolate, to finish

Makes: About 20 truffles
Preparation: 15 minutes + 2 hours 30 minutes to chill
Level: 1

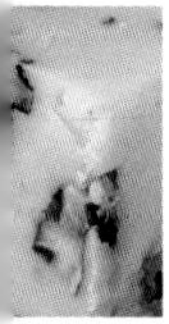

HONEY NOUGAT

Oil a 5 x 12-inch (12 x 30-cm) baking pan. Line with parchment paper. • Place the cream and honey in a saucepan over medium-low heat and bring to a gentle boil. Simmer until the mixture reaches the soft ball stage (235°F–240°F/118°C–120°C). • Remove from the heat and let cool for a few minutes before carefully stirring in the butter and finally the nuts. • Pour the mixture into the prepared pan. Let cool and set, at least 4 hours, preferably overnight. • When set, turn out onto a chopping board and cut into chocolate-sized pieces. • Melt the chocolate in a double boiler over barely simmering water. • Holding each of nougat by the top, dip into the melted chocolate coating half way up the sides. Place each piece onto a tray lined with parchment paper until the chocolate has set.

1 cup (250 ml) heavy (double) cream

1²/₃ cups (400 g) honey

3 tablespoons butter

2 cups (250 g) toasted flaked almonds

5 oz (150 g) milk chocolate, to dip

Makes: About 50 pieces
Preparation: 30–40 minutes
Level: 1

ROCHER

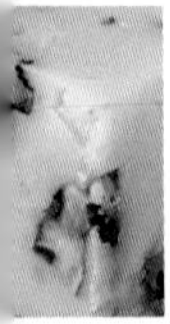

Preheat the oven to 300°F (150°C/gas 2). • Line a baking sheet with parchment paper. • Place the sugar and water in a heavy-based pan over medium heat and bring to a boil. Boil rapidly for 5 minutes. • Remove from the heat and stir in the slivered almonds. • Spread the almonds on the prepared baking sheet and roast place until the nuts are dry, crisp and golden, 15–20 minutes. • Cool the nuts on the baking sheet. • Melt the chocolate in a double boiler over barely simmering water. Stir until the chocolate has melted. • Place the cooled nuts in a bowl and pour the chocolate over the top. Stir gently until the nuts are well coated. • Spoon out tablespoons of the mixture on to a clean baking set completely before serving.

½ cup (100 g) granulated sugar

¼ cup (60 ml) water

2 cups (250 g) slivered almonds

12 oz (300 g) bittersweet (dark) chocolate

Makes: 20–25 pieces
Preparation: 15 minutes
Cooking: 20 minutes
Level: 1

COCOA STICKS

Place cream and corn syrup in a saucepan over medium-low heat and bring to a gentle boil. • Heat the chocolate and cream mixture in a double boiler over barely simmering water. Stir until the mixture is smooth and shiny. • Remove from the heat and set aside until it thickens enough to pipe, about 30 minutes. • Spoon the mixture into a piping bag fitted with a plain $1/4$-inch (5-mm) nozzle. • Line 1–2 baking sheets with parchment paper and pipe lines of the chocolate mixture 1inch (2.5 cm) apart. • Chill in the refrigerator until the sticks are cool and set, about 1 hour. • Cut each strip into 4-inch (10 cm) lengths. Carefully run a knife under each stick and stack them all on a plate. Chill in the refrigerator. • To Finish: Melt the chocolate in a double boiler over barely simmering water. Let cool for a few minutes. • Sift the cocoa into a dessert dish. Place the chocolate in another dessert dish. Roll the sticks first in the chocolate and then in the cocoa. Keep refrigerated until ready to serve.

5 oz (150 g) bittersweet (dark) chocolate, chopped

$1/3$ cup (90 ml) heavy (double) cream

2 tablespoons corn (golden) syrup

To Finish

2 oz (60 g) bittersweet (dark) chocolate, chopped

$1/3$ cup (50 g) unsweetened cocoa powder

Makes: About 50 sticks
**Preparation: 30 minutes
+ 1 hour 30 minutes
to chill**
Level: 2

CHOCOLATE TOFFEE

Preheat the oven to 350°F (180°C/gas 4). • Line a 10 x 15-inch (25 x 38-cm) baking pan with aluminum foil. Butter the foil. • Spread the pecans evenly over the foil. • Place the butter, both type of sugar, and salt in a heavy-based saucepan. Bring to a rolling boil, stirring constantly. • Spoon the syrup over the pecans to coat. Bake until bubbly all over the surface, about 10 minutes. • Immediately sprinkle with the chocolate chips. • Let cool in the pan for 10 minutes then mark with a knife into 1 inch (2.5-cm) squares. Let cool completely. • Peel off the foil and break the toffee into pieces along the markings.

1½ cups (200 g) broken pecans

1 cup (250 g) butter

½ cup (100 g) granulated sugar

2 cups (400 g) firmly packed light brown brown sugar

Pinch of salt

12 oz (350 g) semisweet (dark) chocolate chips

Makes: About 36 pieces
Preparation: 15 minutes
Cooking: 15 minutes
Level: 1

614

■ ■ ■ *Make this toffee as a gift. Wrap each piece in cellophane and tie with a ribbon.*

615

CHOCOLATE DRIZZLED CROCCANT

Preheat the oven to 400°F (200°C/gas 6). • Scatter the nuts on a baking sheet and roast in the oven until are golden, 5–10 minutes. • Rub the nuts in a clean cloth to remove the skins. • Chop in a food processor until finely chopped but not completely ground. • Spread the nuts on the baking sheet again and set aside. • Melt the chocolate in a double boiler over barely simmering water. Let cool for a few minutes. • Bring the sugar and water to a boil in a heavy-based pan over high heat. Brush down the sides with a wet pastry brush from time to time, collecting any crystals that may have formed. • When the sugar begins to bubble rapidly reduce the heat. When it turns golden brown and starts to caramelize, remove from the heat immediately and plunge the pan into a bowl half filled with cold water. • Remove from the water and very carefully pour the caramel into a pitcher (jug). • Pour lines of caramel onto the chopped roasted hazelnuts, carefully covering the lines with more chopped nuts as you go. Let the caramel cool completely and set in the hazelnuts. • When hard, remove the sticks and break into 3-inch (8-cm) lengths. • Drizzle with the melted chocolate. Let the chocolate set and serve with coffee.

1 cup (200 g) granulated sugar
½ cup (125 ml) water
1 cup (120 g) hazelnuts
5 oz (150 g) bittersweet (dark) chocolate

Makes: About 25
Preparation: 30–40 minutes
Cooking: 10 minutes
Level: 2

RICH CHOCOLATE PETIT FOURS

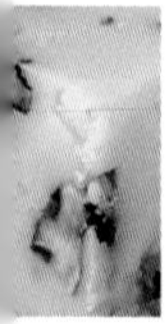

Cut the sponge horizontally into 4 equal layers. • When the ganache is cooled and thick, place one layer of sponge on a plate and spread with layer of ganache $1/2$-inch (1-cm) thick. Cover with another layer of sponge and spread with a layer of ganache. Repeat one more time and top with the final layer of sponge. • Cover and refrigerate for 30 minutes. • In the meantime, melt the remaining ganache and let cool for 10 minutes. • Cut the chocolate sponge into 1-inch (2.5-cm) squares or use a 1 inch (2.5-cm) round cutter to cut out circles. • Place the pieces on a wire rack and spoon the cooled ganache over the top so that the tops and sides are evenly coated. • Chill in the refrigerator for 10 minutes before decorating with a piece of the gold foil.

1 **basic chocolate sponge (see page 696)**

2 **recipes dark chocolate ganache (see page 686)**

Gold foil, to decorate (optional)

Makes: About 24 pieces
Preparation: 45 minutes
Cooking: 15 minutes
Level: 3

LAYER CAKELETS

Preheat the oven to 400°F (200°C/gas 6). • Oil an 8 x 12-inch (20 x 30-cm) baking pan. Line with parchment paper. • Beat the butter and half the sugar in an electric mixer on high speed until light and creamy. • Add the egg yolks one at a time, beating until just combined after each addition. • In a separate bowl, beat the egg whites and remaining sugar on high speed until creamy and glossy and the sugar has completely dissolved. • Mix the cornstarch and almonds in a bowl and fold alternate spoonfuls of the almond mixture and the egg whites into the butter mixture. • Spoon some of the batter (about 3 large serving spoons) into the prepared pan. Spread to 1/8-inch (3-mm) thick. Sift an even layer of cocoa over the top. • Bake until the sponge is cooked and springs back when pressed. • Spoon another layer of the batter over the first and spread to the same thickness. Sift an even layer of cocoa over the top. Bake until the sponge is cooked and springs back when pressed. Repeat until all of the sponge batter and cocoa are used up. • Reduce the oven temperature to 350°F (180°/gas 4). • Cover the cake with aluminum foil and bake until a skewer inserted into the center comes out clean, about 10 minutes. • Turn out onto a wire rack and let cool completely. Cut into 1-inch (2.5-cm) squares or use a 1 inch (2.5-cm) round cutter to cut out circles. • Syrup: Bring the sugar and water to a boil over medium heat. Boil rapidly for 5 minutes. • Remove from the heat and stir in the kirsch. • Brush over the cakelets.

3/4 cup (200 g) butter, softened

1 1/4 cups (250 g) granulated sugar

6 large eggs, separated

1 1/4 cups (180 g) cornstarch (cornflour)

1/2 cup (60 g) ground almonds

1/3 cup (50 g) unsweetened cocoa powder

Syrup

1 cup (200 g) granulated sugar

2 cups (500 ml) water

1/4 cup (60 ml) kirsch

Makes: 12–18 cakelets
Preparation: 35–40 minutes
Cooking: 1 hour
Level: 3

CHOCOLATE ORANGE MERINGUE TARTLETS

Preheat the oven to 350°F (180°C/gas 4). • Grease two 12-cup mini muffin pans. • Roll the pastry out to about $1/8$-inch (2 mm) thick on a floured work surface. Using a 2-inch (5-cm) round cutter, cut out 24 disks. Gently lift each disk and lay it over a muffin cup. Push the pastry into the cups, smoothing the base and pressing into the sides. Trim off any excess pastry. • Line each cup with parchment paper. Fill with baking beans. • Bake for 5–10 minutes. • Remove the baking beans and parchment. Place the cases back in the oven for 2–3 minutes, to cook the base out. When the base is firm to the touch, remove from the oven and let cool completely.

• Filling: Place the chocolate, glucose and cream in a double boiler over barely simmering water. Stir until the mixture is smooth and shiny. • Remove from the heat and stir in the liqueur, orange zest, and butter. Pour the mixture into a bowl and cover with plastic wrap (cling film). Chill in the refrigerator until cool enough to pour into the cases, 30 minutes. • Fill the chocolate cases to two-thirds, leaving room for the meringue.

• Meringue: Preheat the oven to 400°F (200°C/gas 6). • Line a baking sheet with parchment paper. • Whisk the egg whites and sugar in a heatproof bowl over low heat until the sugar has dissolved. • Beat the egg white mixture in an electric mixer until it is white, glossy, and holds soft peaks. • Spoon the

1	recipe chocolate pastry (see page 682)

Filling

12	oz (350 g) white chocolate
$2/3$	cup (150 ml) heavy (double) cream
2	tablespoons glucose
3	tablespoons Cointreau
2	tablespoons butter
	Finely grated zest of 1 orange

Meringue

2	large egg whites
$3/4$	cup (150 g) superfine (caster) sugar

Makes: 24 tartlets
Preparation: 1 hour
 + 30 minutes to chill
Cooking: 20 minutes
Level: 1

meringue into a piping bag fitted with a plain nozzle and pipe onto the chocolate orange filling, bringing the bag up as you pipe to form "witches hats."

- Place the tartlets on the prepared baking sheet.
- Bake until lightly browned, about 5 minutes.

SAVORY DISHES

628

PENNE WITH CHOCOLATE, PISTACHIOS, AND GOAT CHEESE

Penne: Heat the oil in a small saucepan and sauté the onion until just transparent; do not let it color. • Add the penne and stir well over medium heat for 2 minutes. Pour in the wine and milk and season with salt. Bring to a boil and simmer until cooked al dente. • Sauce: Chop the pistachios coarsely in a food processor. • Place the white chocolate in a double boiler over barely simmering water and stir until melted. • Remove from the heat and stir in the mascarpone, goat cheese, and milk. • Drain the penne and place in a heated serving bowl. • Pour the chocolate sauce over the top and sprinkle with the chopped pistachios. Toss well. • Serve hot with the grated dark chocolate sprinkled over the top.

Penne

- 2 tablespoons extra-virgin olive oil
- 1 small white onion, finely chopped
- 12 oz (350 g) penne
- 4 cups (1 liter) dry white wine
- 2 tablespoons milk
- 1 tablespoons coarse sea salt

Sauce

- ½ cup (75 g) shelled pistachios
- 3 oz (90 g) white chocolate
- 4 oz (125 g) mascarpone cheese
- 2 oz (60 g) fresh creamy goat cheese
- 2 tablespoons milk
- 3 oz (90 g) bittersweet chocolate, finely grated

Serves: 4
Preparation: 15 minutes
Cooking: 20 minutes
Level: 1

WILD BOAR IN SPICED CHOCOLATE SAUCE

630

Heat the oil in a large casserole over very low heat. Add the onion, carrot, celery, garlic, and parsley and sauté until the vegetables are softened but have not begun to brown, about 10 minutes. • Chop the meat into bite-sized cubes. Add the meat and brown on all sides over medium heat. Season with salt and pepper. Add the bay leaf, cinnamon, and nutmeg. • Pour in the wine and cook until it evaporates, about 5 minutes. • Add the vinegar and cook until it evaporates, about 3 minutes. • Add the stock, cover, and simmer over low heat until the meat is tender, about 1 hour. Add more stock if the mixture begins to stick to the pan. • Melt the chocolate in a double boiler over barely simmering water. • Add the grappa, walnuts, sultanas, pine nuts, candied peel, and sugar. Mix well and remove from the heat. • Dilute the chocolate mixture with a few tablespoons of the cooking liquid then add to the casserole, mixing well. Simmer for 5–10 minutes. • Serve hot on a bed of hot, freshly made polenta.

■ ■ ■ *This unusual dish was served at the wealthy Medici Court in Renaissance Florence in the 16th century. It really is a bit different and a lot of fun. If you can't get wild boar, replace it with the same amount of venison or beef.*

- ¼ cup (60 ml) extra-virgin olive oil
- 1 medium onion, 1 large carrot, 1 stalk celery, 2 cloves garlic, all finely chopped
- 2 tablespoons finely chopped parsley
- 2 lb (1 kg) wild boar
  Salt and freshly ground black pepper
- 2 bay leaves
- ½ teaspoon cinnamon
- ½ teaspoon ground nutmeg
- ⅔ cup (180 ml) dry red wine
- ¼ cup (60 ml) white wine vinegar
- 1 cup (250 ml) meat stock
- 3 oz (90 g) bittersweet (dark) chocolate
- ¼ cup (60 ml) grappa
- 4 tablespoons walnuts, coarsely chopped
- 2 tablespoons golden raisins (sultanas)
- 3 tablespoons pine nuts
- 3 tablespoons chopped candied citron or lemon
- 2 tablespoons sugar
  Freshly made polenta

Serves: 6
Preparation: 20 minutes
Cooking: 90 minutes
Level: 2

SHRIMP WITH CHOCOLATE SAUCE

632

Heat 2 tablespoons of the oil in a medium saucepan over medium heat. Sauté the onions, bay leaf, thyme, and ham bone, if using, until the onions are lightly browned, 8–10 minutes. • Stir in the tomatoes. Lower the heat, cover, and simmer for 15 minutes. • Pour in the water and simmer until it reduces by half in volume. Strain the sauce through a fine mesh strainer. • Season the shrimp with salt and pepper. • Heat the remaining oil in a large frying pan over medium heat. Fry the shrimp until tender and pink, 5–10 minutes (depending on their size). • Remove from the pan, reserving the oil, and arrange on serving plates. Drizzle the strained sauce over the shrimp. • Mix the garlic, almonds, and chocolate in a small bowl. Pour in 4 tablespoons of the reserved oil and spoon over the shrimp.

½ cup (125 ml) extra-virgin olive oil

2 medium onions, finely chopped

1 bay leaf

1 teaspoon finely chopped thyme

1 small ham bone (optional)

2 lb (1 kg) firm-ripe tomatoes, diced

1 quart (1 liter) water

12 giant shrimp (prawn) tails, each weighing about 2 oz (60 g), cleaned

Salt and freshly ground black pepper to taste

3 cloves garlic, very finely chopped

½ cup (50 g) toasted, finely chopped almonds

4 oz (125 g) semisweet (dark) chocolate, coarsely chopped and melted

Serves: 4
Preparation: 20 minutes
Cooking: 35 minutes
Level: 2

■ ■ ■ *Use Dublin Bay prawns, langoustines, or lobsterettes to add authenticity to this flavorsome Spanish dish.*

MEXICAN TURKEY MOLE

Place the turkey pieces in a large saucepan with the onion quarters, cover with water, and simmer until tender, about 1 hour. • Strain and reserve the stock. • Skin the meat and cut into bite-sized pieces. • Transfer to a large earthenware pot. • Preheat the oven to 350°F (180°C/gas 4). • Sauté the almonds and sesame seeds in a dry frying pan over medium heat until lightly browned. • Transfer to a food processor and chop with the raisins, peppercorns, clove, and cinnamon until finely ground. • Add the chile paste, water, chopped onion, garlic, tomatoes, and bread crumbs and process again until smooth. • Sauté the processed mixture in the oil in a large frying pan over medium heat for about 5 minutes. • Pour $2/3$ cup (180 ml) of the reserved stock into a small saucepan and add the chocolate. • Stir over low heat until the chocolate has melted. • Add to the sautéed mixture and season with salt and pepper. Pour the sauce over the turkey. • Bake until heated through and the flavors have mingled, about 30 minutes. • Serve hot.

2½ lb (1.3 kg) turkey pieces

1 onion, quartered

4 tablespoons blanched almonds

2 tablespoons sesame seeds

2 tablespoons raisins

3 black peppercorns

1 clove

2 teaspoons ground cinnamon

2 teaspoons red chile paste (or more)

$2/3$ cup (180 ml) water

1 onion, finely chopped

2 cloves garlic, finely chopped

3 tomatoes, peeled and chopped

1 cup (60 g) fine dry bread crumbs

1 tablespoon sunflower oil

1 oz (30 g) semisweet (dark) chocolate

Salt and freshly ground black pepper

Serves: 4
Preparation: 45 minutes
Cooking: 1 hour 30 minutes
Level: 2

CHOCOLATE MINI MUFFINS WITH ROBIOLA AND SALAMI

Mini Muffins: Dissolve the yeast in the water and milk in a small bowl. Stir in the sugar and set aside until foamy, 15 minutes. • Place the flour, cocoa, and salt in a large bowl. • Gradually stir in the yeast mixture. • Transfer to a lightly floured work surface and knead for 3 minutes. • Add the chocolate and butter and continue kneading until smooth, evenly colored, and the dough does not stick to your hands, 10–15 minutes • Shape into a ball and cover with a cloth. Set aside to rise in a warm place until the dough has doubled in volume, about 1 hour and 30 minutes. • Preheat the oven to 350°F (180°C/gas 4). • Butter two 12-cup mini muffin pans. • Break the dough into pieces about the size of large walnuts and place them in the muffin cups. • Brush the tops with milk and bake until a toothpick inserted into the center comes out clean, 15–20 minutes. • Let cool on a wire rack. • **Filling:** Cut the muffins in half, and fill each one with a dollop of cheese and a slice of salami.

■ ■ ■ *This New York deli-style snack is deceptively delicious. Use goat's cheese if Robiola is unavailable.*

Mini Muffins

1 oz (30 g) fresh yeast or 2 (1/4-oz/7-g) packages active dry yeast

2/3 cup (180 ml) warm water

7 tablespoons warm milk

1 tablespoon sugar

3 1/3 cups (500 g) all-purpose (plain) flour

4 tablespoons unsweetened cocoa powder

2 teaspoons salt

3 1/2 oz (100 g) semisweet (dark) chocolate, in shavings

7 tablespoons butter (or lard)

1 teaspoon milk, to brush

Filling

1 1/4 cups (310 g) Robiola (or other fresh creamy) cheese

5 oz (150 g) salami (preferably Milano), very thinly sliced

Makes: 20–24 mini muffins
Preparation: 40 minutes + 1 hour 30 minutes to rise
Cooking: 20 minutes
Level: 3

BEEF TENDERLOIN
WITH CHOCOLATE

Season the beef generously with salt and pepper.
• Brown the beef in the butter in a large frying pan over high heat until sealed all over, 8–10 minutes.
• Add the onion and garlic and sauté over medium heat until the onion has softened, about 5 minutes.
• Pour in the water and wine. Cover and simmer over low heat for 15 minutes. • Add the chocolate and simmer until tender, 15–30 minutes more.
• Slice the beef finely and sprinkle with the parsley.

2 lb (1 kg) beef tenderloin, in a single cut

Salt and freshly ground black pepper

3 tablespoons butter

1 small onion, finely chopped

1 clove garlic, finely chopped

1 cup (250 ml) water

½ cup (125 ml) dry white wine

1 oz (30 g) bittersweet (plain) chocolate, finely grated

2 tablespoons finely chopped parsley

Serves: 4–6
Prep: 15 minutes
Cooking: 45 minutes
Level: 2

VENISON IN CHOCOLATE SAUCE

640

Marinade: Place the venison in a large glass bowl with all the ingredients for the marinade and leave overnight. • Remove the venison from the marinade. Filter the liquid and set aside. • Sauce: Place the oil in a large saucepan and sauté the finely chopped red onion, carrot, and celery over medium heat for 5 minutes. • Add the venison, garlic, and parsley and sauté for 3 minutes more. • Gradually pour in the filtered marinade and cook over high heat until the wine has evaporated. • Pour in the stock with the tomato concentrate. Cover and simmer over low heat until the venison is very tender, about 1 hour and 30 minutes. • Mix together the candied fruit, pine nuts, raisins, chocolate, vinegar, and sugar and add to the stew. Stir until the chocolate has melted. • Serve hot with boiled potatoes.

Marinade

- 2 lb (1 kg) venison steak, cut in bite-sized dice
- ³⁄₄ cup (180 ml) dry red wine
- 10 juniper berries
- 1 bay leaf
- 1 shallot, 1 carrot, ½ stalk celery, chopped
- ½ stick cinnamon
- 1 clove

Sauce

- 5 tablespoons extra-virgin olive oil
- 1 red onion, 1 carrot, 1 stalk celery, 2 cloves garlic, all finely chopped
- 2 tablespoons finely chopped parsley
- 2 tablespoons tomato concentrate
- 2 cups (500 ml) beef stock
- 2 tablespoons each mixed candied fruit, pine nuts, golden raisins (sultanas)
- 2 oz (60 g) semisweet (dark) chocolate
- 4 tablespoons each white vinegar and sugar

Serves: 4–6
Preparation: 30 minutes + overnight to marinate
Cooking: 1 hour 40 minutes
Level: 2

642

CHOCOLATE FETTUCCINE WITH BUTTER, SAGE AND MOZZARELLA

Pasta: Sift the flour, cocoa powder, and salt onto a clean work surface (preferably made of wood) and make a well in the center. • Pour the beaten eggs into the well. Use your fingertips to gradually incorporate the eggs into the flour. Take care not to break the wall of flour or the eggs will run. • Gather the dough up into a ball. Knead the dough until smooth and silky, about 20 minutes. • Wrap the dough in plastic wrap (cling film) and let rest for 30 minutes. • Divide the dough into pieces. Roll a piece of dough through a pasta machine at the thickest setting. Continue rolling the dough through the machine, reducing the thickness setting one notch at a time down to the required thickness. You may need to fold the pasta as you work to obtain an evenly shaped sheet. Sprinkle with semolina and cover with a clean dry cloth. Set the machine to cut to 1/4-inch (5-mm) wide and run each sheet through. • Cook the pasta in a large pot of salted, boiling water until al dente. • Sauce: While the pasta is cooking, melt the butter and sage in a small saucepan. • Drain the pasta and toss gently with the butter and sage. Take a large pasta fork and wrap about a quarter of the pasta around it to make a nest. Place 3 mozzarellas in the center and season with freshly ground pink pepper. Repeat with the remaining pasta and mozzarella. • Serve hot.

Pasta

2⅓ cups (350 g) all-purpose (plain) flour

⅓ cup (50 g) unsweetened cocoa powder

Pinch of salt

3 large eggs, lightly beaten

Semolina flour, to sprinkle

Sauce

⅔ cup (180 g) butter

24 fresh sage leaves

12 bocconcini of mozzarella (about the size of a quail's egg), well drained

Freshly ground pink pepper

Serves: 4
Prep: 50 minutes
+ 30 minutes to rest
Cooking: 10 minutes
Level: 2

GNOCCHI WITH GOLDEN RAISINS AND COCOA

Gnocchi: Cook the potatoes in salted, boiling water until tender, 25–30 minutes. • Drain and peel them. Press the potatoes through a potato ricer or mash them and place on a clean work surface. • Work in the eggs and Parmesan and season with salt and pepper. Add enough flour to form a stiff, malleable dough. • Break off pieces of dough and form into logs. Cut into 1-inch (2.5-cm) lengths. Dust with the remaining flour. Do not leave the gnocchi too long before cooking because they will stick. • Cook the gnocchi in small batches in a large pot of salted, boiling water until they bob to the surface. • Sauce: Mix the cocoa, raisins, Parmesan, Ricotta Salata, half the butter, candied lemon peel, cinnamon, and salt and pepper in a large bowl. • Use a slotted spoon to transfer the gnocchi to the bowl and toss them gently until well coated. Drizzle with the remaining melted butter and sprinkle with the Parmesan. • Serve hot.

Gnocchi

- 3 lb (1.5 kg) mealy (floury) potatoes
- 2 large eggs
- 2 tablespoons freshly grated Parmesan cheese

  Salt and freshly ground white pepper
- 3⅓ cups (500 g) all-purpose (plain) flour

Sauce

- 1 tablespoon unsweetened cocoa powder
- 2 tablespoons golden raisins (sultanas), soaked in warm water and drained
- ½ cup (60 g) freshly grated Parmesan cheese
- ½ cup (60 g) freshly grated Ricotta Salata cheese
- ½ cup (125 g) butter, melted
- ⅓ cup (30 g) finely chopped candied lemon peel

  Pinch of ground cinnamon

  Salt and freshly ground white pepper

Serves: 6
Prep: 1 hour
Cooking: 40 minutes
Level: 2

VENETIAN RAVIOLI

Pasta: Sift the flour and salt onto a clean surface and make a well in the center. Break the eggs into the well and mix in with the butter and enough water to make a smooth dough. Knead for 15–20 minutes, until smooth and elastic. Gather the dough up into a ball, wrap in plastic wrap (cling film), and let rest for 30 minutes. • Filling: Sauté the onion in the butter in a large frying pan over medium heat for 5 minutes until softened. • Add the spinach and sauté for 1 minute. • Remove from the heat and transfer to a large bowl. • Mix in the chocolate, raisins, bread crumbs, citron peel, egg, parsley, sugar, and cinnamon. Season with salt and pepper. • The mixture should hold its shape, if it seems too fluid, add more bread crumbs. • Roll the dough out on a lightly floured surface until paper-thin. Cut out 3-inch (8-cm) rounds. • Drop two teaspoons of filling into the centers of the rounds. Fold in half and seal well. • Cook the pasta in small batches in a large pot of salted, boiling water for 3–4 minutes, until al dente. • Use a slotted spoon to transfer the ravioli to a serving bowl and arrange in layers with the melted butter, Ricotta Salata, and sugar.

Pasta

2⅔ cups (400 g) all purpose (plain) flour

Pinch of salt

2 large eggs

2 tablespoons butter, melted

1 tablespoon water

Filling

½ onion, finely chopped

1 tablespoon butter

1 cup (250 g) cooked spinach, finely chopped

2 tablespoons semisweet (dark) chocolate, grated

¼ cup (45 g) raisins

¼ cup (30 g) day-old rye bread crumbs

2 tablespoons chopped candied citron peel

1 large egg

1 tablespoon finely chopped fresh parsley

1 teaspoon sugar

Pinch of cinnamon

Salt and freshly ground black pepper

⅓ cup (90 g) butter, melted

¾ cup (90 g) Ricotta Salata cheese, grated

Pinch of sugar

Serves: 4

Prep: 2 hours + 30 minutes to rest

Cooking: 15 minutes

Level: 3

DRINKS

BROWN COW

650

Place the rum, crème de cacao, crème de menthe, and ice cream in a blender. Blend for a few seconds on low speed until smooth and well mixed. • Pour drink into a champagne flute. Decorate with the chocolate shavings and serve immediately.

1 oz (30 ml) white rum

½ oz (15 ml) dark crème de cacao

¼ oz (7 ml) crème de menthe

1 scoop chocolate ice cream

Chocolate shavings, to decorate

Serves: 1
Preparation: 5 minutes
Level: 1

IRISH CHOCOLATE

Beat half the cream with the confectioners' sugar in a medium bowl with an electric mixer on high speed until soft peaks form. • Bring the remaining cream and milk to a boil in a heavy-based saucepan over medium heat. • Turn the heat down to low and add the chocolate. Stirring until melted. • Add the whiskey and stir until completely combined and smooth. • Pour into warmed mugs and spoon on the whipped cream over the top. • Sprinkle with grated chocolate and serve immediately.

2 cups (500 ml) milk

1 cup (250 ml) heavy (double) double cream, softly whipped

1 lb (500 g) bittersweet (dark) chocolate

1 tablespoon confectioners' (icing) sugar

¼ cup (60 ml) Irish whiskey

Grated chocolate, to sprinkle

Serves: 4
Preparation: 15 minutes
Level: 1

SPICED CHOCOLATE

654

Bring the cream and milk to a boil in a heavy based pan over medium heat. Whisk constantly as the mixture heats to build some froth. • When the milk is simmering, stir in the confectioners' sugar, cinnamon, nutmeg, and chocolate. Stir until the chocolate has melted. • Whisk vigorously for a few minutes until frothy. • Pour into warmed mugs, scooping out the froth. Sprinkle with chile powder and serve immediately.

3 cups (750 ml) heavy (double) cream

½ cup (125 ml) milk

14 oz (400 g) bittersweet (dark) chocolate

2 tablespoons confectioners' (icing) sugar

¼ teaspoon ground cinnamon

Freshly grated nutmeg, to taste

Chile powder, to taste

Serves: 6
Preparation: 15 minutes
Level: 1

WHITE EGG NOG

Beat the egg yolks and sugar in a medium pan with an electric mixer on high speed until pale and creamy. • Add the chocolate, milk, rum, brandy, and nutmeg and beat well. • Bring almost to a boil over medium heat. Let cool and chill in the refrigerator overnight. • Beat the cream in a medium bowl with mixer on high speed until soft peaks form. • Using a clean bowl and beater, beat the egg whites on high speed until soft peaks form. Fold the cream and egg whites into the egg mixture. • Pour into small cups or glasses and sprinkle with additional nutmeg.

2 **large eggs, separated**

3 **tablespoons superfine (caster) sugar**

2 **oz (60 g) white chocolate, melted**

½ **cup (125 ml) milk**

⅓ **cup (90 ml) dark rum**

⅓ **cup (90 ml) brandy**

Freshly grated nutmeg, to taste

½ **cup (125 ml) heavy (double) cream**

Serves: 6
Preparation: 20 minutes + overnight to chill
Level: 1

BITTER HOT CHOCOLATE

Beat the cream and confectioners' sugar in a small bowl with an electric mixer on high speed until soft peaks form. • Bring the milk to a boil in a heavy-based pan over medium heat. Whisk constantly as the mixture heats to build some froth. • When the milk is simmering, add the chocolate and stir until melted. • Pour into warmed mugs and top with the whipped cream. • Dust with cocoa and serve immediately.

3 cups (750 ml) milk

12 oz (300 g) bittersweet (dark) chocolate

½ cup (125 ml) heavy (double) cream, softly whipped

1 tablespoon confectioners' (icing) sugar

Unsweetened cocoa powder, to dust

Serves: 4
Preparation: 15 minutes
Level: 1

CHOCOLATE MONKEY

Place the banana liqueur, crème de cacao, chocolate syrup, ice cream, and milk in a blender. Process for a few seconds until smooth. • Pour into long glasses. Top with whipped cream and a drizzle of chocolate syrup.

1¼ oz (45 ml) shots banana liqueur

1 oz (30 ml) dark crème de cacao

¼ cup (60 ml) chocolate syrup + extra, to drizzle

3 scoops chocolate ice-cream

1 cup (250 ml) milk

¼ cup (60 ml) whipped cream, to top

Serves: 4
Preparation: 15 minutes
Level: 1

657

HOT ALMOND CHOCOLATE

Bring the milk and half the cream to a boil in a medium saucepan over medium heat, whisking constantly. • When the milk is simmering, stir in the chocolate, confectioners' sugar, and cocoa. Stir until the chocolate has melted. • Pour a tablespoon (15 ml) of amaretto into 4 warmed glasses. Pour the chocolate mixture over the top, scooping in the froth. • Beat the remaining cream until soft peaks hold. Spoon over chocolate drinks and sprinkle with toasted almonds. • Serve immediately, garnished with the amaretti cookies.

2   cups (500 ml) milk

1   cup (250 ml) heavy (double) cream

3   oz (90 g) milk chocolate

2   teaspoons (confectioners' (icing) sugar

¼   cup (30 g) unsweetened cocoa powder

2   oz (60 ml) amaretto liqueur

Toasted almonds, to decorate

8   amaretti cookies (biscuits), to garnish

Serves: 4
Preparation: 15 minutes
Level: 1

LUXURIOUS CHOCOLATE

660

Set out 4 cups on a tray. Divide the chocolate shavings equally between the cups. • Bring the milk to a boil in a heavy based pan over a medium heat whisking constantly to build the froth. As soon as the mixture reaches a boil remove from the heat. • Divide the hot milk evenly among the 4 cups, shaking out the froth into each. Serve hot with sugar on the side.

8 oz (250 g) bittersweet (dark) chocolate shavings

2 cups (500 ml) warm milk

Serves: 4
Preparation: 15 minutes
Level: 1

■ ■ ■ *This is really a do-it-yourself hot chocolate. You can add as much or as little milk as you like.*

MOCHA WHIRL

Place the ice cream, coffee, and cocoa in a blender. Process for a few seconds until smooth. • Pour into glasses and serve.

4 scoops vanilla ice cream

½ cup (125 ml) strong brewed coffee, cold

3 tablespoons unsweetened cocoa powder

Serves: 4
Preparation: 5 minutes
Level: 1

662

CHOCOLATE BANANA SMOOTHIE

Place the banana, chocolate syrup, milk, and crushed ice in a blender. Process for a few seconds until just slushy. • Pour into 4 glasses and serve.

1   **ripe banana**

1   **cup (250 ml) chocolate milk**

½   **cup (125 ml) chocolate syrup (see page 692)**

1   **cup (250 ml) crushed ice**

Serves: 2
Preparation: 5 minutes
Level: 1

CHOCOLATE FRAPPE

664

Place the sugar, vanilla pod, and water in a saucepan over medium heat. Bring to a boil then reduce the heat and simmer for 5 minutes. • Sift the cocoa into a small bowl. • Remove the syrup from the heat and pour enough of the syrup into the cocoa to make a paste. Stir until there are no lumps then add the rest of the syrup a little at a time. Stir until smooth. Keep the vanilla pod in the mixture. Let cool then chill in the refrigerator. • Strain the syrup when chilled. • Fill 4 tall glasses with the crushed ice. Pour the syrup over the crushed ice and finish with a squeeze of lime juice. Serve immediately.

2 cups (400 g) light brown sugar

1 vanilla pod

3/4 cup (85 g) unsweetened cocoa powder

1 1/4 cups (300 ml) boiling water

4 cups (1 liter) crushed ice

2 limes

Serves: 4
Preparation: 30 minutes
Level: 1

CHOCOLATE MARTINI

Place the vodka, chocolate liqueur, and crème de cacao into a cocktail shaker half filled with crushed ice. Shake well. Add the sugar syrup to the shaker and gently swirl. • Strain the mixture into 4–8 mini martini glasses. Top each martini with shaved chocolate and serve.

666

- ¼ cup (60 ml) freezing chocolate vodka
- ¼ cup (60 ml) chocolate liqueur
- ¼ cup (60 ml) dark crème de cacao
- 1 oz (30 ml) sugar syrup
- 1 tablespoon bittersweet (dark) chocolate, in shavings

Serves: 4
Preparation: 10 minutes
Level: 1

ICED CHOCOLATE

Beat the malt powder and milk in a medium bowl until well combined. • Place scoop 2 scoops of ice cream into each of 2 tall glasses. Pour the milk over the ice cream and top with a generous spoonful of cream. Top with chocolate shavings. • Serve Immediately.

668

4   teaspoons malt powder

2   cups (500 ml) milk

4   scoops chocolate ice cream

1   cup (250 ml) whipped cream

    Chocolate shavings, to top

Serves: 2
Preparation: 10 minutes
Level: 1

CREAMY WHITE CHOCOLATE

Bring the milk to a boil in a heavy-based saucepan over medium heat, whisking continuously. • When the milk is simmering, remove from the heat add the coffee liqueur and chocolate. Stir until the chocolate has melted. • Pour into warmed glasses and top with the whipped cream. • Dust with cinnamon and serve immediately.

3　cups (750 ml) milk

8　oz (250 g) white chocolate, grated

2　tablespoons coffee liqueur

½　cup (125 ml) heavy (double) cream, softly whipped

　　Cinnamon, to dust

S
erves: 4
Preparation: 15 minutes
Level: 1

COOL CHOCOLATE COCONUT CREAM

Place the sugar, vanilla pod, and water in a sauce pan over medium heat. Bring to a boil then simmer for 5 minutes. • Sift the cocoa powder into a small bowl. • Remove the syrup from the heat and pour enough of it into the cocoa to make a paste. Stir until there are no lumps then add the rest of the syrup a little at a time mixing well. Leave the vanilla pod in the mixture and let cool. Strain the syrup when it is completely cold. • Beat the cream and cream of coconut in a medium bowl until soft peaks form. • Divide the crushed ice among 4 tall glasses. • Pour a quarter of the rum into each glass. Pour in the chocolate syrup and top with spoonfuls of the coconut cream. • Garnish each drink with the toasted coconut and serve.

2 cups (400 g) light brown sugar

1 vanilla pod

1¼ cups (300 ml) boiling water

¾ cup (85 g) unsweetened cocoa powder

2 oz (60 ml) dark rum

½ cup (125 ml) heavy (double) cream

⅓ cup (90 ml) cream of coconut

2 cups (500 ml) crushed ice

Toasted coconut shavings, to garnish

Serves: 4
Preparation: 10 minutes
    + 30 minutes to cool
Level: 1

DOUBLE CHOCOLATE MILKSHAKE

Divide the chocolate syrup evenly among 4 tall glasses and swirl. Place the glasses in the freezer until the milkshake is ready. • Place the milk, ice cream, and chocolate syrup in a blender and process for a few seconds until smooth. • Pour into the prepared glasses and serve immediately.

- ¼ **cup (60 ml) chocolate sauce**
- 3 **cups (750 ml) milk**
- 4 **scoops chocolate ice cream**
- ¼ **cup (60 ml) chocolate syrup (see page 692)**

Serves: 4
Preparation: 10 minutes
Level: 1

HOT MOCHA

Bring the milk and cream to a boil in a saucepan over medium heat, whisking constantly to build the froth. • When the milk is simmering, add the chocolate and confectioners' sugar. Stir until the chocolate has melted. • Pour a quarter of the coffee into each warmed mug. Pour the chocolate mixture in over the top, scooping in the froth. • Sprinkle with grated chocolate and serve immediately.

2 **cups (500 ml) milk**

2 **teaspoons confectioners' (icing) sugar**

5 **oz (150 g) semisweet (dark) chocolate, chopped + extra, grated, to decorate**

½ **cup (125 ml) heavy (double) cream**

2 **oz (60 ml) strong espresso coffee**

Serves: 4
Preparation: 15 minutes
Level: 1

675

BASIC RECIPES

CHOCOLATE PASTRY CREAM

678

Place the chocolate in a large bowl and set aside.
• Beat the egg yolks and one-third of the sugar with
an electric mixer on high speed until pale and
creamy. • With mixer on low speed, beat in the
flour. • Place the remaining sugar and milk in a
saucepan over medium heat and bring to the boil.
• Pour the hot milk mixture onto the egg mixture
gradually, stirring continuously. Pour the mixture
back into the pan and simmer over low heat for
2 minutes. • Pour this egg mixture onto the
chocolate. Stir until the chocolate has
completely melted. • Cover and let cool.

6   large egg yolks
³/₄ cup (150 g) granulated
     sugar
¹/₃ cup (50 g) all-purpose
     (plain) flour
2   (500 ml) cups milk
5   oz (150 g) bittersweet
     (dark) chocolate, finely
     chopped

Makes: About 3 cups
     (750 ml)
Preparation: 20 minutes
Level: 1

CHOCOLATE CUSTARD

Place the chocolate in a large bowl and set aside.
• Beat the egg yolks and one-third of the sugar with an electric mixer on high speed until pale and creamy. • Bring the milk to a boil in a pan over medium heat. When the milk is simmering, remove from the heat. Pour half of the hot milk into the egg mix, whisking continuously. Pour back into the pan with the remaining milk and return to the heat. Stir constantly until it begins to thicken or coats the back of a metal spoon. • Remove from the heat and pour over the chocolate. Stir until the chocolate has melted and the mixture is thick and smooth.

6   large egg yolks

½   cup (100 g) superfine (caster) sugar

2   (500 ml) cups milk

8   oz (250 g) bittersweet (dark) chocolate, chopped

Makes: About 3 cups (750 ml)
Preparation: 15 minutes
Level: 1

CHOCOLATE PASTRY

Place the flour and cocoa into a small bowl. • In an electric mixer fitted with the hook attachment, place the flour mixture, butter, and sugar and mix on slow until the pastry resembles fine crumbs. • Add the egg and continue mixing until the dough comes together. • Turn the pastry out onto a floured work surface and gently knead, bringing all the pastry together. It is important not to over work the pastry at this stage. • Roll the pastry into a ball, wrap in plastic wrap (cling film) and chill in the refrigerator for 20 minutes. • The pastry is now ready to use.

682

1²/₃ cups (250 g) all-purpose (plain) flour

½ cup (75 g) unsweetened cocoa powder

¾ cup (200 g) butter, cut into pieces

½ cup (100 g) caster sugar

1 large egg, lightly beaten

Makes: About 1½ pounds (750 g)
Preparation: 20 minutes + 20 minutes to chill
Level: 1

CHOCOLATE FRANGIPAN

684

Melt the chocolate in a double boiler over barely simmering water. Remove from the heat and let cool for a few minutes. • Beat the sugar and butter with an electric mixer on high speed until creamy. • Add the eggs one at a time, beating until just combined after each addition. • With mixer on low, slowly pour in the chocolate and beat until well combined. Briefly turn the speed to high, after scraping down the sides of the bowl. • Gradually add the flour and almonds to the batter. • Cover and refrigerate for 30 minutes before using.

8 oz (250 g) semisweet (dark) chocolate

½ cup (125 g) butter

½ cup (100 g) superfine (caster) sugar

3 large eggs

¼ cup (30 g) all-purpose (plain) flour

1 cup (120 g) finely ground almonds

Makes: About 3 cups (750 g)
Preparation: 30 minutes + 30 minutes to chill
Level: 1

DARK CHOCOLATE GANACHE

686

Place the chocolate in a large bowl and set aside.
• Bring the cream to a boil in a saucepan over
medium heat.• Pour the hot cream the chocolate.
Stir until the chocolate has melted and it is smooth
and shiny.• Transfer to a smaller bowl, cover with
plastic wrap (cling film) pressed onto the ganache
to prevent a crust forming.• Refrigerate
until needed.

**12 oz (300 g) bittersweet
(dark) chocolate, grated**

**1¼ cups (300 ml) heavy
(double) cream**

Makes: About 2¼ cups
(750 ml)
Preparation: 15 minutes
Level: 1

CHOCOLATE FROSTING

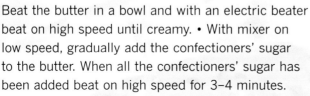

688

Beat the butter in a bowl and with an electric beater beat on high speed until creamy. • With mixer on low speed, gradually add the confectioners' sugar to the butter. When all the confectioners' sugar has been added beat on high speed for 3–4 minutes. • Beat in the cocoa powder and slowly add the milk. • When all the ingredients have been added, turn the mixer to high speed and beat for 30 seconds, scraping down the sides and re-beating. • The frosting should be dark in color and of spreadable consistency.

3 cups (450 g) confectioners' (icing) sugar
1 cup (250 g) butter
1 cup (150 g) usweetened cocoa powder
²/₃ cup (150 ml) milk

Makes: About 3 cups (750 g)
Preparation: 20 minutes
Level: 1

CHOCOLATE SAUCE

Place the chocolate and half the milk in a saucepan over medium heat and bring to a boil. • Dissolve the cornflour in the remaining milk and mix into the chocolate along with the sugar. • Stir constantly over low heat until thickened. • Remove from the heat and whisk until really smooth.

690

- **12** oz (300 g) bittersweet (dark) chocolate, grated
- **2** (500 ml) cups milk
- **½** cup (100 g) superfine (caster) sugar
- **2** teaspoons cornstarch (cornflour)

Makes: About 3 cups (750 ml)
Preparation: 10 minutes
Level: 1

CHOCOLATE SYRUP

692

Bring the sugar, vanilla pod, and water to a boil in a saucepan over medium heat. Reduce the heat to low and simmer for 5 minutes. • Place the cocoa in a small bowl. • Remove the syrup from the heat and pour enough of it into the cocoa to make a paste. Stir until there are no lumps then add the rest of the syrup a little at a time. • Keep the vanilla pod in the mixture and let cool. Strain the syrup when it is completely cold. It is ready for use.

2 cups (400 g) light brown sugar

$^3/_4$ cup (85 g) unsweetened cocoa powder

1$^1/_4$ cups (300 ml) boiling water

1 vanilla pod

Makes: About 2 cups (500 ml)
Preparation: 20 minutes
Level: 1

CHOCOLATE CURLS

Melt the chocolate in a double boiler over barely simmering water. • Remove the pan from the heat. Dry the base of the bowl; it is essential that no water drips onto the chocolate. • Pour the chocolate onto a marble surface and, using a stepped palate knife, quickly spread the chocolate over the marble as evenly and thinly as you can. Leave the chocolate to set completely. • Using a pastry scraper, start at the edge of chocolate furthest from you and about 1 inch (2.5 cm) from the top. Hold the scraper at a 45-degree angle to the marble. Push away from you into the chocolate. The chocolate should curl up onto the scraper. • To get variation in the curl, alter the angle of the scraper, vary the length of the push, and twist the scraper as you are pushing. Experiment to get the effect you are after. • When you have used most of the chocolate, it can be scraped up and re-melted and curled until all the chocolate has been used.

12 oz (300 g) bittersweet (dark), milk, or white chocolate, grated

Preparation: 20 minutes
Level: 2

■ ■ ■ *These curls can be very effective for decoration. The method is the same for milk, dark and white chocolate.*

BASIC CHOCOLATE SPONGE

Preheat the oven to 350°F (180°C/gas 4). • Butter and flour a 9-inch (23-cm) springform pan. • Melt the chocolate in a double boiler over barely simmering water. Set aside to cool. • Place the flour, cocoa, baking powder, baking soda, and salt in a large bowl. • Beat the butter and sugar in a large bowl with an electric mixer at medium speed until creamy. • Add the eggs, one at a time, beating until just blended after each addition. • With mixer at low speed, gradually beat in the dry ingredients, alternating with the chocolate, milk, and oil.
• Spoon the batter into the prepared pan. • Bake until a toothpick inserted into the center comes out clean, 50–60 minutes. • Cool the cake in the pan on a rack for 10 minutes. Loosen and remove the pan sides and let cool completely.

12 oz (350 g) bittersweet (dark), chocolate, coarsely chopped

2 cups (300 g) all-purpose (plain) flour

1/4 cup (50 g) unsweetened cocoa power

2 teaspoons baking powder

1/2 teaspoon baking soda (bicarbonate of soda)

1/4 teaspoon salt

1/3 cup (90 g) butter

1 1/4 cups (250 g) superfine (caster) sugar

4 large eggs

1/2 cup (125 ml) milk

2 tablespoons vegetable oil

Makes: One 9-inch (23-cm) sponge
Preparation: 20 minutes
Cooking: 50–60 minutes
Level: 2

INDEX

Bars and brownies

Basic recipes

Candy

Cookies

Drinks

Savory dishes

Tea and coffee cakes